HEAT-ZONE
Gardening

HEAT-ZONE
Gardening

How to choose plants that thrive in your region's *warmest* weather

DR. H. MARC CATHEY
President Emeritus, American Horticultural Society

WITH LINDA BELLAMY

TIME® LIFE BOOKS

Time-Life Books is a division of Time Life Inc.

TIME LIFE INC.

PRESIDENT and CEO: George Artandi

TIME-LIFE BOOKS

PRESIDENT: Stephen R. Frary

TIME-LIFE CUSTOM PUBLISHING

Vice President and Publisher	Terry Newell
Vice President of Sales and Marketing	Neil Levin
Director of New Product Development	Quentin McAndrew
Director of Editorial Development	Jennifer Louise Pearce
Director of Special Sales	Liz Ziehl
Managing Editor	Donia Ann Steele
Marketing Manager	Inger Forland
Production Manager	Carolyn M. Clark
Quality Assurance Manager	James King

Editorial Staff for *Heat-Zone Gardening*

Project Manager	Linda Bellamy
Design	Leonard G. Phillips
Picture Coordinators	Ruth Goldberg, Kimberly Grandcolas
Special Contributors	Celia Beattie, Lina B. Burton, Ruth Goldberg, Catharine Hackett, Darcie Johnston, Lynn McGowan, Carole Ottesen, Holly H. Shimizu, Mary-Sherman Willis

ACKNOWLEDGMENTS

The authors would like to thank Monrovia, the Horticultural Research Institute of the American Nursery and Landscape Association, Goldsmith Seed Company, the American Horticultural Society, and Time-Life Books for their expertise and generous support of this project. And to Emanuel Shemin, for his faith and support from the very beginning.

First printing. Printed in China.

Library of Congress Cataloging-in-Publication Data

Cathey, Marc
    Heat-Zone Gardening : how to choose plants that thrive in your region's warmest weather / Marc Cathey.
      p. cm.
    ISBN 0-7835-5279-3
    1. Landscape gardening—United States. 2. Heat-zone gardening—United States. 3. Landscape plants—United States. I. Title.
    SB473.C345 1998
    635.9'52—dc21   97-31250
                                      CIP

Table
OF CONTENTS

THE HEAT ZONE
Concept

Our country is one complete garden,
each section adding its chorus to
the great symphony.

— *Jens Jensen,*
Siftings

"*WILL THIS PLANT SURVIVE IN MY CLIMATE?*"
is one of the first questions most gardeners ask when
planning a garden. In any given year, the hapless gardener may
be forced to deal with unseasonable cold fronts, hailstones,
bone-dry stretches of drought, torrential downpours, killer heat
waves, and many other vagaries of the weather. And, according
to scientists, our weather will become even more unpredictable
in the next century.

Until now, gardeners have relied solely on the cold-zone ratings
to determine a plant's regional hardiness. Cold hardiness, however, is only one factor in a plant's chances of survival.
Recognizing that summer heat can be equally devastating to
many plants—including annuals, biennials, and other plants
that are usually not considered heat-sensitive, such as vegetables and wildflowers—the American Horticultural Society
(AHS) has developed a revolutionary new garden concept based
on a plant's tolerance to heat. In this chapter you'll learn all
about the AHS Plant Heat-Zone Map—why it will have increasing importance as we face global climatic changes and how it
can help you choose plants wisely, anywhere under the sun.

Gardening IN THE 21ST CENTURY

IN THE WAKE OF A POSTWAR BUILDING BOOM THAT HAS TRANSFORMED MUCH OF OUR NATURAL LANDSCAPE INTO PARKING LOTS, STRIP MALLS, AND SPRAWLING SUBURBIA, AMERICA IS EXPERIENCING A FULL-BLOWN GARDENING RENAISSANCE.

Gardens, scholars say, are the first signs of commitment to a community.

—*Anne Raver*

More of us are gardening than ever before—and across the country gardeners are sharing a commitment to "garden lightly on the earth." Over the past 30 years, we've seen rising interest in ecological, water-thrifty, heirloom, organic, and natural habitat approaches to gardening—all reflecting a growing awareness of the environment. These trends are sure to intensify as we enter the next century.

Rather than a high-maintenance lawn, a visitor is greeted by the sight of a brick patio surrounded by easy-care perennials and grasses in this Maryland garden. The brick's concentric circles are like the ripples on the surface of a still pond.

With an eye toward conserving energy and resources, our gardens are more efficient than in the past (requiring far less upkeep), and our designs are more practical. No longer content with a handful of high-maintenance plants and water-demanding turf grass, we're eager to experiment with unfamiliar species, heat- and drought-tolerant cultivars, and new, more effective gardening techniques.

And, blessed with an amazing diversity of native plants and climates, American gardeners are turning to the natural landscape for inspiration. Like old-time plant explorers, many of us are taking to the back roads (or visiting our local native plant nurseries and botanic gardens) with field guides in hand—and hardworking American wildflowers such as

Polygonatum (Solomon's-seal), *Penstemon* (beardtongue), and *Thalictrum* (meadow rue) are winning our hearts and finding

their way into our gardens alongside more familiar azaleas, geraniums, and impatiens.

But whatever our gardening styles—from dramatic cacti collections and northern California coastal gardens to Texas bluebonnet meadows and tranquil East Coast glades—the challenges we now face come from sources much larger, and less familiar, than our own backyards.

Our Changing Climate

Global warming—the gradual heating up of the earth's atmosphere due to an increase in atmospheric carbon dioxide—holds an obvious significance for gardeners everywhere. Climatologists warn of far-reaching changes in regional climate and local weather caused by an increase in the global average temperature of half a degree Celsius over the last century. This warming trend is caused by many factors, but at least part of the problem lies in human activities such as the burning of fossil fuels in electric power plants and automobiles, and the razing of tropical forests. Moreover, because populations and industry will continue to grow, current projections forecast a continued increase in temperature of about .54°F (0.3°C) per decade over the next century.

While this increase may seem too slight to matter very much, we are already facing dramatic changes in the global climate. Five out of the 10 hottest years ever documented have occurred since 1990, with 1995 breaking all heat records for recorded weather history. And, as a result of this warming trend,

Making the right garden for your region means taking cues from the surrounding landscape. (STARTING AT FAR LEFT) A garden in the Southwest uses cactus, and *Encelia farinosa* (brittlebush). Orange-flowered bromeliads thrive outdoors year round in Florida. Annual *Lupinus texensis* (Texas bluebonnet) does well in its home state's sandy, poor soil. Perennial grasses like *Miscanthus sinensis* 'Variegata' grow well in temperate regions.

Virginia's wide range of temperatures, from well below freezing in the winter to scorching hot in summer, calls for plants that can tolerate these conditions, such as the billowing ornamental grasses like *Pennisetum* (fountain grass), native *Hydrangea quercifolia* (oakleaf hydrangea) with its beautiful white flower panicles, pink *Spiraea* 'Anthony Waterer', and other colorful perennials.

the rhythm of the seasons is slowly being altered as extended periods of frost-free days eat away at the edges of "winter." In the northeastern United States, for example, the frost-free season now begins approximately a week earlier than in the past.

Throughout the country, longer and more intense heat waves and at least occasional periods of drought remind us that our water resources can no longer be taken for granted. As groundwater levels diminish or become polluted from chemical runoff, and as rainfall becomes more erratic, gardeners in all regions of the country can expect to see increasing

water costs as well as community-imposed restrictions on water use for gardening purposes.

Wherever you live—and whatever the outcome of predicted climatic change—waterwise, heat-tolerant garden design makes good gardening sense. And whether you are planning a more efficient garden out of necessity, to increase the value of your property, or in response to environmental concerns, the new AHS Plant Heat-Zone Map will be an invaluable tool for choosing the right plant for the right place—both now and into the 21st century.

Slightly shaded under an ironwood tree in this dry Arizona garden *(ABOVE)*, prickly pear and barrel cactus grow among colorful desert flowers like red *Salvia greggii* and yellow *Baileya multiradiata* (desert marigold). In Florida's steamy summer heat *(LEFT)*, tender tropical bromeliads nestle at the base of an old *Ligustrum* among bright pink impatiens.

How to
USE THE MAP

The AHS Plant Heat-Zone Map establishes guidelines for the heat tolerance of plants, and can be used by gardeners across the country in selecting the best plants for their climate. It indicates the longest periods of heat that can be expected in all regions of the United States.

The map shows 12 different zones, each representing a range of summer heat. These ranges are defined by average annual days above 86°F (30°C) and are based on the high temperatures recorded each year from 1974 to 1995 in the United States. (The temperature 86°F is the point at which plants experience damage to cellular proteins.) Although the zones are generally distributed as expected, by latitude and topography, there are also island zones that are cooler than surrounding areas because of differences in elevation. In the higher regions of the Appalachians, for example, the small town of Boone, North Carolina, is several zones cooler than lower elevations throughout the state. Likewise, many urban areas are in a warmer zone than the surrounding countryside. Denver, Colorado, for example, is AHS heat zone 7, while the area adjacent to the city is AHS heat zone 6.

Armed with both the U.S. Department of Agriculture (USDA) hardiness zones and the AHS heat zones for your area, as well

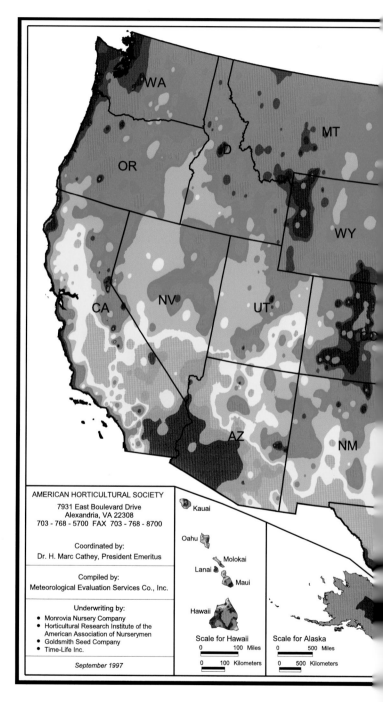

AMERICAN HORTICULTURAL SOCIETY
7931 East Boulevard Drive
Alexandria, VA 22308
703 - 768 - 5700 FAX 703 - 768 - 8700

Coordinated by:
Dr. H. Marc Cathey, President Emeritus

Compiled by:
Meteorological Evaluation Services Co., Inc.

Underwriting by:
- Monrovia Nursery Company
- Horticultural Research Institute of the American Association of Nurserymen
- Goldsmith Seed Company
- Time-Life Inc.

September 1997

Kauai

Oahu

Molokai

Lanai

Maui

Hawaii

Scale for Hawaii
0   100 Miles

0   100 Kilometers

Scale for Alaska
0   500 Miles

0   500 Kilometers

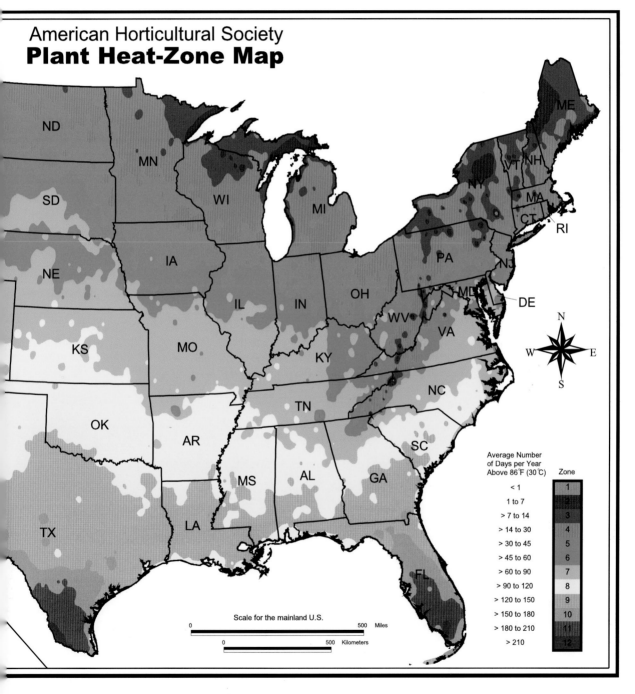

American Horticultural Society
Plant Heat-Zone Map

Average Number of Days per Year Above 86°F (30°C)	Zone
< 1	1
1 to 7	2
> 7 to 14	3
> 14 to 30	4
> 30 to 45	5
> 45 to 60	6
> 60 to 90	7
> 90 to 120	8
> 120 to 150	9
> 150 to 180	10
> 180 to 210	11
> 210	12

Scale for the mainland U.S.

0   500   Miles

0   500   Kilometers

It is not nice to garden anywhere. Everywhere there are violent winds, startling once-per-five-centuries floods, unprecedented droughts, record-setting freezes, abusive and blasting heats never known before. There is no place, no garden, where these terrible things do not drive gardeners mad.

—*Henry Mitchell,*
The Essential
Earthman

as individual plant zone ratings *(see Plant Profiles, pages 66-182)*, you can quickly select the best plants for your garden by considering:

→ Will this plant thrive for years in my site?

→ Will this plant survive my winters, but be severely stressed by the high temperatures of my summers?

→ Will this plant do well during my summers, but not survive a possible plunge in winter temperatures?

→ Are there any cultivars or species of this plant that are more cold or heat tolerant?

Keep in mind, however, that many factors come into play when determining satisfactory growth over the summer. Wind, air pollution, soil type, moisture,

and the amount of sunlight all affect the adaptability of plants. Some plants may languish and eventually die if planted in unfavorable conditions, such as near light-reflecting asphalt or mirrored buildings, in dry soil beneath a roof overhang or on steep, wind-blown banks. *(See pages 24-27.)*

About the Plant Heat-Zone Map

The elements of this map parallel the USDA Plant Hardiness Map:

ZONES The United States was divided into 12 zones based on the average number of days each year that a given region experiences "heat days"—from cool-summer areas with an average of less than 1 day per year above 86°F (zone 1) to subtropical areas with an average of more than 210 days per year above 86°F (zone 12).

SUMMER PERFORMANCE In assigning heat zones to individual plants *(see Plant Profiles, pages 66-182)*, adaptability to summer heat was selected as the most important factor. In this age of "gardening lightly on the earth," it is the goal of some gardeners to plant a garden, water it until established, and then leave the plantings to fend for themselves.

Keep in mind, however, that the performance of plants in particular heat zones can be distorted by the lack of water (even for a brief period of time) or other basic care at critical stages in a plant's life. The heat-zone ratings used throughout this book are based upon the assumption that basic good gardening principles are followed, including:

→ Proper soil cultivation and planting, and the use of soil amendments, compost, or other organic nutrients as needed.

→ Siting for optimal growing conditions, with adequate sun or shade and protection from drying winds.

→ The appropriate use of mulch to conserve soil moisture and block weed growth.

→ Adequate water supplied to the roots of plants at all times. Newly planted perennials, shrubs, and trees may take several months or even years to establish themselves in a site, requiring more water initially for root development. Once safely established, plants should be able to grow with diminishing amounts of water. *(See pages 42-47 for information on waterwise landscapes.)*

PLANT CLASSIFICATION Many plants can survive in climates that are cooler or warmer than the recommended zones. However, the ratings we have used in this book indicate that the plants perform very well within their assigned zones. For the purposes of our zone ratings, mere survival does not represent satisfactory performance.

Tall pink hollyhocks and *Echinacea* (coneflower), red bee balm, and other flowering annuals and perennials *(FACING PAGE)* need full summer sun to produce abundant blooms and a sturdy upright growth habit. Their needs are met in this southern Colorado garden. But farther south, in Florida *(ABOVE)*, *Polystichum setiferum* (soft shield fern) must be protected from the blazing heat.

15

Choosing CLIMATE-ADAPTED PLANTS

Pansies *(TOP)* can survive a mild winter, but will succumb to high summer heat. Long-lived herbaceous peonies *(MIDDLE)* need a period of cold winter dormancy, while caladiums *(BOTTOM)* cannot survive outdoors north of USDA hardiness zone 10.

Some things gardeners must simply accept, such as the amount of rainfall or the range of temperatures within their region. Wherever you live, the key to a successful garden rests on choosing plants that are adapted to your climate.

Good gardeners must be skillful matchmakers. No matter how hard you try, plants suited to the cooler summers of Burlington, Vermont (AHS heat zone 4), will never perform well in the sweltering summer temperatures of New Orleans, Louisiana (AHS heat zone 9). Likewise, warm-climate plants, such as *Zingiber officinale* (common ginger) won't survive winters above USDA hardiness zone 9, and may struggle if planted in the "cooler" summer regions above AHS heat zone 8.

Many plants, especially those native to arid climates, require a hot, dry season to ripen their wood, bulb, or rhizome. While these plants can be grown in cooler, wetter climates, they may fail to fruit or flower. On the other hand, *Zephyranthes candida* (rain lily) will only flower after a drop in temperature that signals the arrival of cooler autumn weather.

Fortunately, many species are highly adaptable and will grow in a wide range of climates. Easygoing *Rudbeckia hirta* (coneflower) and *Achillea* (yarrow) will grow happily in a wide range of conditions and are found in USDA hardiness zones 4-9 and AHS heat zones 9-2. The *Yucca*—a plant native to the deserts of Mexico—will grow in USDA hardiness zones 4-9 and AHS heat zones 9-1, and includes varieties that can withstand even severe frost. *(See page 58 for a list of climate-adaptable native plants.)*

> For a plant to adapt to life in the Southwest, it must be able to tolerate occasional below-freezing temperatures in winter and several months of scorching temperatures. Summertime highs average in the 90s in the "cooler" desert areas and well over 100° in the hot spots, where daytime soil surface temperatures can reach 190°.
>
> — *Carole Ottesen,*
> The Native Plant Primer

Climate and Hardiness

A plant's cold hardiness has long been an indication of its ability to survive. The most critical factor in selecting plants for your climate is their degree of winter hardiness. While a hardy, cool-climate plant, such as *Paeonia lactiflora* (garden peony), will survive winter temperatures as low as -40°F (USDA hardiness zone 4), other plants, such as *Magnolia grandiflora* (southern magnolia), will not survive winter temperatures below 0°F (USDA hardiness zone 7). Aided by the USDA Plant Hardiness Map, which was most recently updated to 11 zones in 1990, gardeners have learned through experience where the great variety of hardy plants can be grown over the winter.

The second most critical factor—and one that is increasingly important—is your plants' performance over the summer months. A plant's ability to adapt to summer heat not only applies to hardy perennials but also to annuals, woody shrubs, biennials, bulbs, wildflowers, and other heat-sensitive summer plants such as pansies and delphinium. Of course, plants grown as annuals in one zone may perennialize in a warmer region.

Alstroemeria (Peruvian lily), petunias, caladiums, coleus, and *Alpinia purpurata* (red ginger), for example, may thrive for several years in warmer regions, such as southern Florida and southwestern California (AHS heat zones 12-10), but must be grown as annuals in cooler regions. On the other hand, heat-sensitive woody plants, such as *Picea glauca* var. *albertiana* (dwarf Alberta spruce), and *Pieris japonica* (lily-of-the-valley shrub) will successfully overwinter in the South, only to struggle in the hot summers of regions in AHS heat zones 12-8.

But wherever you're gardening, the new AHS Plant Heat-Zone Map and plant ratings will take the guesswork out of choosing heat- and drought-tolerant plants—saving you time, energy, and money in the long run.

Native *Yucca baccata* (Spanish bayonet), Mediterranean *Centranthus ruber* (red valerian) *(at bottom right)* and lavender *(at back)*, and a prickly *Berberis* 'Rosy Glow' can all adapt to the same conditions of cool wet winters, dry hot summers, and well-draining soil in this New Mexico garden.

Getting STARTED

You've studied gardens in magazines and clipped photographs of plants that caught your eye. Over the course of several weekends, you've visited local nurseries and public gardens. Now the list of gardenworthy contenders is several pages long—and it's time to make the final cuts. The following steps will help you get started.

Hosta fluctans

Hosta (HOS-ta)
PLANTAIN LILY

USDA Hardiness: zones 4-9
AHS Heat: zones 9-2
Height: 15 inches to 4 feet
Plant type: perennial
Soil: moist, well-drained, slightly acid
Light: partial to bright full shade

The many forms of plantain lilies are prized mainly for their spreading clumps of attractive foliage, making them ideal for textural and color accents in perennial beds and borders. Trumpet-shaped flowers appear in summer. Good drainage is essential, especially in winter. Although most hostas thrive in deep shade, variegated and blue forms need bright shade to hold their color. Hosta tolerates sun in cooler areas, with abundant moisture. Hostas for hot, muggy climates include *H. fortuneii* 'Albomarginata'.

Sample plant profile

STEP 1 Determine the zone you live in on both the USDA Plant Hardiness Map and the AHS Plant Heat-Zone Map. (The USDA Plant Hardiness Map will help you determine which plants will survive the winter, based on the average minimum temperature in your region.) For example, gardeners in the Washington, D.C., area live in USDA hardiness zone 7 and AHS heat zone 7. Washington, D.C., falls within the Mid-Atlantic region—an area with hot, humid summers where temperatures may reach 95°F to 100°F during the "dog days" of summer, and where minimum winter temperatures may average 0°F to 10°F.

STEP 2 Next, determine if a particular plant is suited to grow in your region by finding the plant listed in the *Plant Profiles (pages 66-182)*. There you'll find that the sample plant *Hosta* is suited to USDA hardiness zones 4-9 and AHS heat zones 9-2.

STEP 3 The final step is to check your information to determine if the chosen plant will thrive in both the lowest and the highest temperatures in your region. In this case, the gardener in Washington, D.C., can grow *Hosta* with ease, because zone 7 falls within both its hardiness and heat-zone ranges.

In general, we can determine that *Hosta* is a fairly easygoing plant that will flourish in areas with warm to cooler summers. It would struggle, however, in regions with extremely long, hot summers and would not survive winter temperatures below -20°F.

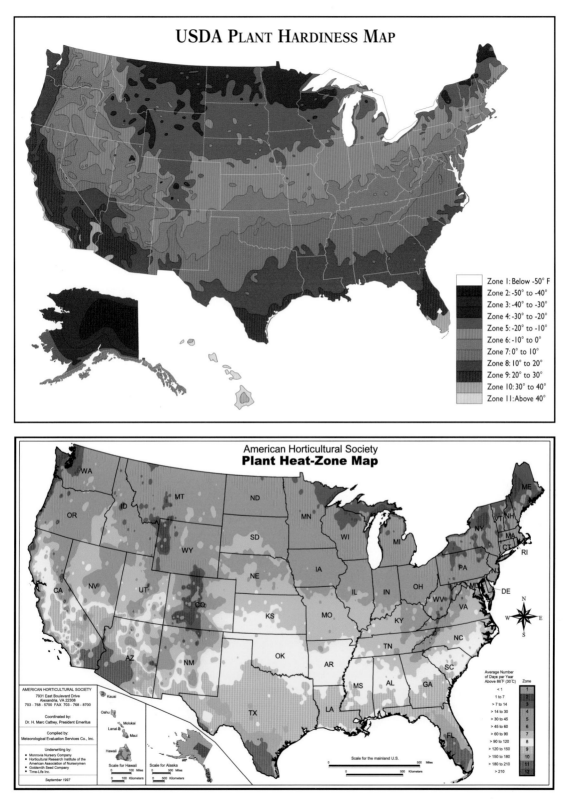

USDA Plant Hardiness Map

	Zone 1: Below -50° F
	Zone 2: -50° to -40°
	Zone 3: -40° to -30°
	Zone 4: -30° to -20°
	Zone 5: -20° to -10°
	Zone 6: -10° to 0°
	Zone 7: 0° to 10°
	Zone 8: 10° to 20°
	Zone 9: 20° to 30°
	Zone 10: 30° to 40°
	Zone 11: Above 40°

American Horticultural Society
Plant Heat-Zone Map

WA MT ND MN ME
OR ID WI NY VT NH
SD MI MA
WY NE IA PA CT RI
NV UT CO IL IN OH NJ
CA KS MO WV MD DE VA
AZ NM OK AR KY NC
TN SC
TX MS AL GA
LA
FL

AMERICAN HORTICULTURAL SOCIETY
7931 East Boulevard Drive
Alexandria, VA 22308
703 - 768 - 5700 FAX 703 - 768 - 8700

Coordinated by:
Dr. H. Marc Cathey, President Emeritus

Compiled by:
Meteorological Evaluation Services Co., Inc.

Underwriting by:
• Monrovia Nursery Company
• Horticultural Research Institute of the American Association of Nurserymen
• Goldsmith Seed Company
• Time-Life Inc.

September 1997

Kauai
Oahu
Molokai
Lanai Maui
Hawaii

Scale for Hawaii
0   100 Miles
0   100 Kilometers

Scale for Alaska
0   500 Miles
0   500 Kilometers

Scale for the mainland U.S.
0   500 Miles
0   500 Kilometers

Average Number of Days per Year Above 86°F (30°C)	Zone
< 1	1
1 to 7	2
> 7 to 14	3
> 14 to 30	4
> 30 to 45	5
> 45 to 60	6
> 60 to 90	7
> 90 to 120	8
> 120 to 150	9
> 150 to 180	10
> 180 to 210	11
> 210	12

GARDENING
in Your
ZONE

Nature writes. Gardeners edit.

— *Roger Swain*

*T*HOUGHTFUL PLANNING, A BIT OF OLD-FASHIONED HARD WORK, *and ingenuity are the basis of every successful garden, whether it's a small rooftop garden in Manhattan, a collection of semitropicals in a Savannah courtyard, or a Texas wildflower meadow.*

It is always better—and easier—to work with nature than against it. Step by step, this chapter shows how to build on the challenges of your landscape—in any climatic zone. You'll learn how to become a savvy garden strategist, making the most of whatever your landscape has to offer. For example, you can plant a marginally hardy fruit tree in a sunny, sheltered spot by the back door, grow a cook's garden of herbs in decorative pots and troughs on a tiny city terrace, or create shade on a treeless lot with quick-growing, leafy vines scrambling across an arbor.

Assessing YOUR LANDSCAPE

Responsible gardening begins right in your own yard. Whether you're starting your garden from a bare, bull-dozed lot, reviving an existing garden, or merely redesigning a troublesome area, the first step in creating a healthy, environ-mentally successful garden is to assess your landscape.

Before you've lifted your trowel or put the first tender new seedling in the ground, get to know everything you can about your landscape and write it down. Note the climatic zones for both cold har-diness and heat, the type of soil in your garden, typical high and low tempera-tures, patterns of rainfall, sun, shade, and wind, as well as any existing plant material or built features. You should also take into account special climatic influ-ences or potential problems such as heat pockets, steep slopes or berms, roots or rub-ble, perpetually wet areas, compacted soil, or large trees and shrubs that may have outgrown their site.

Ask yourself detailed questions about your landscape. Does an eroding slope lose topsoil during summer thunderstorms? Is

Naturalized wildflowers like *Clematis montana* 'Rubens' (anemone clematis) *(ABOVE)*, import-ed from China, and natives like pink *Oenothera speciosa* (pink evening primrose) from Texas and Kansas *(RIGHT)* fit comfortably in a low-maintenance, naturalized landscape.

your soil quick-draining and sandy, or does it become rock-hard in the summer sun? Are there high-maintenance features such as trimmed edgings or large expanses of lawn that you would like to eliminate?

Back to Nature

Before making up your final plant list, note any wildflowers growing in your community, as well as naturalized plants, such as maple seedlings, that sprout up on their own. Unlike wildflowers, naturalized plants are nonnatives species imported into this country that will self-propagate with vigor once they're settled in a congenial habitat.

Often you'll find naturalized and native plants growing along country back roads or embankments. In the warm, humid climate of Georgia, for example, naturalized *Daucus carota* (Queen Anne's lace) often colonizes in open, sunny fields, while the exotic-looking native vine *Passiflora incarnata* (passionflower) thrives at the woodland's edge. Many of these plants make fine, low-maintenance additions to your garden, creating a living link with the natural landscape of your region.

Others, such as *Lysimachia* (loose-

A multicolored carpet of flowering rock plants *(LEFT)* spreads over and around the stones holding up a sloping bank in this Denver garden. Lavender-blue Stokes' asters and native goldenrod *(BELOW)* brighten a natural garden at the end of summer.

strife) and *Rosa multiflora*, may become invasive if planted in favorable garden conditions. Before using naturalized plants in your garden, contact local nature centers, garden clubs, and state agriculture departments to learn which plants are considered invasive in your area.

Keep in mind that collecting native plants from the wild is not only illegal in many states, but also harmful to the natural habitat. It's best to buy greenhouse-propagated plants from reputable nurseries, garden clubs, or native plant societies.

Micro-
CLIMATES

A niche between stepped, stone retaining walls *(RIGHT)* provides a warm, sheltered microclimate ideal for rock plants such as pink arabis.

While both hardiness and heat zones are important in determining what will grow in your garden, you should also pay close attention to microclimates—variations in temperature, light intensity, and moisture that may exist within a single plot of land. Shaped by regional climate, topography, and the features of your property, your microclimate (and growing conditions) may be completely different from your neighbor's down the street.

In fact, a large suburban lot may have several microclimates. The location of buildings and fences, trees and shrubs, banks, hilltops and valleys, bodies of water, and hardscape features such as driveways, patios, and sidewalks can all produce a wide range of microclimates within a single garden.

Observant gardeners soon learn how to make the challenges of microclimates work for them in the garden. Sun-loving, colorful prairie plants such as *Coreopsis*

The landscaping of this yard *(RIGHT)* takes advantage of several different microclimates. Evergreen trees underplanted with hostas and ferns break the path of blustery north winds. On the south side of the house, deciduous trees create cool pockets of shade and easy-care raised beds hold sun-loving herbs and vegetables. A variety of heat-tolerant perennials and dwarf fruit trees edge the drive.

verticillata, Castilleja integra (Indian paintbrush), *Rudbeckia fulgida* (black-eyed Susan), *Penstemon barbatus* (bugler penstemon), and *Echinacea purpurea* (purple coneflower) will all flourish in an open strip of land along the driveway. Shady, low-lying areas that puddle after summer thunderstorms provide the perfect spot for a collection of fragrant mints, while the crevices between stones are ideal niches for tiny alpines and rock-garden plants such as *Sedum, Portulaca* (moss rose), and *Arabis* (rock cress).

South-facing fences and walls absorb heat from the sun and reflect it into adjacent areas. These warm, sheltered spots are excellent places to grow marginally hardy climbers, shrubs, and fruit trees. If the soil is free-draining, the same area may be used for a small culinary garden stocked with sun-loving herbs such as *Salvia officinalis* (sage), *Thymus* (thyme), and *Rosmarinus* (rosemary)—all natives of the sun-baked Mediterranean region. On the other hand, the north-facing side of a wall provides a cool, shady microclimate for true shade-lovers such as the gold-dappled *Aucuba, Brunnera macrophylla* 'Variegata', *Hosta, Polygonatum* (Solomon's-seal), and *Dicentra spectabilis* (Japanese bleeding heart).

City Gardens

Urban gardeners are faced with a special set of environmental challenges. In general, city gardens are several degrees warmer than their rural or suburban counterparts within the same region and climatic zones. In early spring, warmer temperatures work to the advantage of urban gardeners. Bulbs and other spring-flowering plants will often bloom several weeks earlier than the same plants grown in an outlying suburban garden. During the summer months, however, stifling heat, increased air pollution, and towering buildings that block out light and channel drying winds can all wreak havoc on city gardens. Plants grown in these conditions may suffer from soot and grime that accumulate on the leaf surfaces, interfering with photosynthesis and eventually weakening the entire plant.

The sunny walls of city buildings shield tall plants like these hollyhocks from buffeting winds. They also reflect heat and trap warm air. *Stachys byzantia* (lamb's ears) is a hardworking ground cover well suited to this Georgetown street garden.

Tough annuals for urban gardens include red salvia and zinnias *(ABOVE, LEFT)* and white nicotiana and red impatiens *(ABOVE, RIGHT)*. Perennials *(BELOW)* also make dependable city plants. White-flowered hostas and pink Japanese anemones bloom behind yellow *Coreopsis* 'Moonbeam' and blue plumbago.

When choosing trees and shrubs for an urban garden, try to include a large number of pollution-tolerant varieties such as *Berberis thunbergii* (Japanese barberry), *Cotinus coggygria* (smoke tree), and *Koelreuteria paniculata* (golden rain tree). Less expensive, quick-growing annuals such as *Cleome, Mirabilis* (four-o'clock), *Alyssum,* petunias, *Salvia coccinea* (scarlet sage), *Impatiens* (balsam), zinnias, and *Nicotiana* (flowering tobacco) can be used as colorful accents and replaced later in

the summer if necessary. Dependable perennials for a city garden include shade-loving *Hosta* and *Pulmonaria* (lungwort), and sun-loving *Sedum spectabile, Iris* (bearded iris), *Pelargonium* spp. (geraniums), and *Veronica spicata* (spiked speedwell). Ground covers that tolerate poor soil and pollution include *Lamium* and *Hedera helix* (English ivy).

Gardeners who tend narrow plots surrounded by large, light-blocking walls or buildings must also contend with the difficulties of deep shade. *(See page 29.)* Try thinning your planting beds to reduce competition for light, water, nutrients, and oxygen. Painting walls and fences a light color, so they reflect available light, helps considerably as well. Even a slight increase in ambient light can greatly enhance a plant's growth and bloom.

The Windy Garden

While breezes in sultry, humid regions offer a respite from summer heat, the extremely strong, dry winds of the Plains and Southwest damage plants and may actually pull moisture from the soil, causing droughtlike conditions. Coastal gardens are particularly susceptible to wind damage, as are gardens in higher elevations, on rooftops or balconies, or on open expanses of land.

A protective windbreak may be in order if you garden in a particularly windy region and your plants seem to be suffering. Not only do strong winds rob soil and foliage of moisture, they can also shred leaves and stunt growth. The most effective windbreak is semipermeable, such as a hedge, a row of trees, or a slatted fence. Unlike a solid wall of stone or brick, which produces strong downdrafts on the sheltered (or leeward) side, a semipermeable barrier filters and dissipates the force of fast-moving air.

> ❧
>
> March, 1790—
> A cold wind in
> this month
> killed all the
> peaches at
> Monticello.
>
> ❧
>
> — *Thomas Jefferson*

In general, a windbreak will protect an area of at least double its height. Trees and shrubs that may be used to thwart the wind include *Pseudotsuga menziesii* (Douglas fir), *Cupressus arizonica* (Arizona cypress), *Abies concolor* (Colorado fir), *Pinus strobus* (eastern white pine), *Elaeagnus angustifolia* (Russian olive), *Cupressus macrocarpa* (Monterey cypress), *Thuja occidentalis* 'Nigra' (American arborvitae), and *Picea abies* (Norway spruce).

Evergreen conifers (*LEFT*) offer a range of colors and shapes, from golden yellow dwarf *Thuja orientalis* 'Aurea Nana' (Berckman's Golden arborvitae), or globular blue-gray *Picea abies*, to deep blue-green *Pinus sylvestris* (Scotch pine). Their year-round presence makes them excellent windbreaks.

27

Sun
AND SHADE

Plants in this shady garden *(ABOVE)* receive almost no direct sun, but plenty of ambient light reaches them under the high tree canopy. Such a site makes a good home for woodland plants like azaleas. Sunlight drenches this garden *(ABOVE, RIGHT)*, and reflects off the stone paving. Sun-lovers like yellow *Coreopsis occidentalis* (lance-leaved tickseed) and orange-red *Alstroemeria aurantiaca* (Peruvian lily) can take the heat.

Whether choosing a site for a new garden or selecting plants for your landscape, one of your first tasks is to evaluate the light conditions at hand. When assessing how much sun a site receives, consider light variations during the day and in different seasons, as well as any shade that may be cast from structures such as sheds, trellises and walls, and hedges, shrubs, and trees.

It's wise to plan ahead for any changes in sun or shade patterns that may occur during the current growing season or even from one year to the next. In early spring, for example, bulbs will receive plenty of sunlight if planted beneath deciduous trees. Later in the season, after the trees have leafed out, the same area will be well suited to shade-loving, woodland plants.

Keep in mind that the structure of your garden will change as the season progress-es. Young trees and shrubs will cast shade over an expanding area as they continue to grow through the years. Remember to factor in a plant's mature height, spread, and growth rate. By midsummer, tall or densely leaved plants may shade short, sun-loving vegetables and flowers.

North-facing slopes, because they receive less sunlight, are cooler than south-facing slopes. South- or west-facing walls and fences, as well as light-reflective hardscapes such as driveways or patios, create heat pockets several degrees warmer than other areas of your landscape.

Light intensity is as important as the amount of light a site receives. In general, full sun indicates a location that receives at least 6 hours of direct sunlight between 9:00 a.m. and 4:00 p.m. As a rule of thumb, 3 hours of direct midday sun in the hottest zones are equivalent to 6 hours of sunlight in cooler zones. If you garden in a warmer climate or at higher elevations where the light is extremely intense, it's best to site full-sun plants in an area that receives morning sun and afternoon shade.

Partial shade describes an area with between 4 and 6 hours of direct sun each day, while full shade is the equivalent of fewer than 4 hours of direct sun. A large variety of woodland plants thrive in the dappled light of a partial-shade garden, including *Aquilegia* (columbine), *Polygonatum* (Solomon's-seal), *Fothergilla gardenii*, *Phlox divaricata* (wild sweet William), and most ferns. Plants that will grow in full shade include *Eupatorium rugosum* (white snakeroot), *Aucuba*, *Lamium maculatum*, *Convallaria* (lily of the valley), *Dennstaedtia punctilobula* (hay-scented fern), and the ornamental grass *Hakonechloa macra* 'Aureola'.

Dry shade challenges even the best of gardeners. This condition often occurs beneath trees with canopies so dense that rainfall is prevented from reaching the soil inside its dripline. If possible, thin and selectively prune low-hanging tree branch-

es to let in more light and rain, or increase the moisture retention of your soil by adding amendments such as leaves, compost, or rotted manure.

Plants that thrive in dry shade environments include *Hedera helix* (English ivy), *Vinca minor* (periwinkle), night-blooming *Matthiola longipetala* (evening stock), *Mahonia aquifolium* (Oregon grape), *Phlox stolonifera* (creeping phlox), *Brunnera macrophylla* (Siberian forget-me-not), *Ilex cornuta* 'Burfordii' (Burford holly), *Aquilegia canadensis* (wild columbine), *Aster divaricatus* (white wood), and *Myrica cerifera* (wax myrtle).

If you garden in arid climates where dry shade may be accompanied by high heat and low humidity, try planting *Hosta lancifolia* (narrow-leaved hosta), *Epimedium* (barrenwort), *Helleborus foetidus* (hellebore), and *Skimmia*.

Spring-blooming daffodils thrive beneath deciduous trees which remain leafless during the bulbs' active growth period. The daffodils' foliage takes up nourishment through photosynthesis and stores it in the bulbs. By late spring, the daffodil foliage has withered, and the bulbs become dormant until the next year.

Ground-WORK

An indication of the type of soil conditions favored by nasturtiums is this clump of naturalized nasturtiums growing in fast-draining, alkaline sandy gravel on the California coast.

Good soil is the foundation of all successful gardens. There are literally thousands of variations on the basic types of soil across the country—from porous, fast-draining, gravelly soil common to California's Coastal Range to the rich, sweet loam of the South's Cumberland Plateau.

Not only does soil vary from region to region, but different areas of your property may have very different types of soil. Closer to your house, where organically rich topsoil was probably scraped away during construction, you may find a layer of compacted hardpan not far below the surface. If your property includes an established woodland, the soil is likely to be a rich blend of composted leaves, twigs, and other organic matter deposited over time.

It is important to know your basic soil type before deciding which plants to try in your garden. While it's always a good idea to create the best possible soil for your plants, there are a variety of plants for any soil type. Native plants will be particularly well adapted to the soil in your region. As a rule of thumb, it is easier to match plants to your soil than it is to modify your entire soil structure to fit a plant's requirements.

If you're starting a new garden, it's a good idea to send samples of your soil to a testing service, such as your local county cooperative extension. This service will report on nutrients and pH—a measurement of the soil's acidity or alkalinity based on a scale of 1 (very acid) to 14 (very alkaline), with pH 7 as the neutral midpoint. In general, pH readings of 6.5 to 7.0 suit the widest range of plants.

Soil texture greatly affects a plant's health. In well-structured soil, the particles form a connective web of pores, where water, nutrients, and air circulate and are made easily accessible to foraging roots. An ideal soil for many plants is loam—a lightly textured, friable balance of sand, organic matter, and clay.

> When fully 'cooked' it looks like the blackest, richest soil in the world—or a devil's food cake.
>
> — Eleanor Perenyi, on 'Compost'

Sandy soil is free-draining and often infertile, and will dry out quicker than other soils due to its large, loose-fitting particles. On the other hand, clayey soil is densely packed and nutrient-rich, and tends to flood after a hard rain. The waterlogged conditions of clay can eventually destroy many plants: If drainage is too slow, vital oxygen

Hemerocallis (daylily)

will be replaced by water in the pores of the soil. Plants may then weaken and wilt, and eventually suffocate.

Improving Your Soil

Gardeners have long sung the praises of compost. Most agree that there is never enough to go around, and many gardeners keep more than one compost bin in use during the growing season. Unless you're blessed with deep, rich loam, you'll probably want to amend your soil with compost, leaf mold, peat moss, or other types of organic matter. These amendments will improve the texture of your soil as well as provide a nutritious boost for growing plants.

Both sandy and clayey soils can be greatly improved by the addition of organic matter. Keep in mind that periodically you'll need to add fresh organic matter, as it is continuously decomposing. Generous amounts of compost, aged manure, or leaf mold worked into the top 12 to 18 inches of sandy soil act as a sponge between large sand particles, greatly increasing moisture retention. Clayey soils benefit from the addition of coarse, fibrous organic matter, which helps to aerate the soil and increase drainage.

Water-holding polymers are a recently developed soil additive particularly suited to dry, sandy soil. The most effective of these polymers—cross-linked polyacrylamides—are small beads that expand into gelatinous material when wet. Polymers absorb and store up to 400 times their weight in water. Roots are then slowly dampened as the polymers release the stored water.

Hard work unloading soil-improving leaf mold pays off. Decomposed leaves are rich in nutrients and increase the soil's capacity to retain moisture.

31

The Many
USES OF MULCH

Think of organic mulch as nature's elegantly designed climate-control system for your soil. In winter, a protective mulch acts as a thermal blanket by insulating against sudden freezing and thawing. And during the hot summer months, hardworking mulch regulates soil temperature, retains root-zone moisture, reduces light reflectivity (which, in turn, keeps leaves and stems cool), blocks the growth of water-guzzling weeds, prevents runoff, and improves the texture and water-holding capacity of the soil as the mulch begins to decompose.

As an added bonus, mulch can be used as a design feature to create distinct zones within your landscape. A small mulched area around trees and shrubs will protect them from lawn mower damage, while shredded hardwood mulch on flower beds and borders clearly defines and separates planted areas from the lawn. Mulch is also an inexpensive, attractive ground cover for paths or utility areas in the landscape.

Types of Mulch

Acidic pine needles are well suited to many woodland plants, including azaleas, ferns, rhododendrons, and camellias. Shredded bark, straw, dried grass clippings, hairy vetch, and leaf mold are all effective mulches for a variety of flowers and vegetables. For decorative and landscaping purposes, coarse bark and shredded hardwood are two of the most popular mulches.

Many herbs, alpine wildflowers, and other plants native to hot, arid climates tend to prefer light-colored sand or gravel mulch. These mulches are less moisture-retentive and will reflect light and heat, helping to create the hot, dry conditions suited to these plants. This is especially useful in climates where the summers are hot and very humid. In areas of frequent, misty rains and cloud

cover, heavy mulches may lead to plant disease and rot.

The most commonly used inorganic mulches are black plastic and landscape fabric. Keep in mind that neither will provide nutrients to the soil, as do organic mulches. Black plastic should be used with caution, as it excludes air and moisture from the soil beneath and can be unsightly unless covered with mulch. It will, however, prevent weed growth and help the soil retain warmth through the night—particularly useful in cooler climates to hasten the warming of the soil. Landscape fabric is expensive and labor-intensive to install, but it is useful in controlling erosion on steep slopes and preventing weeds.

Applying Mulch

The best time to add mulch to your garden is in the spring, after the soil has warmed and you have removed all perennial weeds and weed roots. In general, a 2- to 3-inch layer works well for temperature control and moisture retention. When applying mulch around perennials and low-growing shrubs, rake it an inch or two away from the plant stems and trunks to

prevent rot. If you garden in warm, humid climates, keep in mind that the decomposition process takes place much quicker than in cooler, drier climates. You should either use coarser mulch or be prepared to replenish fine-textured mulch during the growing season.

If you are planting annuals or vegetables by seed, a good rule of thumb is to apply mulch after seedlings are up and growing, since putting mulch down too early may prevent spring sunlight from warming the ground sufficiently for germination. Also, mulching is not recommended for wildflower gardens where the majority of native flowering plants are spring-blooming annuals. These plants self-seed in early spring and then disappear by May. Mulch would only thwart the growth of the next year's seedlings.

The gravel mulch (*FAR LEFT*) in this arid Albuquerque, New Mexico, garden helps preserve the dry conditions and cool roots that cholla cactus, santolina, *Chrysothamnus nauseosus* (rabbit bush), and blue *Penstemon strictus* (Rocky Mountain penstemon) need to thrive. Bark mulch (*ABOVE*) makes a good, inexpensive walking surface in the pathways of this formal garden. However, you will have to add fresh bark every year.

Techniques
FOR SUMMER SURVIVAL

Sun-loving herbs such as yellow santolina, low-growing thyme, and purple *Veronica officinalis* can tolerate a good deal of heat and drought, but in the warmest regions they will do better if you add humus or peat to improve the soil's moisture retentiveness.

Almost every gardener, at some point, will face the challenges of gardening during periods of intense heat or spells of drought. *(See U.S. drought map, page 43.)* Too much sun and heat, particularly in periods of little or no rainfall, will cause many plants to dry out, wilt, temporarily stop growing (a condition known as heat-check), or eventually die back as the soil temperature increases.

Choosing plants appropriate to your heat zone is especially critical to your plants' health during periods of intense heat and/or diminished rainfall. You may be able to "stretch" a plant's zone by creating a cooler microclimate within your landscape. But if faced with a heat wave, water restrictions, periods of drought, or other inclement summer conditions, such plants may not survive. Keep in mind, as well, that young plants and transplants are the most vulnerable and will require extra water and perhaps a bit of improvised shade until their root systems are well established.

While many plants thrive in direct sun, extremely high temperatures, coupled with periods of little or no rainfall, will stress all but the toughest of plants. When planting and maintaining your garden, there are a few special techniques you can use to help keep plants healthy in the face of summer's extremes.

PRUNING When setting out new plants, lightly prune or pinch back any unnecessary or leggy growth, weak or broken stems, or dried foliage. This will strengthen the plant, reduce transpiration, and decrease water demand.

PLANTING When planting, keep the

> I have learned much from other people's gardens, and the lesson I have learned most thoroughly is never to say 'I know'— there is so infinitely much to learn.
>
> — *Gertrude Jekyll*

number of plants in an area to a minimum. With fewer plants, there will be more room for roots to develop and less competition for available moisture. In warm, humid climates, the improved air circulation will help prevent fungal diseases.

FERTILIZING Fertilize with a light hand. Overfertilization accelerates a plant's growth rate and, in turn, increases its requirement for water. Frequent and heavy applications of nitrogen and potassium will promote fast, soft growth in plants, making them more susceptible to the stresses of drought and high summer temperatures. Phosphorous, on the other hand, encourages root growth and the development of stocky, tough plants. Plants that thrive in drought conditions, such as *Rosmarinus officinalis* (rosemary), *Santolina* (lavender cotton), and *Cistus* (rock rose), should not be fertilized at all.

ANTITRANSPIRANTS While most often used to protect tender plants going into winter, antitranspirants work equally well in reducing water loss from plants during the summer. Wax- or latex-based antitranspirant sprays reduce water loss by sealing the microscopic openings, or stomata, in a plant's foliage. Apply antitranspirants during periods of moderate temperatures, before summer gets under way, and keep in mind that you'll need to reapply the spray as your plants grow.

LINERS To keep the root zones of shallow-rooted plants cool and moist, lay perforated plastic sheeting beneath the planting holes. The plastic liner will help prevent water from leaching out into the surrounding dry soil. You can also place strips of plastic sheeting between rows of plants or around a single plant to increase water retention.

For mass plantings in the summer, choose water-thrifty plants that do not compete for moisture when water levels are low, such as yellow *Achillea filipendulina* 'Moonshine' and lavender-blue salvia 'May Night'.

Creating SHADE

Unlike its cultivated cousins, *Rhododendron periclymenoides* (Pinxterbloom azalea) has a loose and open form, and subtle color that suit a woodland garden perfectly.

Shade acts as a soothing balm to the summer garden. In regions with weeks of fierce heat, gardeners consider naturally occurring shady areas a lucky happenstance— and a necessity for plants and gardeners alike. In gardens where shade doesn't exist, it is created. Trees are planted, arbors are covered with scrambling vines, and fabric row covers shelter tender transplants from the scorching midday sun.

Gardeners in all climates can appreciate the practical benefits of shade gardening. Less watering, weeding, mulching,

and pruning are required, and the cooling effect of large trees can drastically cut air-conditioning costs. In addition, many of our most beautiful and unusual native plants are shade-loving, including *Erythronium* (trout lily), *Dicentra* (bleeding heart), *Polygonatum* (Solomon's-seal), *Passiflora lutea* (passionflower), and clove-scented *Rhododendron viscosum* (swamp azalea), which flourishes throughout the forested East Coast and as far west as Mississippi.

EASY-CARE SHADE TREES

Acer rubrum 'October Glory' (red maple)

Betula nigra 'Heritage' (Heritage river birch)

Carpinus caroliniana (American hornbeam)

Cladrastis kentukeya (yellowwood)

Fraxinus pennsylvanica 'Marshall's Seedless' (green ash)

Ginkgo biloba (ginkgo)

Nyssa sylvatica (black tupelo, sour gum)

Quercus phellos (willow oak)

Q. rubra (red oak)

Sophora japonica (Japanese pagoda tree)

Tilia cordata (littleleaf linden)

Zelkova serrata (Japanese zelkova)

Trees

Trees are the real workhorses of a garden. Not only do they provide a soaring vertical element to the garden, they also screen buildings and roads, buffer traffic noise, clean the air by taking in carbon dioxide and putting out oxygen, and serve as

the single greatest cooling agent in a hot summer landscape. (The temperature beneath a venerable old oak may be as much as 10 to 15 degrees cooler than in a sunny area.) In addition, deep-rooted trees use very little water from the topsoil, tapping groundwater or moist subsoil instead.

While trees may be the most expensive plants in your land-

scape, they are also long-lived and require very little maintenance once established.

For the most advantageous summer cooling, plant large shade trees on the south or southwest side of your house. *(See list, opposite)*

Keep in mind that the quality of shade will vary, depending upon the density and size of the leaves as well as the tree's shape. The

> A large shade tree may release into the atmosphere 100 gallons of water on a hot day, and its cooling effect is equal to that of five average-sized air conditioners running 24 hours constantly.
>
> ❧
>
> — *Thomas Christopher,*
> Waterwise Gardening

(TOP, LEFT TO RIGHT) Betula jaquemonti 'White Spire' (white-barked Himalayan birch) has chalk-white bark and its foliage turns bright yellow in fall. *Cladrastis* (yellowwood) is covered in pendant flower clusters in the summer. *Acer rubrum* (red maple) turns deep red in autumn. Red wild columbine *(ABOVE)* and blue *Phlox divaricata* (wild blue phlox) spread in a sun-dappled shade garden.

The airy branches and fine foliage of a ficus *(ABOVE, LEFT)* makes a lacy silhouette in this La Jolla, California, garden. The climbing rose 'New Dawn' *(ABOVE, RIGHT)*, growing up an arbor in this Alabama garden, can become a long-lived architectural feature.

pyramidal evergreen *Juniperus virginiana* 'Canaertii' (eastern red cedar), for example, casts a narrow, dense shadow year round, while the red maple's high canopy of overlapping foliage creates a wide circle of summer shade—just the spot for a garden bench or swing. Smaller ornamental trees such as *Cornus kousa* (Kousa dogwood) and *Cercis canadensis* (redbud) can be used to broaden your plant palette. When sited in the midst of perennials, these trees create a small area of dappled light preferred by many woodland natives and spring-flowering bulbs. Small, quick-growing trees ideal for patio shade in arid climates include the drought-tolerant southwestern natives *Cercis occidentalis* (western redbud), *Cercidium* 'Desert Museum' (paloverde), and *Chilopsis linearis* (desert willow).

Climbing Vines

Climbing vines are colorful, versatile, and given to great effects in a brief amount of time. Grown on arbors, pergolas, or trellises, vines not only cast cooling shade onto a garden's hot spots but also provide vertical accents, bursts of color, screening, and privacy.

For the impatient gardener, annual

vines are particularly useful as temporary summer shade: Many species leaf out, bud, and grow 20 feet or more in a matter of weeks. And, if you're dissatisfied with the performance of one species, you can always sample another the next year. Annual climbers that quickly grow to a height of 10 feet or more include purple-flowered *Dolichos lablab* (hyacinth bean), *Phaseolus coccineus* (scarlet runner bean), *Cobaea scandens* (cup-and-saucer vine), *Passiflora coccinea* (red passionflower), *Humulus japonicus* (Japanese hop), and the scented, night-blooming *Ipomoea alba* (moonflower).

For more permanent shade, choose perennial species such as *Aristolochia durior* (Dutchman's-pipe), *Parthenocissus*

quinquefolia (Virginia creeper), *Clematis, Akebia quinata* (fiveleaf akebia), *Wisteria floribunda* (Japanese wisteria), *Campsis radicans* (trumpet creeper), and *Polygonum aubertii* (silver-lace vine). Evergreen or semi-evergreen vines include *Bignonia capreolata* (trumpet flower), *Ficus pumila* (creeping fig), and *Gelsemium sempervirens* (yellow jasmine). Keep in mind that perennial vines need periodic upkeep and pruning to keep them looking their best.

The annual vine, *Dolichos lablab* (hyacinth bean) *(ABOVE, LEFT)* is growing in Thomas Jefferson's garden at Monticello just as it did in his day. Wisteria vines *(ABOVE, RIGHT)* straddle an arbor, casting shade in the summer.

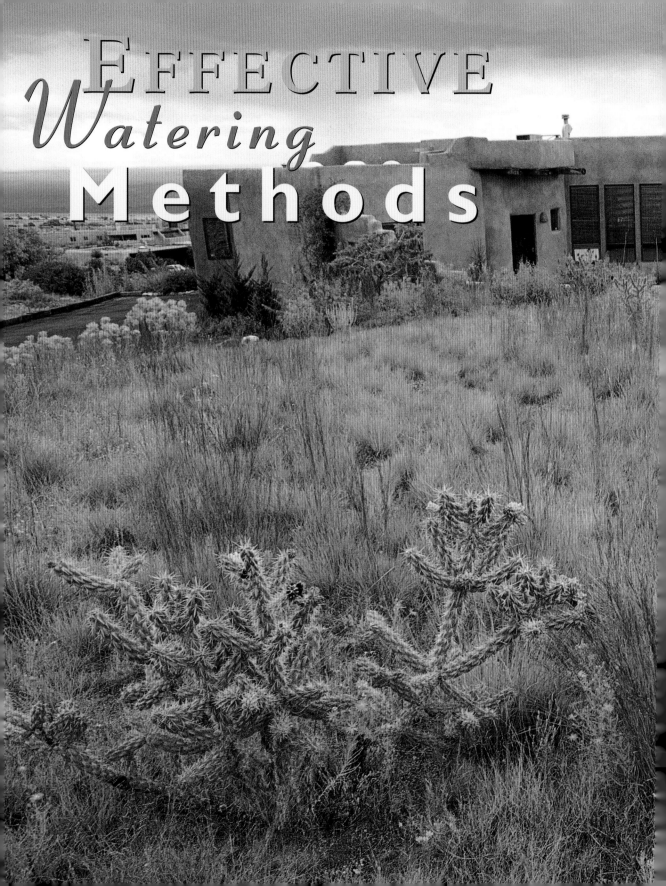

EFFECTIVE
Watering
Methods

There are two ways to face the rainless weeks.
One is to water, and the other is merely not to.

—Elizabeth Lawrence,
A Southern Garden

THERE ARE NO HARD-AND-FAST RULES FOR WATERING.

Knowing how—and when—to irrigate your garden has become increasingly complicated in a world of overburdened water supplies and weather extremes.

It is a thing of the past to simply pick up a garden hose and water copiously—and daily. In the future, more of us will be gardening hand in hand with local legislation that periodically restricts our use of water for landscaping purposes. The wise gardener must ensure that water is used only when needed, and plants must be chosen with their watering needs in mind.

Waterwise GARDENING

Watering is the gardener's most critical chore. Plants simply cannot survive without water—whether provided by the grace of nature or the gardener's hose. Unfortunately, the amount of water available for landscaping purposes is declining as both population and industry continue to grow. In addition, unpredictable weather patterns, including erratic rainfall or extended drought during the growing season, are now common throughout most of the United States, and it is likely that our water

resources will be even more taxed during the next century. *(See map, opposite.)*

For gardeners who live in humid climates, watering may be necessary only during the occasional heat wave or prolonged dry spell. Those who garden in marginal or arid regions, however, must be prepared to provide supplemental water to their landscape throughout most of the growing season unless they grow plants adapted to such conditions.

Wherever we garden, it is becoming increasingly important to use water responsibly. Even in areas with ample precipitation, municipal water levels may be dangerously low. In Florida (heat zones 11-9), for example, a warm, moist climate provides almost year-round gardening opportunities in the central and southern parts of the state, where over 55 inches of rain falls per year (in comparison to a scant 8 inches per year in some areas of California). However, while summers are moist, winters (the peak tourist season) are most often dry. The strain on water supplies during the winter is extreme, and as a result, many districts in Florida have passed legislation restricting landscape water use.

Assessing Your Water Needs

Whether due to climate, limited time, or community-imposed water restrictions, today's gardeners must learn to water their gardens sparingly. The first step toward efficient watering is to create an irrigation plan based on the specific needs of your garden. How large is your garden or landscape? How much rainfall does your area receive? Are you subject to periods of drought or heavy flooding? Do you have sandy, fast-draining soil that will require more frequent watering, or is your garden on a new site that has compacted, impenetrable soil? Are restrictions imposed on landscape irrigation in your community? Finally, just how much supplemental watering is practical in terms of your own energy, your concern for the environment, and rising water costs?

After careful consideration, you may decide to save a small area near your house for a few water-demanding favorites, and plant the remainder of your landscape with low-maintenance, native American plants or new, drought-resistant varieties of perennials, trees, and shrubs. Keep in mind, however, that even water-thrifty species and cultivars will require supplemental irrigation until they are well established, and other plants will need extra watering during prolonged dry spells.

DROUGHT POTENTIAL IN THE CONTINENTAL UNITED STATES

ARID
Subject to extended periods of drought

MARGINAL
Subject to both extended and brief periods of drought

HUMID
Subject to occasional periods of drought

HUMID
Sufficient water at all times

Creating Water Zones
IN YOUR GARDEN

Plant thirsty hydrangeas (*ABOVE*) in a high-water-use zone. Drought-tolerant yellow *Achillea* (yarrow), *Miscanthus* (eulalia), and sage (*BELOW*) all thrive in a low-water-use zone.

An important part of waterwise design is planning your landscape in terms of water use—a process known as "zoning." This concept is both practical and simple: By grouping plants with similar water needs, irrigation will be more efficient, and thus less work for the gardener.

Unlike regional climatic zones, water zones are created by gardeners to match the needs and conditions of their particular landscape. In general, it's best to plan for as few zones as possible to simplify your watering chores, whether you water with hoses, sprinklers, or an installed irrigation system. Most gardens can be divided into high, moderate,

and low zones based on water needs.

When planning your garden's zones, you can create transitions between each zone with plants that tolerate a range of moisture levels. Excellent plants for transitional areas include *Hemerocallis* (daylily), *Boltonia asteroides, Lamium, Miscanthus sacchariflorus* (silver banner grass), *Monarda* (bee balm), and the shrubs *Viburnum tinus* and *Clethra alnifolia* (summersweet).

High-Water-Use Zones

In general, high-water-use beds are located closer to the house, where plants are easier both to water and to enjoy. This soothing, green oasis is just the place for all your thirstier species, shallow-rooted plants, lawn grass, and container plantings, which dry out quickly and may need daily watering in warmer climates. Here you might also place shrubs such as *Rhododendron canadense* (native to damp, open woods in the northeastern United States), *Hydrangea macrophylla*, and the intensely fragrant *Daphne odora*. Moisture-loving perennials for this zone include *Amsonia tabernaemontana* (bluestar), *Iris ensata* (Japanese iris), *Hosta*,

Dicentra eximia (bleeding heart), *Primula* (primrose), *Phlox divaricata* (wild blue phlox), *Astilbe*, *Lobelia cardinalis* (cardinal flower), and plumed *Matteuccia struthiopteris* (ostrich fern). If you're planning a kitchen garden, it should also be included here, as vegetables require a great deal of moisture to support their rapid growth.

Moderate-Water-Use Zones

Moderate zones are areas where you water mainly during times of climatic stress, such as heat waves, high winds, or prolonged dry spells. For the most part, plants chosen for these areas should thrive on average rainfall and be fairly adaptive to occasional dry soil, unlike plants in high-water-use zones, which require consistently moist soil. You may select from a variety of plants for these areas in your garden, including *Gypsophila paniculata* (baby's-breath), *Dianthus barbatus* (sweet William), *Anemone canadensis* (meadow anemone), *Iberis amara* (rocket candytuft), *Bergenia purpurascens* (saxifrage), *Chrysopsis falcata* (yellow aster), and the shrubs

Hamamelis virginiana (witch hazel) and *Cornus mas* (Cornelian cherry).

Low-Water-Use Zones

With careful planning, low-water-use areas can be even more striking (and require much less work) than other parts of your garden. Once plants are established, they should thrive on natural rainfall as much as possible. These areas can be stocked with native trees, shrubs, and wildflowers, as well as drought-resistant plants from other regions. In low-water-use beds and borders, which are often located farther from your house than other water-zone areas, try to include plants with striking flowers, foliage, or texture. The shrubs *Potentilla fruticosa* 'Katherine Dykes', *Berberis thunbergii* 'Rose Glow' (barberry), and *Buddleia davidii* (butterfly bush) will give your garden substance. Interesting, colorful perennials might include *Salvia azurea* ssp. *pitcheri* (Pitcher's sage), *Sedum spectabile* 'Autumn Joy', silvery-leaved *Perovskia atriplicifolia* (Russian sage), *Liatris spicata* (spike gay-feather), *Echinacea purpurea* (coneflower), *Yucca filamentosa*, and red-flowered *Achillea millefolium* 'Fire King' (yarrow).

Dianthus barbatus (sweet William) *(TOP)* IS amenable to moist conditions and the occasional dry spell. *Sedum* 'Autumn Joy' *(MIDDLE)* IS drought tolerant, and both hosta and astilbe *(BOTTOM)* thrive in high-water-use zones.

The Fine Art
OF WATERING

A watering can with a specially-fitted nozzle is the best way to gently spot-water tender young plants until they mature and toughen.

Knowing when to water your plants is an acquired skill, one that requires careful observation of your garden's soil, weather, and plants. While seasoned gardeners may have learned from experience when their plants need water, most of us benefit from a few basic guidelines.

An important part of waterwise gardening is knowing how to "read" your landscape for signs of water shortage. All plants show signs of stress when they are suffering from a lack of water. You may notice reduced growth; poor flower or fruit production; drooping, limp, or slightly curled leaves; or subtle changes in foliage color. Parched lawns are easy to spot: growth slows down, grass blades change to a dull, bluish hue (and eventually turn brown), and the turf will retain footprints when walked upon.

Keep in mind that some heat-sensitive plants, such as basil and hydrangeas, may wilt dramatically in strong midday or afternoon sun, even though the soil around their roots remains moist. If wilted plants perk up in the cool of the

An in-ground sprinkler system is used in late afternoon to avoid excess water evaporation in this Calistoga, California, garden.

evening, you'll know that no supplemental watering is needed.

The best way to ensure a water-thrifty landscape is to include a majority of drought-resistant plants in your garden plan. *(See list, page 48.)* Even then, however, you'll need to pay particular attention to any newly planted trees, shrubs, and perennials. Consistent, deep watering is critical until transplants have established a root system and can fend for themselves—a year or so for perennials, and two or more years for shrubs and trees. As plants mature, progressively deeper (and less frequent) watering will encourage the roots to penetrate down into the soil, helping them survive an occasional heat wave or dry spell in good condition. Once established, drought-resistant plants may need only minimal watering—or even none at all—depending upon your soil and climate. Many water-thrifty plants may actually be damaged by too much water. *Tropaeolum* (nasturtium) and *Lantana,* for example, will produce fewer flowers and more foliage if kept constantly moist. In fact, all plants will eventually rot if persistently overwatered.

It's always best to check your plant's root-zone moisture level if you're unsure when to water. Checking the moisture level is also important whenever there are high winds, temperatures above 86°F, or periods of little or no rainfall. You can do this by digging down 4 to 6 inches with a trowel and feeling the soil. If the soil is dry, a deep watering is in order. A good rule of thumb for thirstier plants (those in high- and moderate-water-use zones) is to irrigate to a depth of 12 inches—twice a month for woody plants, and every 7 to 10 days for perennials. The best time to water is during the early morning, when temperatures are cooler and evaporation will be minimal.

Sun-loving, drought-tolerant lantana *(LEFT)* is allowed to dry out between waterings, and thus blooms profusely. However, the nasturtium *(RIGHT)* produces few blooms as a result of being overwatered.

47

Plants for a Dry Garden

Perennials

Achillea
(yarrow)

Anaphalis
(pearly everlasting)

Euphorbia corollata
(flowering spurge)

Chrysopsis mariana
(Maryland golden aster)

Galega officinalis
(goat's rue)

Helianthus mollis
(downy sunflower)

Hemerocallis
(daylily)

Kniphofia
(torch lily)

Liatris punctata
(spotted gay-feather)

Oenothera spp.
(evening primrose)

Rudbeckia
(coneflower)

Sedum spp.
(stonecrop)

Solidago spathulata
(goldenrod)

Tulbaghia violacea
(society garlic)

Trees and Shrubs

Acer platanoides
(Norway maple)

Betula jacquemontii
(Himalayan birch)

Cercis siliquastrum
(Judas tree)

Crataegus pedicellata
(scarlet hawthorn)

Forestiera neomexicana
(desert olive)

Mahonia aquifolium
(Oregon grape)

Myrica pensylvanica
(bayberry)

Myrtus communis
(myrtle)

Philadelphus spp.
(mock orange)

Prunus maritima
(beach plum)

Quercus coccifera
(Kermes oak)

Schinus molle
(pepper tree)

Spiraea spp.
(spirea)

Symphoricarpos spp.
(snowberry)

Ground Covers

Bergenia
(bergenia)

Carpobrotus acinaciformis
(Hottentot fig)

Cytisus procumbens
(broom)

Euphorbia amygdaloides
var. *robbiae*
(wood spurge)

Gazania
(gazania)

Iberis sempervirens
(candytuft)

Liriope muscari
(lilyturf)

Potentilla fruticosa
(shrubby cinquefoil)

Sedum acre
(gold-moss sedum)

Stachys byzantina
(lamb's ears)

Teucrium chamaedrys
(germander)

Trachelospermum
(star jasmine)

Vinca major
(periwinkle)

These plants revel in the sun and tolerate dry conditions. (*TOP ROW FROM LEFT*) Prairie plants such as purple *Liatris* (gay-feather), pink cosmos, and orange calendulas make a splash in this Colorado garden. Other prairie flowers include pink daisy-like *Echinacea* (coneflower) and yarrow. Grassy *Liriope muscari* 'Big Blue' ('Big Blue' lilyturf) grows in full sun as well as full shade. (*MIDDLE ROW FROM LEFT*) Tough yellow-blooming ice plants scramble over rocks and gravel. *Spiraea* x *bumalda* 'Goldflame' likes dry soil and open areas. *Forestiera neomexicana* (desert olive) is native from Texas to Colorado. (*BOTTOM*) A carpet of orange-red gazania spreads to a daylily border.

Choosing
A WATERING SYSTEM

A sprinkler (ABOVE) attached to a hose is one of the most versatile ways to irrigate your garden. Soaker hoses, on the other hand, can be threaded almost imperceptibly through your plants, as among the tulips at right, with less water loss through evaporation than sprinklers.

The best way to ensure a waterwise garden is to select plants that will thrive, for the most part, on the amount of rainfall you receive in your climatic zone. But since there will inevitably be times when you'll need to irrigate, the next step is to choose the most efficient watering system for your particular landscape.

Watering plants with a watering can or hand-held hose, while time-consuming, is still one of the best methods for irrigating container plantings, window boxes, raised beds, small urban gardens, or a few individual plants in hard-to-reach corners of your property. On the other hand, watering larger landscapes with a hand-held, high-pressure hose is both time-consuming and wasteful. Instead, you may choose from a variety of sprinklers or irrigation hoses for all your larger watering jobs.

SPRINKLERS When choosing a sprinkler, try to select a water distribution pattern that is well suited to your landscape's needs. Large areas of lawn, for example, would best be watered by forceful, far-reaching sprinklers such as oscillating or pulse-jet systems. Smaller areas, on the other hand, might require a static sprinkler that delivers low-pressure spray over a small, circular area. A fan-shaped misting sprinkler is ideal for seedlings, delicate flowers, and ground covers. When using a sprinkler system, keep in mind that sprinklers deliver water through the air rather than directly to plants' roots, where it is most needed. As a result, there may be up to a 70 percent water loss through evaporation. In most instances, slow-release drip or soaker irrigation systems offer a more efficient way to water.

oscillating

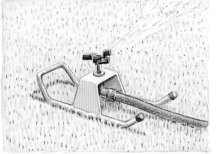

pulse-jet

static

fan

SPRINKLERS FOR YOUR GARDEN

Sprinklers are the best method of watering large areas, such as lawns or ground covers. Humidity-loving plants and young seedlings also benefit from sprinkling. If your soil is clayey, choose a sprinkler that delivers water gently. Otherwise, wasteful water runoff may be a problem.

SOAKER HOSES AND DRIP IRRIGATION

Among the most popular and effective methods of irrigation, soaker hoses and drip systems deliver water slowly and efficiently to the root zone. Experts estimate that, when used correctly, these systems can save up to 70 percent in outdoor water use. The slow release of water (approximately half a gallon per hour) allows moisture to soak in deeply, encouraging deep rooting and healthy plant growth. And, because the foliage doesn't get wet, there are fewer problems with fungal diseases. Soaker hoses ooze water along the entire length of their porous walls, while drip-irrigation systems emit water through tiny spouts along the length of the hose.

Both drip and soaker systems can be installed by the home gardener. You'll find a wide variety of basic, low-cost kits that include all the valves, feeder lines, and other attachments necessary to set up either type of system. If you travel often, have a weekend home, or are simply too busy to monitor your watering daily, you may choose to purchase an automatic timer that controls the irrigation system according to a programmed schedule.

A drip irrigation system (LEFT) through a bed of young pepper plants gently irrigates the tender root systems without getting foliage wet. This can greatly reduce the incidence of mildew and other destructive funguses.

The New
American
GARDEN

In this great country, although we may
speak the same language and
watch the same television programs
and read the same magazines,
we really live in very different climates.
How could our gardens ever be the same?

— *Carole Ottesen,*
The Native Plant Primer

WHOLE NEW SPIRIT IS CHANGING
the American garden. With less time for
garden chores, as well as an increased commitment
to "garden lightly on the earth," we're making the
best possible use of what our landscapes—and climates—have to offer. American gardeners are asking
more questions and spending more time planning
before planting. And, when it comes to good garden-
making, we're taking our cues from nature. We're
unabashedly mixing native plants with hardworking
species from around the world, with one firm
requirement: Each plant must be well suited to our
gardens, wherever we happen to live.

The Right Plant
FOR THE RIGHT PLACE

If even a fraction of America's 38 million gardeners turned a quarter of their landscape into a re-wilded spot that recalls, at least roughly, its pre-settlement state, there would be a measurable impact. If every gardener gave just one tenth of an acre back, the instant net gain would be 3.8 million acres of native plants.

—Ken Druse
The Natural Habitat Garden

Native plants like pink *Eupatorium maculatum* (Joe-Pye weed) *(LEFT)* and prickly-pear cactus *(RIGHT)* have become valuable additions to the garden.

American gardeners are taking a down-to-earth approach to garden design. More and more, we're veering away from all those prima donnas of the plant world and seeking out plants that will largely take care of themselves.

Practical plants, however, are anything but boring. True to our great democratic spirit, American gardeners think nothing of mixing native Texas bluebonnets, Kansas gay-feathers, and Carolina allspice with South American *Portulaca* or the latest new cultivar of Japanese *Hosta*. And, while our hearts may be won by a plant's beauty, we realize that all is lost if it fails to thrive. With this in mind, we're careful to choose "the right plant for the right place"—those plants uniquely suited to

Mertensia virginica
(Virginia bluebell)

our climatic zones and our garden's growing conditions.

Native Plants

Native American plants—those species indigenous to our country's forests, prairies, coastlines, and deserts—are as tough and independent as American pioneers. Beautiful, tolerant of neglect, and easy to maintain, native plants are the foundation of environmentally responsible gardens from coast to coast. American gardeners have one of the richest plant populations of any continent—North America has over 6,000 species of gardenworthy wildflowers, as well as thousands of native trees, grasses, and shrubs.

Keep in mind, however, that the

native plant palette for Virginia is not the same as that for New Mexico. The first step in selecting native plants and wildflowers for your garden is to compare your growing conditions to those where the plants grow wild. Do the plants naturally thrive in warm, humid woodlands or on salt-sprayed, sandy coastlines? Do they prefer stream banks or sunny, dry hillsides? Spring-flowering *Erythronium americanum* (trout lily), which grows wild in the leafy litter of the

Rhododendron maximum
(rosebay rhododendron)

forest floor, for example, can't be expected to live if planted in a hot, sun-baked area of your garden.

Some native plants are more adaptable than others and can be cultivated successfully over a wide geographical area and range of climates. *(See list, page 58.)* For example, *Rhododendron maximum* (rosebay rhododendron) is native to mountain ranges extending from Maine down through the southern Appalachians and will grow happily in

This Rocky Mountain garden with dry sandy soil is home to native flowers, starting in spring with pale yellow *Scutellaria* (scullcap), lavender *Salvia* (sage), golden yellow *Eschscholzia californica* (California poppy), and a local native, purple *Penstemon strictus* (Rocky Mountain penstemon).

partially to deeply shaded woodland gardens in USDA hardiness zones 3-8 and
AHS heat zones 9-1. Other
plants, including most
endangered species, have a
narrow range of adaptability. Although *Sequoia* (red-
wood), for example, falls
within USDA hardiness

zones 7-9 and AHS heat zones 9-3, only
in its native site on the western slopes of
the Sierra Nevadas in California do we
find that the seedling becomes the majes-
tic tree we all admire.

Keep in mind that collecting native
plants from the wild is not only harmful
to the habitat but it may
also disrupt the reproduc-
tive cycles of endangered
plant species. When shop-
ping for native plants,
look for the term "nursery
propagated" in catalogs or
on plant labels, and if in doubt, simply
ask how a nursery gets its plants.
According to the National Wildflower
Research Center in Austin, Texas, 600
North American native plant species are
in danger of extinction, and thousands
more are threatened by the loss of native
habitats and irresponsible collectors who
dig up plants from the wild. *(For sources
of more information on native plants, see
Sources, page 183.)*

Hardworking Nonnatives

The key to finding the best plants for your
garden lies in knowing their origins. As a
rule of thumb, when choosing nonnative
plants for your garden, seek out those
that come from climates similar to yours.
Many species indigenous to the

Mediterranean, as well as parts of Australia, New Zealand, and South Africa, are well suited to gardens in California and parts of the Southwest. *Origanum* (marjoram), *Lavandula stoechas* (French lavender), *Laurus nobilis* (bay laurel), *Rosmarinus officinalis* (rosemary), *Cistus* spp. (rock roses), *Capparis spinosa* (caper bush), *Ficus carica* (fig), *Salvia argentea* (silver sage), and *Eucalyptus* spp. are just a few hardworking nonnatives that thrive with very little care in regions with poor soil and hot, dry summers—as well as in sun-baked niches in more temperate climates.

Gardeners in the central and eastern areas of the country share a continental climate with parts of Europe, China, and Japan. Many of our most popular low-maintenance plants derive from these regions. *Hosta, Hemerocallis* spp. (daylilies), and *Hydrangea macrophylla* all hail from Japan, while *Lilium lancifolium* (tiger lily), *Pyracantha* (firethorn), and *Rhododendron fortunei* are natives of China. European natives suited to easy-care American gardens include *Calendula officinalis* (pot marigold), *Campanula* spp. (Canterbury bells), *Hesperis matronalis* (sweet rocket), *Digitalis purpurea* (fox-glove), *Achillea* (yarrow), and *Viola tricolor* (Johnny-jump-up).

Digitalis purpurea (fox-glove) traveled from Europe and Britain to the United States with the earliest settlers, as it was valued as a medicinal plant. It has since settled comfortably into American gardens, like this one in Virginia.

WILDFLOWERS AND NATIVE PLANTS

CLIMATE-ADAPTABLE NATIVE PLANTS

Lobelia cardinalis

Many species of native plants can be grown in a wide range of climates. Threadleaf coreopsis, for example, will bloom all summer in sunny gardens in the Midwest, Southwest, and eastern North America, in USDA hardiness zones 4-9 and AHS heat zones 12-1.

Allium cernuum
(nodding onion)

Amsonia tabernaemontana
(bluestar)

Aquilegia canadensis
(wild columbine)

Baptisia australis
(wild blue indigo)

Coreopsis verticillata
(threadleaf coreopsis)

Dicentra eximia
(wild bleeding heart)

Filipendula rubra (meadowsweet)

Helianthus x *multiflorus* 'Flora Pleno' (sunflower)

Heuchera micrantha
(common alumroot)

Iris prismatica
(slender blue flag)

Lobelia cardinalis
(cardinal flower)

Lysimachia ciliata
(fringed loosestrife)

Oenothera fruticosa
(sundrops)

Penstemon digitalis
(beardtongue)

Rudbeckia hirta
(gloriosa daisy)

Tiarella cordifolia
(foamflower)

Yucca filamentosa
(Adam's-needle)

HEAT-LOVING, LONG-BLOOMING WILDFLOWERS

Many garden-worthy wildflowers will bloom for a month or more, providing continuous color during even the hottest summer days.

Boltonia asteroides 'Snowbank'
(boltonia)

Callirhoe involucrata
(prairie winecup)

Coreopsis verticillata
(threadleaf coreopsis)

Echinacea purpurea
(purple coneflower)

Eschscholzia californica
(California poppy)

Gaillardia x *grandiflora*
(Indian blanket)

Gaura lindheimeri
(gaura)

Geranium maculatum
(wild geranium)

Helianthus annuus 'Italian White' (sunflower)

Heuchera sanguinea
(coral bells)

Liatris microcephala
(small blazing star)

Linum perenne ssp. *lewisii*
(blue flax)

Lobelia siphilitica
(great blue lobelia)

Lupinus texensis
(Texas bluebonnet)

Gaillardia aristata

Mirabilis multiflora
(giant four-o'clock)

Oenothera caespitosa
(white evening primrose)

Penstemon canescens
(beardtongue)

Phacelia campanularia
(California bluebell)

Phlox paniculata
(garden phlox)

Ratibida pinnata
(prairie coneflower)

Romneya coulteri
(Matilija poppy)

Rudbeckia subtomentosa
(sweet black-eyed Susan)

Stokesia laevis

Ruellia humilis
(wild petunia)

Silene armeria
(catchfly)

Solidago caesia
(wreath goldenrod)

Stokesia laevis
(Stokes' aster)

Verbena canadensis
(rose verbena)

Zinnia grandiflora
(Rocky Mountain zinnia)

HUMIDITY-LOVING NATIVE PLANTS

Jefferson grew *Helianthus angustifolius* at Monticello

Hot weather in the United States ranges from steamy "dog days" in the Deep South to scorching, dry summers in the Southwest. Plants that perform well in arid climates may suffer from rot or fungal diseases in moister regions. The following native plants are well suited to hot, humid summer gardens.

Amsonia hubrectii
(Arkansas bluestar)

Baptisia australis
(blue false indigo)

Chrysopsis mariana
(Maryland golden aster)

Eupatorium fistulosum
(Joe-Pye weed)

Euphorbia corollata
(flowering spurge)

Helianthus angustifolius
(swamp sunflower)

Heuchera americana
(alumroot)

Hibiscus coccineus
(red mallow)

Iris fulva
(red flag iris)

Lobelia cardinalis
(cardinal flower)

Oenothera fruticosa
(sundrops)

Phlox subulata
(moss pink)

Tiarella cordifolia
(foamflower)

Verbena canadensis
(rose verbena)

Verbena canadensis

Designing for
THE 21ST CENTURY

Faced with changing climatic conditions, increased population and development, and the rising costs of water, a primary focus of 21st-century garden design will be water thriftiness.

In an attempt to reduce their dependency on supplemental water, American gardeners have already begun to redefine what constitutes good garden design.

Great expanses of irrigation-dependent lawn and high-maintenance plantings are gradually being transformed into natural landscapes that primarily include indigenous trees, shrubs, and perennials. Self-sufficient wildflowers are finding their way into perennial beds; front yards are being redesigned as woodland oases with native trees and shrubs; and more gardeners are turning to waterwise designs such as courtyard gardens, container plantings, and rock gardens. The prototype of this new gardening style—the New American Garden—was installed at the U.S. National Arboretum in Washington, D.C., in 1987.

Lawns

While lawns provide soothing unity to the landscape, the traditional beauty of a well-groomed lawn is not without costs in upkeep and labor. Lawns planted in conventional turf grass demand more water than any other planting. In addition, fertilizers, herbicides, and pesticides regularly used in lawn maintenance may prove harmful to the environment. Many pesticides destroy beneficial insects as well as pests, and the chemical mix of herbicides and nonorganic fertilizers may eventually filter into underground aquifers, polluting valuable reserves of groundwater.

The size and shape of a lawn affect both maintenance and irrigation needs. Clearly, a smaller lawn area demands less water and upkeep. Areas that are difficult to maintain, such as driveway

> The lawn may well not survive a long period of environmental activism—and no other single development would do more for the American garden. For as soon as someone decides to rip out a lawn, he or she becomes, perforce, a gardener, someone who must ask the gardener's questions: What is right for this place? What do I want here? How can I go about creating a pleasing outdoor space on this site? How can I use nature here without abusing it?
>
> —Michael Pollan

boundaries, irregularly shaped strips of lawn, or steep banks, can be replanted with drought-resistant species, ground covers, or native plants. You may also consider replacing high-maintenance turf with native grasses such as buffalo grass or blue grama or taller meadow grasses. These durable grasses require few nutrients and little or no watering, even during extended periods of drought and soaring summer temperatures.

In a shady location where grass is hard to grow, such as this wooded property in Virginia, evergreen *Vinca minor* (periwinkle) *(ABOVE, LEFT)* makes a good, low-maintenance ground cover. Buffalo grass *(ABOVE, RIGHT)* has become a popular lawn grass in the arid West, as in this Santa Fe, New Mexico, lawn. An added bonus, it only reaches 4 to 6 inches and needs little mowing.

Creating a Flowery Lawn

An easy-care, pretty solution to difficult land-scape areas, such as a narrow strip of lawn running beside your driveway or an awkwardly shaped side yard, is to slowly replace areas of high-maintenance turf grass with low-growing wildflowers or ground covers.

Begin by adding multiples of a single species planted in irregular drifts. If you like the effect, add more low-growing plants such as *Viola labradorica*, *Crocus ancyrensis*, *Tulipa*

Ice plant lawn

humilis, *Chionodoxa*, and *Antennaria alpina* (alpine everlasting).

If you decide to use taller plants, you might try *Iris tenax* (Oregon iris), *Lupinus texensis* (Texas bluebonnet), *Achillea millefolium* (common yarrow), *Phacelia campanularia* (California bluebell), *Aster novae-angliae* 'Purple Dome' (New England aster), *Eschscholzia californica* (California poppy), or *Callirhoe involucrata* (prairie winecup).

The irregularly shaped, gravel-filled stones of this patio near Denver, Colorado, becomes the perfect site for rock plants that like quick-draining soil and dry conditions. Tucked between the stones are various dianthus, blue *Veronica prostrata* (hare-bell speedwell), and red-dish pink *Phlox subulata* (moss pink).

Hardscapes

Paved areas in the landscape—often referred to as hardscapes—are clean, durable, and virtually maintenance-free. Patios or terraces provide a transition between house and garden, and in small city gardens, paved surfaces create a more polished look for garden "rooms."

Hardscapes are especially beneficial to gardeners in hot, dry climates. Paving provides a low-maintenance alternative to lawns or other plantings that require irrigation. In addition, hardscapes decrease the amount of moisture lost from the soil by evaporation, and any water runoff from paved areas can be directed to nearby planting beds.

When choosing paving materials, keep in mind that light-colored stones or concrete may create a glare in strong sunlight. Concrete can, however, be tint-ed in a variety of colors to achieve a more subdued effect. Brick is one of the most popular kinds of garden paving. Often used in city gardens, brick can be laid in a variety of patterns and attains an aged, mossy look in shady areas.

Ready-cut stone—usually limestone, granite, sandstone, or slate—is especially suited to naturalistic settings. A stone terrace can be softened by the effect of low-growing plants tucked into small pockets of soil between the stones. The dry, open space of a stone terrace is an ideal setting for many sun-loving plants, including the Mediterranean natives *Lavandula*, *Thymus serpyllum* (creeping thyme), *Helichrysum* spp., *Santolina chamaecy-parissus* (lavender cotton), and *Rosmarinus officinalis* 'Prostratus' (pros-trate rosemary).

Slopes

Gardening on slopes will try the patience of even the most stalwart gardener. Not only are slopes difficult to mow and maintain, they are inevitably dry and often nutrient-deficient. In regions where summer brings periodic downpours, valuable topsoil is often swept away by fast-flowing water. In addition, rainwater has no chance to percolate down to the root zones of plants. And, if water eventually penetrates to the roots, it may tend to pool at the base of the slope.

There are a number of plants, however, that can be used to control erosion and water runoff. Plants with fibrous, spreading roots such as *Calamintha grandiflora* (calamint), *Phlox subulata*, *Galium verum* (bedstraw), *Ruta* (rue), and *Origanum vulgare* (wild marjoram) will all help control erosion. Wildflowers that thrive on sunny, dry banks include *Aster novae-angliae* (New England aster), *Melampodium* (blackfoot daisy), *Eschscholzia californica* (California poppy), *Penstemon strictus* (Rocky Mountain penstemon), and *Coreopsis lanceolata* (lanceleaf coreopsis). If the base of your slope is typically moist, try wildflower plantings of *Iris fulva* (copper iris), *Asclepias incarnata* (swamp milkweed), *Iris versicolor* (blue flag), *Hibiscus coccineus* (rose mallow), and *Lobelia cardinalis* (cardinal flower).

You can easily create a small rock garden among stone outcroppings on your slope. Waterwise plants that will

thrive in dry crevices on a sunny south- or west-facing slope include *Silene pindicola* (campion), *Cerastium tomentosum* (snow-in-summer), and *Achillea ageratifolia;* South African natives *Delosperma nubigerum* (ice plant), *Osteospermum fruticosum* (South African daisy), and *Pelargonium* spp.; and many Mediterranean natives, including *Salvia officinalis* (sage), *Cistus* spp. (rock rose), *Santolina chamaecyparissus* (lavender cotton), *Aphyllanthes monspeliensis*, *Thymus* spp. (thymes), and *Aurinia saxatilis* (basket-of-gold).

If your slope is extremely steep, however, you may want to consult a professional landscape architect for advice. Changing the grade of a landscape by terracing or constructing retaining walls is an ambitious project best left to a professional.

The steep rocky bank along a stairway leading to the front of this Colorado house is host to a vast assortment of flowering sedums, such as pink *S. spurium* (two-row stonecrop) and yellow *S. kamtschaticum*. The best way to plant this type of garden is to insert the plants between the stones as they are being set in place.

Container Gardens

Container gardens make it possible to grow plants far beyond the confines of your site and climate. New Englanders can enjoy flame-tinted *Croton* and sweet-scented gardenias all summer, then carry them into the house or greenhouse before the first frost. Likewise, gardeners in hot, dry climates can satisfy their yen for thirstier plants by selecting a few favorites for special treatment. Extra water, shade protection at midday, and the use of spacious planters filled with rich, moisture-retentive soil can help ensure the health of water-thirsty container plants grown in an arid climate.

Providing adequate water is the most important chore for a container gardener, as the soil in pots and planters will dry out much quicker than soil in the garden. It is best to check

A stone basket *(ABOVE)* with *Hebe* 'Variegatum' and creeping *Lysimachia nummularia* 'Aurea' (golden creeping Jenny) makes a composition in yellow. In a wooden tub *(ABOVE, RIGHT)*, spiky agave and *Hesperaloe parviflora* (red hesperaloe) contrast with the fluffy pink spirea. Purple-blue trailing lobelia *(RIGHT)* spills out of a formal stone urn.

your plants each morning and apply water if the top 2 inches of soil feel dry to the touch. If planters are located in full sun, many plants will wilt slightly in the afternoon and pick up again as the sun sets.

Keep in mind that terra-cotta pots will dry out more quickly than plastic. To reduce evaporation, place your planted pot inside a larger container and insulate the space between with perlite or sphagnum moss. Water evaporating from the outer pot will help cool the soil in the inner pot.

Large terra-cotta pots dot this Virginia garden, adding spots of color. At the center is a potted *Paulownia tomentosa* (princess tree) and in the back, a multi-stemmed potted *Populus alba* (white poplar). Tender potted plants can be brought inside for winter.

SMALL TREES AND SHRUBS FOR CONTAINER PLANTING

Many trees and shrubs thrive when planted in large containers, at least 16 inches in diameter. Use a loamy, light-weight soil mix, and be prepared to water often during hot, dry weather. Apply a slow-release fertilizer at the time of planting to provide low, sustained nutrients for 3 to 6 months. Trees and shurbs may need to be repotted as they grow larger. Wheeled bases are available for large planters so that potted trees can be moved about to create a bit of shade wherever you like.

Acacia baileyana
(golden mimosa)

Acer palmatum
(Japanese maple)

Arbutus unedo
(strawberry tree)

Buddleia davidii
(butterfly bush)

Cercis canadensis 'Forest Pansy'
(redbud)

Chamaecyparis obtusa
(Hinoki false cypress)

Citrus limon
(lemon)

Clethra barbinervis
(Japanese clethra)

Cornus alba 'Sibirica'
(Siberian dogwood)

Gleditsia triacanthos 'Inermis'
(thornless honey locust)

Hamamelis virginiana
(witch hazel)

Hydrangea macrophylla
(French hydrangea)

Ilex vomitoria 'Pendula'
(weeping yaupon holly)

Laburnum x *watereri* 'Vossii'
(golden-chain tree)

Lagerstroemia indica
(crape myrtle)

Nandina domestica
(heavenly bamboo)

Thuja occidentalis
'Emerald Green'
(American arborvitae)

Plant Profiles

Flowers really do intoxicate me.

❧

— Vita Sackville-West

*P*RESENTED HERE IS A SELECTION OF PLANTS THAT INCLUDES*
both North American native plants as well as easy-care plants from around the
world. The plants were chosen for their ornamental qualities, ease of cultivation, and
availability. Each genus is listed by its Latin botanical name, followed by the common
name. (If you know a plant only by its common name, refer to the index.) Each brief
description includes the plant's cold and heat-zone ranges, mature height, type, soil, and
light and maintenance needs.*

*Keep in mind that new heat- and drought-resistant cultivars are constantly being intro-
duced, while some cultivars may no longer be available. For that reason, these entries
concentrate on information regarding the genus. Refer to the USDA Plant Hardiness and
the AHS Plant Heat-Zone maps on page 19 to determine the climatic zones for your region
before selecting plants from our Plant Profiles.*

*In the coming months, you will see the addition of heat zones on plant labels as well as
in reference books and nursery catalogs. Each plant will be assigned four numbers. For
example, hosta will be 4-9 (USDA hardiness zone) and 9-2 (AHS heat zone). If you live in
USDA hardiness zone 7 and AHS heat zone 7, for example, hosta would be an excellent
choice for your climate.*

*It will take several years for a majority of our garden plants to be coded. After almost 40
years, we are still perfecting the zone ratings for the USDA Plant Hardiness Map. Plants
vary in their heat stress tolerance, not only from species to species, but also from cultivar
to cultivar. In addition, unusual seasons—fewer or more hot days than normal—will
invariably affect results in your garden, as will extremely dry or humid conditions. Due to
the many factors that complicate a plant's reaction to heat, we expect gardeners to find
that many plants will survive outside their designated heat zone.*

Abelia (a-BEE-lee-a)

ABELIA

USDA Hardiness: zones 5-9
AHS Heat: zones 12-6
Height: 3 to 6 feet
Plant type: shrub
Soil: moist, well-drained, acid
Light: partial shade to full sun

Abelia's fountainlike sprays of small, pointed, richly green leaves are bronze when young and often turn bronze or bronzy purple again in fall. Tiny bell-shaped or tubular

Abelia x *grandiflora*

flowers, which attract bees and butterflies, bloom from early summer to frost. In the northern parts of its range, abelia is semi-evergreen. *A.* x *grandiflora* (glossy abelia) is a rounded shrub 3 to 6 feet high (to 8 feet in the South) and equally wide, with small pinkish white flowers. Abelia has few pests and diseases, and flowers best when provided with at least a half-day of sunlight each day. It tolerates less-than-ideal soil. Abelia will tolerate humidity.

Acacia (a-KAY-sha)

ACACIA, SILVER WATTLE

USDA Hardiness: zones 9-11
AHS Heat: zones 12-1
Height: 20 to 60 feet
Plant type: tree
Soil: well-drained to dry
Light: full sun

Acacias are natives of Australia, where they thrive in the dry, tropical climate. Typically, each flower is composed of a mass of stamens

Acacia dealbata

that form a dense cluster. Though not long-lived, these trees are remarkably fast growers and may reach 30 feet in only 5 years. *A. dealbata* (silver wattle) grows 30 to 60 feet tall with silvery leaves and silvery bark, and extremely fragrant yellow flowers. Acacias require warm climates and, once established, tolerate both drought and seaside conditions.

Abies (AY-beez)

FIR

USDA Hardiness: zones 3-7
AHS Heat: zones 7-2
Height: 30 to 50 feet or more
Plant type: tree
Soil: moist to dry, well-drained
Light: full sun

Ideal as a pyramid-shaped screen or vertical accent, the upper branches of white fir grow upright in habit; the middle and lower, horizontal to descending. *A. concolor*

Abies concolor

(white fir, Colorado fir) reaches 30 to 50 feet high by 15 to 30 feet wide, having a central trunk with whorled branches and producing bluish green, grayish green, or silvery blue needles up to 2½ inches long; 'Compacta' is a densely branched dwarf cultivar usually 3 feet high. Although white firs tolerate dry, rocky soils, they grow better in deep, sandy or gravelly loams. They withstand drought, heat, cold, and air pollution better than other firs. They tolerate light shade but fare best in full sun. Mulch well with shredded bark, woodchips, or leaves.

Acanthopanax (a-kan-tho-PA-naks)

FIVE-LEAF ARALIA

USDA Hardiness: zones 4-8
AHS Heat: zones 9-3
Height: 8 to 10 feet
Plant type: shrub
Soil: well-drained
Light: full sun to full shade

Five-leaf aralia is an excellent plant for difficult sites. The arching, wide-spreading stems form a broad, rounded

Acanthopanax sieboldianus

shrub, but it can be sheared to produce a dense hedge. Its bright green compound leaves appear in early spring and persist late into fall. *A. sieboldianus* has five to seven leaflets per leaf and light brown stems; 'Variegatus' has leaves with creamy white margins. Five-leaf aralia tolerates a wide range of soil types, from acid to alkaline and from sandy to clay, and it stands up well to air pollution and drought.

Acanthus *(a-KAN-thus)*
BEAR'S-BREECH

USDA Hardiness: zones 8-11
AHS Heat: zones 12-1
Height: 3 to 4 feet
Plant type: perennial
Soil: well-drained, acid
Light: full sun to partial shade

Bear's-breech forms spreading clumps of broad, shiny, deeply lobed leaves up to 2 feet long and tall, stiff spikes of tubular flowers borne well above the foliage in summer.

Acanthus mollis 'Oakleaf'

The flowers and seed heads are effective in arrangements. Give bear's-breech the full sun it loves except where summers are hot, when some shade is advisable. Tolerant of moderate drought, bear's-breech abhors wet winter soil. Once established, this plant is difficult to remove from a site, as bits of fleshy roots inadvertently left behind easily grow into new plants.

Achillea *(ak-il-EE-a)*
YARROW

USDA Hardiness: zones 4-9
AHS Heat: zones 9-2
Height: 6 inches to 4½ feet
Plant type: perennial
Soil: well-drained, poor
Light: full sun

Flat-topped flower clusters form above green or gray-green fernlike foliage. Long-lasting when cut, the flowers also dry well. *A. filipendulina* (fernleaf yarrow) has yellow

Achillea 'Moonshine'

flower clusters up to 5 inches across; *A.* 'Coronation Gold' is a hybrid with 3-inch deep yellow flower clusters. *A. millefolium* (common yarrow) has cultivars in shades from pink to red; 'Red Beauty' has broad crimson flower clusters. Yarrow tolerates southern heat and dry conditions.

Acer *(AY-ser)*
MAPLE

USDA Hardiness: zones 2-9
AHS Heat: zones 10-3
Height: 6 to 75 feet
Plant type: shrub, tree
Soil: moist, well-drained
Light: full sun to partial shade

This genus includes a diverse group of deciduous plants ranging from towering trees with brilliant fall foliage to small, picturesque specimens ideal as centerpieces for or-

Acer griseum

namental beds. Most maples can withstand occasional drought; red maples grow naturally in wet soil. *A. rubrum* 'Autumn Blaze' is said to be slightly more drought tolerant than true red maple cultivars. *A. palmatum* 'Bloodgood' is a heat-tolerant cultivar; 'Dissectum' (threadleaf maple) often shows leaf burn in hot, dry climates; find a spot sheltered from strong winds, late spring frosts, and searing sun.

Aconitum *(ak-O-NY-tum)*
MONKSHOOD

USDA Hardiness: zones 3-8
AHS Heat: zones 8-3
Height: 2 to 5 feet
Plant type: perennial
Soil: moist, well-drained, fertile
Light: partial shade to full sun

Flowers resembling tiny helmets bloom along the tips of stiffly erect stems. Monkshood's coarsely textured clumps of lobed leaves blend well at the edges of wood-

Aconitum columbianum

lands or in the back of a border among ferns and hostas. The roots are poisonous. Plant monkshood in early fall, 18 inches apart, with the crowns just below the surface in soil enriched with organic matter. Leave undisturbed. Propagate from fresh seed.

Acorus calamus 'Variegatus'

Acorus *(AK-o-rus)*
SWEET FLAG

USDA Hardiness: zones 3-11
AHS Heat: zones 12-2
Height: 1 to 5 feet
Plant type: perennial
Soil: moist
Light: full sun to partial shade

The creeping rhizomes of sweet flag thrive in wet soils along stream banks or in aquatic gardens. The grass-like leaves smell of tangerine; the rhizomes have a spicy cinnamon aroma prized in potpourri. Once used in herbal medicine, sweet flag is now considered hazardous. It is being researched as an insecticide. *A. calamus* (sweet flag) has sword-shaped leaves up to 5 feet tall and tiny yellow-green flowers. *A. gramineus* is a heat-tolerant species. Plant sweet flag in a constantly moist site, even under as much as 2 inches of water. It can be propagated from seed, but the seed must not be allowed to dry out. Otherwise, divide rhizomes in spring or fall.

Aeonium *(ee-OH-nee-um)*
AEONIUM

USDA Hardiness: zones 9-11
AHS Heat: zones 9-4
Height: 1 to 3 feet
Plant type: perennial
Soil: light, well-drained
Light: full sun

Aeoniums bear fleshy leaves in attractive rosettes and flower clusters in shades of yellow. *A. arboreum* 'Schwartzkopf' bears golden yellow flowers and dark, shiny, purple-black leaves. *A. tabuliforme* produces pale yellow flowers. Aeoniums thrive in California coastal conditions, where their soil and light needs are best met, and they enjoy high humidity and mild temperatures. They can be grown farther inland, but may require some shade for protection from midday heat. They do not tolerate frost.

Aeonium arboreum
'Schwartzkopf'

Adiantum capillus-veneris

Adiantum *(ad-ee-AN-tum)*
MAIDENHAIR

USDA Hardiness: zones 7-11
AHS Heat: zones 9-3
Height: 12 to 24 inches
Plant type: perennial
Soil: moist, well-drained, acid
Light: partial to full shade

Delicate maidenhair ferns provide a fine-textured embellishment to shade gardens when massed as ground covers, used as fillers among larger plants, or allowed to cascade over the edges of banks and walls. They also do well as container specimens for patio use. *A. capillus-veneris* (southern maidenhair) has deep green deciduous fronds with glossy purple-black stems and broad, triangular leaflets composed of tiny fan-shaped segments. Sow maidenhair spores or set out divisions of the fern's slender rhizome in spring; spores take 6 weeks to germinate. Keep ferns moist; plants that dry out completely may shed their fronds, although these will regrow when moisture reaches normal levels.

Aesculus *(ES-kew-lus)*
BUCKEYE

USDA Hardiness: zones 3-7
AHS Heat: zones 8-4
Height: 20 to 40 feet
Plant type: tree
Soil: moist, well-drained, slightly acid
Light: full sun to partial shade

The buckeye is a low-branched, round-topped tree with deep green five-fingered compound leaves that turn a vibrant orange in fall. The pest-resistant buckeyes cast deep shade, discouraging the growth of grass below. The seeds are poisonous. *A. glabra* (Ohio buckeye, fetid buckeye) grows 20 to 40 feet tall with an equal spread, bears medium to dark green leaflets 3 to 6 inches long that open bright green, followed by flower panicles up to 7 inches long. *A. x carnea* (red horse chestnut) grows to 40 feet and bears flowers ranging from flesh-colored to scarlet.

Aesculus x *carnea*

Agapanthus
(ag-a-PAN-thus)
LILY-OF-THE-NILE

USDA Hardiness: zones 8-11 or
    tender
AHS Heat: zones 12-1
Height: 18 inches to 5 feet
Plant type: bulb
Soil: moist, well-drained
Light: full sun

Agapanthus x 'Headbourne
Hybrids'

Domed clusters of five-petaled, star-shaped flowers with prominent stamens rise on leafless, hollow stalks from graceful clumps of straplike evergreen leaves that persist after the flowers fade. *A. africanus* 'Albus' (African lily) has clusters of 30 or more white flower stars in the summer. *A.* x 'Headbourne Hybrids' has sky blue to deep blue blooms on 3- to 4-inch stalks; can be evergreen in warmer climates. In colder areas, grow plants in pots, moving them indoors before frost. They bloom best when slightly potbound.

Agave *(a-GAH-vay)*
CENTURY PLANT

USDA Hardiness: zones 9-11
AHS Heat: zones 12-5
Height: 18 inches to 40 feet
Plant type: perennial
Soil: well-drained to dry, sandy
Light: full sun

Century plant's rosettes of coarse, spiny evergreen leaves are accentuated—generally at the end of the plant's long life—by erect, often extremely tall stalks bearing

Agave parryi

heavy spikes of fragrant flower bells. *A. americana* (American aloe) has arching, blue-green leaves in mounds 6 feet wide. *A. attenuata* (foxtail agave) has rosettes of waxy, pale green leaves up to 5 feet across. *A. parryi* has rosettes of powdery gray-green leaves up to 3 feet across. Protect young plants from frost and winter moisture.

Agastache *(a-GAH-sta-kee)*
GIANT HYSSOP

USDA Hardiness: zones 4-11
AHS Heat: zones 12-5
Height: 2 to 5 feet
Plant type: perennial
Soil: moist, well-drained
Light: full sun to light shade

Clumps of erect stems lined with fragrant leaves and tipped with spikes of colorful, edible flowers make giant hyssop a bold border accent. *A. barberi* has red-purple

Agastache foeniculum

flowers with a long season of bloom; 'Firebird' has copper-orange blooms; 'Tutti-Frutti', raspberry-pink to purple flowers. *A. foeniculum* (anise hyssop, blue giant hyssop, anise mint, licorice mint) has licorice-scented leaves and purple-blue flowers; 'Alba' has white blossoms. *A. foeniculum* prefers a dry, open site in full sun or partial shade. It is well suited to sandy soils and tolerates summer heat. Start seed indoors 10 to 12 weeks before the last frost. Established plantings self-sow; or propagate by division in spring or fall.

Ageratum *(aj-er-AY-tum)*
FLOSSFLOWER

USDA Hardiness: zones 10-11
AHS Heat: zones 12-1
Height: 6 to 30 inches
Plant type: annual
Soil: moist, well-drained
Light: full sun

A profusion of fluffy flowers with threadlike petals crown clumps of heart-shaped leaves. With soft colors and a compact mounding habit, dwarf varieties create excellent garden edgings. Taller

Ageratum houstonianum
'Fine Wine'

varieties combine well with other flowers in the middle or back of a border. *A. houstonianum* bears tiny blue or bluish purple flowers in dense, fuzzy clusters from summer through fall; 'Capri' bears blue flowers with white centers, and it is heat tolerant; 'Summer Snow' grows 6 to 8 inches tall with pure white flowers that begin early and continue to frost. Flossflowers brown in extreme heat; dead material should be removed and the soil fertilized.

Agonis (a-GO-nis)
PEPPERMINT TREE

USDA Hardiness: zone 10
AHS Heat: zones 12-6
Height: 25 to 35 feet
Plant type: tree
Soil: well-drained to dry
Light: full sun to partial shade

Agonis flexuosa

The peppermint tree is a fast-growing evergreen for warm climates. Its leaves are willowlike and are borne on graceful, arching branches. It is a good choice for a wide-spreading lawn tree, street tree, or large container plant. *A. flexuosa* grows to 35 feet, with an equal spread of deep green leaves; small white, fragrant flowers appear in early summer, followed by woody capsules; bark is an attractive reddish brown and vertically fissured. The peppermint tree requires a nearly frost-free location; it will die back to the ground if temperatures fall below 25°F. It thrives in warm coastal locations and is tolerant of most soils and moisture conditions.

Ajuga (a-JOO-ga)
BUGLEWEED

USDA Hardiness: zones 3-9
AHS Heat: zones 8-2
Height: to 12 inches
Plant type: perennial
Soil: well-drained, acid loam
Light: full sun to light shade

Ajuga reptans

An excellent ground cover, ajuga creates dense mats of attractive foliage that suppress weeds. The foliage, in shades of green, deep purple, bronze, or creamy white mottled dark pink, is topped by whorled flowers. *A. genevensis* (Geneva bugleweed) has blue, pink, or white summer flowers; *A. pyramidalis* (upright bugleweed) bears blue late-spring flowers; *A. reptans* (common bugleweed) bears violet flowers. Bugleweed grows equally well in sun or shade and is often evergreen in mild winters. However, plants may be prone to fungal disease in hot, humid conditions.

Akebia (a-KEE-bee-a)
CHOCOLATE VINE

USDA Hardiness: zones 4-8
AHS Heat: zones 8-3
Height: 20 to 40 feet
Plant type: perennial
Soil: well-drained
Light: full shade to full sun

Akebia quinata

Chocolate vine is equally good at covering ground or walls, quickly twining around anything close at hand. With its semi-evergreen foliage, it offers multiseason interest to the landscape. Purple fruit pods dangle abundantly from the plant in fall; in the spring, small fragrant flowers peep out from the new foliage. *A. quinata* (five-leaf akebia) has dark blue-green leaves and dark purple flowers, followed by purple fruit pods up to 4 inches long that ripen in late summer. A tough, vigorous plant, chocolate vine tolerates nearly any growing condition and can easily choke out other plants. Pruning is required to keep it under control.

Alcea (al-SEE-a)
HOLLYHOCK

USDA Hardiness: zones 3-9
AHS Heat: zones 10-3
Height: 4 to 9 feet
Plant type: biennial, perennial
Soil: well-drained
Light: full sun

Alcea rosea

Hibiscus-like, 3- to 4-inch-wide colorful flowers blooming in spires at the tips of hollyhock's erect stems make a bold statement in a summer border. *A. rosea* (garden hollyhock) has single- or double-petaled flowers in shades of white, yellow, pink, or purple. Although hollyhocks are a short-lived perennial, they are most commonly grown as biennials. Sow seed in spring or late summer for bloom in the second season. To coax a second bloom in fall from mature plantings, cut stems to the ground after plants bloom in summer and feed with any good garden fertilizer.

Alchemilla mollis

Alchemilla (al-kem-ILL-a)
LADY'S-MANTLE

USDA Hardiness: zones 3-8
AHS Heat: zones 7-1
Height: 12 to 18 inches
Plant type: perennial
Soil: moist, well-drained loam
Light: full sun to light shade

Lady's-mantle's sprays of tiny blossoms rise from low mats of attractive deeply lobed foliage that make it a good ground cover. The flowers are an excellent filler in arrangements and also dry well. *A. conjuncta* has pale green ⅛-inch flowers and star-shaped green leaves edged with silver; USDA zones 4-8. *A. mollis* has 2- to 3-inch clusters of chartreuse blossoms above crinkled, velvety leaves; USDA zones 4-7. In hot climates, select locations with partial shade.

Aloe (AL-oh)
ALOE

USDA Hardiness: zones 10-11
AHS Heat: zones 12-3
Height: 2 to 4 feet
Plant type: annual
Soil: well-drained, sandy
Light: full sun to light shade

Aloe barbadensis

Aloe produces rosettes of fleshy, pointed leaves that twist and arch to create architectural border specimens. Where aloe can be grown outdoors, plants produce a flower stalk in summer, but potted plants maintained indoors seldom bloom. The sap inside aloe leaves soothes burns and skin irritations. *A. vera* [also classified as *A. barbadensis*] (medicinal aloe, Barbados aloe, unguentine cactus) has mottled gray-green leaves up to 3 feet long and 3- to 4-foot-tall flower stalks with dense clusters of yellow to orange or red flowers. Water aloes infrequently.

Allium cernuum

Allium (AL-lee-um)
FLOWERING ONION

USDA Hardiness: zones 3-9
AHS Heat: zones 9-5
Height: 6 inches to 5 feet
Plant type: bulb
Soil: moist, well-drained, sandy
Light: full sun to partial shade

Related to edible culinary species, flowering onions produce showy flower clusters, usually in dense spheres or ovals composed of hundreds of tiny blooms packed tightly together, but sometimes in loose, dangling or upright airy domes of larger flowers. Alliums are striking as cut flowers or in dried bouquets. Some flowering onion species will naturalize, and a few are suitable for forcing. Rodent pests find the bulbs unappealing. Plant flowering onions in fall in northern zones, in spring or fall in warmer areas. Protect bulbs with winter mulch north of USDA zone 5. Allium will tolerate heat and dry soil.

Aloysia (a-LOYZ-ee-a)
LEMON VERBENA

USDA Hardiness: zones 8-11
AHS Heat: zones 12-6
Height: 2 to 8 feet
Plant type: shrub
Soil: average, well-drained
Light: full sun

Aloysia triphylla

The lemon-lime aroma of lemon verbena's leaves perfumes the garden from spring through fall. Use fresh leaves in cooking and dried leaves for tea. *A. triphylla* (lemon verbena) has whorls of lemon-scented leaves and loose clusters of tiny white to lilac late-summer flowers. Where frost is a possibility, cut stems to 6 to 12 inches in fall and provide protective winter mulch. Potted plants drop their leaves in winter and do best if moved outdoors during warmer months. Propagate lemon verbena from seed or from cuttings taken in summer.

Althaea officinalis

Althaea (al-THEE-a)
MARSH MALLOW

USDA Hardiness: zones 3-9
AHS Heat: zones 9-1
Height: 4 to 5 feet
Plant type: perennial
Soil: moist
Light: full sun

Marsh mallows create colorful border backdrops and temporary screens in marshy, wet garden sites. The tender young leaves, flowers, and the nutlike seeds contained in the plant's ring-shaped fruits can be used in cooking. Roots release a thick mucilage, which was once used in the original marshmallow confection. Sow seeds of marsh mallow in spring or divide in spring or fall, setting plants 2 feet apart. Keep marsh mallow's woody taproot constantly moist. Pick leaves and flowers just as the flowers reach their peak.

Amelanchier alnifolia

Amelanchier (am-el-ANG-kee-er)
SERVICEBERRY

USDA Hardiness: zones 4-9
AHS Heat: zones 8-3
Height: 15 to 40 feet
Plant type: large shrub, tree
Soil: moist, well-drained, acid
Light: full sun to partial shade

Serviceberry provides year-round landscape interest. White flower clusters appear in early spring; leaves emerge purplish gray and change to deep green in summer and from yellow to apricot and red in fall. The smooth gray bark is attractive all winter. Serviceberry is often found growing wild beside stream banks, at the edge of woodlands, or along fence rows. In the garden, it tolerates a broad range of moisture conditions.

Amaranthus caudatus

Amaranthus (am-a-RAN-thus)
AMARANTH

USDA Hardiness: zone 0
AHS Heat: zones 12-1
Height: 18 inches to 6 feet
Plant type: annual
Soil: dry to well-drained
Light: full sun

Amaranths are large, brilliantly colored tropical plants that add a bold touch to borders with their long-lasting tasseled flowers and colorful leaves. *A. caudatus* (love-lies-bleeding) grows 3 to 5 feet tall with huge drooping tassels of red flowers up to 2 feet long; 'Viridis' grows 2 to 3½ feet, with greenish yellow flower tassels. *A. cruentus* (purple amaranth, prince's-feather) produces drooping red or purple flower spikes. Seed requires very warm temperatures and can be started indoors 4 to 6 weeks prior to the last frost. In warm areas sow seed directly. Thin to allow 1 to 2 feet between plants. Water sparingly.

Amsonia tabernaemontana

Amsonia (am-SO-nee-a)
BLUESTAR

USDA Hardiness: zones 3-9
AHS Heat: zones 8-4
Height: 2 to 3 feet
Plant type: perennial
Soil: moderately fertile, well-drained
Light: full sun to partial shade

Amsonia produces pale blue star-shaped blossoms on willowlike leaves, providing a lovely foil for later-blooming perennials. *A. tabernaemontana* bears steel blue flower clusters; *A. t.* var. *salicifolia* blooms slightly later than the species. Amsonias grown in shade have a more open habit than those grown in sun. In poor to moderately fertile soil, amsonia stems rarely need staking; avoid highly fertile soil, which produces floppy growth.

Anaphalis triplinervis

Anaphalis (an-AFF-al-is)
PEARLY EVERLASTING

USDA Hardiness: zones 3-9
AHS Heat: zones 8-3
Height: 1 to 3 feet
Plant type: perennial
Soil: moist, well-drained loam
Light: full sun to light shade

Anaphalis bears flat clusters of fluffy ¼-inch flower buttons atop erect stems lined with narrow silvery leaves. It provides a gray-white accent in borders and is excellent for drying. *A. margaritacea* (common pearly everlasting) is 2½ feet tall, with slender leaves that are green on top and woolly gray underneath. *A. triplinervis* has pearly flowers above silvery gray leaves that turn a soft gray-green toward the end of summer. *A. margaritacea* tolerates drought.

Anemone (a-NEM-o-nee)
WINDFLOWER

USDA Hardiness: zones 5-9
AHS Heat: zones 9-3
Height: 3 to 18 inches
Plant type: bulb
Soil: moist, well-drained
Light: full sun to light shade

Anemone apennina

Windflowers carpet a border with drifts of daisylike flowers held above whorls of attractively divided leaves resembling flat parsley. Single or double rows of petals surround a prominent cushion of anthers in a contrasting color, often with a halo of cream or white separating it from the main petal color. *A. apennina* can be grown north of USDA zone 6 by setting tubers out in spring, then lifting them for storage in fall. Anemones need constant moisture, though not soggy conditions, to bloom at their best. Some need shade in USDA zones 7-9.

Andropogon gerardii

Andropogon (an-dro-PO-gon)
BLUESTEM

USDA Hardiness: zones 2-7
AHS Heat: zones 12-9
Height: 2 to 8 feet
Plant type: ornamental grass
Soil: dry, sandy to moist
Light: full sun

Bluestems are perennial bunch grasses found in prairies, open woods, and lowlands over much of the United States. The narrow leaves are blue-green in spring and summer and copper or maroon in fall. *A. gerardii* (big bluestem, turkeyfoot) bears purplish late-summer flower clusters. *A. glomeratus* (bushy bluestem) has silvery green to pinkish flowers surrounded by salmon sheaths in fall followed by fluffy white seed heads. *A. gerardii* grows best in a sandy loam and withstands periodic flooding. Bluestems tolerate clay soil and drought once established. Propagate by seed or division in the spring.

Anethum (a-NEE-thum)
DILL

USDA Hardiness: zones 0
AHS Heat: zones 12-1
Height: 3 to 4 feet
Plant type: annual
Soil: average to rich, well-drained
Light: full sun

Dill's aromatic feathery leaves and flat, open clusters of yellow summer flowers add delicate texture to garden beds. Dill also thrives in window-sill gardens. Both

Anethum graveolens

the seeds and the leaves are culinary staples; immature flower heads flavor cucumber pickles. *A. graveolens* (dill) has soft 3- to 4-foot stems lined with fine, threadlike foliage; 'Bouquet' is a compact cultivar producing more leaves than flowers. Sow dill seed in the garden and thin seedlings to stand 8 to 10 inches apart. Plants may need staking. Dill self-sows readily; remove flower heads to prevent self-sowing and to encourage leaf production.

Angelica gigas

Angelica *(an-JEL-i-ka)*
ANGELICA

USDA Hardiness: zones 4-9
AHS Heat: zones 8-2
Height: 3 to 8 feet
Plant type: biennial or short-lived
    perennial
Soil: rich, moist
Light: partial shade to full sun

Tall columns of coarse-textured, licorice-scented leaves and broad, flat clusters of tiny summer flowers make angelica a bold border specimen or backdrop. *A. gigans* grows to 6 feet tall, with 8-inch clusters of burgundy flowers. Angelica leaves, stems, and seeds are used in cooking, although some herbalists believe they may be carcinogenic. Do not attempt to collect angelica in the wild, as it closely resembles poisonous water hemlock. Sow very fresh angelica seed in the garden in spring or fall. Angelica self-sows readily; transplant seedlings before taproots become established.

Anthemis *(AN-them-is)*
CHAMOMILE

USDA Hardiness: zones 3-8
AHS Heat: zones 8-3
Height: 2 to 3 feet
Plant type: perennial
Soil: well-drained to dry, poor
Light: full sun

Chamomile bears daisylike blossoms 2 to 3 inches across amid mounded, aromatic gray-green foliage; these are excellent as border fillers or as cut flowers. Some anthemis are evergreen. *A. sancti-johannis* (St. John's chamomile) bears bright orange flowers on evergreen shrubs. *A. tinctoria* (golden marguerite, dyer's chamomile) has upturned, pale cream to deep gold petals rimming golden brown centers and is tolerant of both drought and heat; 'Kelwayi' has bright yellow flowers; 'Moonlight', pale yellow; 'E.C. Buxton', creamy white.

Anthemis tinctoria

Antennaria rosea

Antennaria *(an-te-NAY-ri-a)*
PUSSY-TOES

USDA Hardiness: zones 3-8
AHS Heat: zones 7-1
Height: 2 to 16 inches
Plant type: perennial
Soil: dry to moist, well-drained
Light: full sun

Pussy-toes form low-growing mats of attractive fuzzy leaves. Used as ground covers, they effectively control erosion on sunny banks. The fuzzy flower heads are silvery white or pink. *A. alpina* (alpine everlasting) is a western mountain native with white summer flowers; USDA zones 4-8. *A. rosea* (rose pussy-toes) is a western native with small, light pink flower clusters in spring; USDA zones 3-7. Grow alpine everlasting in moist, well-drained soil and the other species in dry soil. Antennarias make good ground covers and in ideal conditions may become invasive.

Anthriscus *(an-THRIS-kus)*
CHERVIL

USDA Hardiness: zones 0
AHS Heat: zones 6-1
Height: 1 to 2 feet
Plant type: annual, biennial
Soil: average, well-drained
Light: light to full shade

One of the fine herbs of French cuisine, chervil's finely divided leaves resemble parsley with a hint of warm anise flavor. *A. cerefolium* (chervil, salad chervil) forms mounds 1 to 2 feet tall of lacy bright green leaves topped by small, open clusters of tiny white flowers in summer. Chervil is an ideal outdoor container plant. Plant chervil in a location with plenty of shade and moisture. Sow seeds successively for a continuous supply of fresh leaves. Seeds sown in fall produce a spring crop. Remove flowers to encourage greater leaf production; alternatively, allow plants to go to seed and self-sow.

Anthriscus cerefolium

Antirrhinum
(an-tir-RYE-num)

SNAPDRAGON

USDA Hardiness: zones 8-11
AHS Heat: zones 12-1
Height: 6 inches to 4 feet
Plant type: tender perennial
Soil: well-drained, fertile
Light: full sun to partial shade

Antirrhinum majus

Snapdragons, with their wide range of heights and flower colors and long season of bloom, have been cultivated since ancient times. Short varieties add color to rock gardens and edgings, while taller types are well suited to the middle and rear of borders. *A. majus* bears terminal clusters of flowers that open from the bottom up. Each bloom has five lobes, divided into an upper and a lower lip. Varieties are classified by height: small (6-12 inches), intermediate (12-24 inches), and tall (2-4 feet). Start seed indoors in late winter for transplanting in mid- to late spring. Perennial in USDA zones 8 to 11.

Arabis *(AR-a-bis)*

ROCK CRESS

USDA Hardiness: zones 3-7
AHS Heat: zones 8-1
Height: 6 to 12 inches
Plant type: perennial
Soil: well-drained loam
Light: full sun

Arabis alpina

Low-growing rock cress, with its flat-faced single- or double-petaled ½-inch flowers, makes an excellent creeping ground cover for the border or rock garden. *A. alpina* 'Flore Pleno' has white, fragrant double-petaled flowers. *A. caucasica* (wall rock cress) 'Rosabella' is a compact 5-inch plant with rosy pink flowers. *A. procurrens* has sprays of white flowers above mats of glossy evergreen leaves. Rock cress is easily grown, but humid weather and standing water will cause rot. *A. procurrens* thrives in light shade as well as full sun.

Aquilegia *(ak-wil-EE-jee-a)*

COLUMBINE

USDA Hardiness: zones 4-7
AHS Heat: zones 9-3
Height: 8 inches to 3 feet
Plant type: perennial
Soil: moist, well-drained, acid loam
Light: full sun to shade

Aquilegia canadensis

The flowers of this beautiful and delicate wildflower come in many colors and bicolors, appearing in spring on erect stems; they are nodding or upright. Many species have a life span of only 3 to 4 years. *A. caerulea* (Rocky Mountain columbine) has blue and white flowers. *A. canadensis* (Canadian columbine) has nodding yellow and red flowers; *A. flabellata* 'Nana Alba' (fan columbine) grows pure white nodding flowers; *A. x hybrida* 'Crimson Star' bears bright red and white upright flowers. Columbines require good drainage. In full sun provide steady moisture; plants are intolerant of heat and drought.

Aralia *(a-RAY-lee-a)*

ARALIA

USDA Hardiness: zones 4-9
AHS Heat: zones 12-9
Height: 1 to 45 feet
Plant type: perennial, shrub, tree
Soil: dry to moist, acid, fertile
Light: partial to full shade

Aralia elata 'Variegata'

Aralias are perennials that grow in open woods over much of the United States. Their large compound leaves impart a lush appearance to a garden, and their berries attract birds to the garden. *A. elata* (Japanese angelica) is a large shrub or tree that grows to 45 feet. *A. nudicaulis* (wild sarsaparilla) bears greenish white flowers from late spring to early summer and purplish fall berries. Aralias thrive in open woods and require little care once they have become established. Wild sarsaparilla prefers a dryish soil, while spikenard prefers a moist, fertile one. Mulch for winter protection. Aralia will tolerate humidity.

Arbutus (ar-BEW-tus)

STRAWBERRY TREE

USDA Hardiness: zones 8-9
AHS Heat: zones 9-4
Height: 8 to 12 feet
Plant type: large shrub, tree
Soil: well-drained, acid
Light: full sun to partial shade

The strawberry tree provides interest to southern and West Coast gardens throughout the year. The leaves are evergreen, the bark is deep reddish brown and exfoliates, and the branches become attractively gnarled with age. Small urn-shaped flowers grow in 2-inch clusters in the fall, and the orange-red berrylike fruit ripens the following season. Plant where leaves will be protected from drying winds. The strawberry tree tolerates a wide range of soil conditions as long as drainage is good. It requires watering only during periods of drought. It is also tolerant of seaside conditions.

Arbutus unedo

Ardisia (ar-DEES-ee-a)

ARDISIA

USDA Hardiness: zones 7-10
AHS Heat: zones 12-3
Height: 8 inches to 6 feet
Plant type: shrub, ground cover
Soil: moist, well-drained, acid, fertile
Light: full shade

A lovely low evergreen for shady areas, ardisia has glossy dark green serrated leaves with small star-shaped flowers borne in summer, followed by berries that persist into winter. *A. crenata* (Christmas berry, coralberry, spiceberry) has lustrous foliage and bright red berries; *A. japonica* (marlberry) is a ground cover with lustrous dark green leaves, white flowers, and red berries, and is variably hardy to USDA zone 5 but best in USDA zones 7-9; 'Hakuokan' has broad, white leaf margins. Amend soil with leaf mold, peat moss, or compost. Provide protection from harsh winter winds. Variegated forms are less cold hardy than the green ones.

Ardisia crenata

Arctostaphylos uva-ursi

Arctostaphylos (ark-toh-STAF-i-los)

BEARBERRY

USDA Hardiness: zones 2-8
AHS Heat: zones 9-3
Height: 6 to 12 inches
Plant type: ground cover
Soil: well-drained, acid, sandy
Light: full sun to light shade

Bearberry's long trailing stems lined with tiny dark green oval leaves spread into low mats of evergreen foliage, making bearberry an ideal ground cover to control erosion on difficult rocky or sandy banks. Dangling flower clusters lining the stems in spring are followed by bright red oval berries in fall. Bearberry figures in herbal medicine. *A. uva-ursi* (common bearberry) produces slender arching stems to 5 feet long with tiny urn-shaped red-tinged white flowers. Sow bearberry seeds or set out rooted cuttings in spring, spacing plants 1 to 2 feet apart. Bearberry will tolerate dry conditions as long as it receives periodic deep watering.

Arenaria (a-ren-AIR-ee-a)

SANDWORT

USDA Hardiness: zones 5-9
AHS Heat: zones 9-6
Height: 2 to 8 inches
Plant type: perennial
Soil: moist but well-drained, sandy
Light: full sun to partial shade

Sandwort forms mats of small, dainty evergreen foliage crowned with star-shaped tiny white flowers. Its low, spreading habit makes it ideal tucked into wall crevices and between pavers. *A. montana* has white flowers with yellow centers. *A. verna* ssp. *caespitosa* [now formally listed as *Minuartia verna* ssp. *caespitosa*] (Irish moss) has mosslike leaves and ⅜-inch white flowers. Plant sandwort 6 to 12 inches apart. Water well during dry spells in the growing season. Propagate by division in late summer or early fall.

Arenaria montana

Arisaema *(a-ris-EE-ma)*

DRAGONROOT

USDA Hardiness: zones 4-9
AHS Heat: zones 9-3
Height: 1 to 3 feet
Plant type: tuber
Soil: moist, acid
Light: partial to full shade

Arisaema, which includes over 150 wild species, produces a fleshy spike called a spadix nestled within an outer leaf-like spathe, which folds over the spadix like a hood. Use

Arisaema triphyllum

arisaemas in wildflower or woodland gardens or along stream banks, where they will slowly spread out and naturalize. The popular *A. triphyllum* (Jack-in-the-pulpit) is the best-known arisaema. Plant arisaemas in fall, setting tubers 4 inches deep and 1 foot apart in soil that is constantly moist but not soggy.

Armeria *(ar-MEER-ee-a)*

THRIFT, SEA PINK

USDA Hardiness: zones 5-7
AHS Heat: zones 9-4
Height: 6 inches to 2 feet
Plant type: perennial
Soil: well-drained, sandy loam
Light: full sun

Thrifts produce spherical clusters of flowers on stiff stems above tufts of grassy evergreen leaves. *A. alliacea* [also called *A. plantaginea*]

Armeria maritima

(plantain thrift) has rosy pink or white flower clusters; 'Bee's Ruby' has intense ruby red flower clusters. *A. maritima* (common thrift) bears white to deep pink flowers on 1-foot stems; 'Alba' is a dwarf cultivar with white flowers on 5-inch stems; 'Bloodstone' has brilliant red flowers; 'Laucheana', rose-pink flowers. Thrifts require fast-draining soil; too much moisture will cause them to rot.

Aristolochia *(a-ris-to-LO-kee-a)*

DUTCHMAN'S-PIPE

USDA Hardiness: zones 6-8
AHS Heat: zones 12-3
Height: 30 feet
Plant type: vine
Soil: moist, well-drained
Light: partial to full shade

Dutchman's-pipe is a vigorous deciduous twining vine with long, glossy, dark green, heart-shaped leaves and dark

Aristolochia macrophylla

flowers that look like small pipes with fluted edges. Valued for its fast growth, aristolochia has long been used for shading a porch, covering a trellis for privacy, or concealing an unsightly wall. *A. macrophylla* [also classified as *A. durior*] (pipe vine) bears purplish brown, yellow-throated flowers in early summer. Aristolochia does well in bright to medium or partial shade. It tolerates any average garden soil but performs with more vigor if compost is applied to its base in spring. Water during droughts.

Armoracia *(ar-mo-RAH-kee-a)*

HORSERADISH

USDA Hardiness: zones 3-10
AHS Heat: zones 12-1
Height: 2 to 4 feet
Plant type: perennial
Soil: moist, well-drained
Light: full sun to light shade

Spring clumps of oblong leaves with ruffled, wrinkled edges grow from horseradish's fleshy taproot, followed by clusters of tiny white summer

Armoracia rusticana

flowers. The pungent root is used in cooking, and was a medicinal plant before it became popular as a condiment. *A. rusticana* (horseradish, red cole) has thick, branching white-fleshed roots a foot long or longer, with leaves to 2 feet and flower stalks to 4 feet; 'Variegata' has leaves streaked white. Plant pieces of mature root at least 6 inches long in spring or fall. Set root pieces 3 to 4 inches deep and 1 to 2 feet apart. Horseradish can be invasive, as new plants grow from any root pieces left in the garden.

Arnica cordifolia

Arnica (AR-ni-ka)
ARNICA

USDA Hardiness: zones 5-8
AHS Heat: zones 8-2
Height: 6 to 24 inches
Plant type: perennial
Soil: well-drained, sandy, acid
Light: full sun

Slender flower stalks rise from arnica's rosettes of narrow aromatic leaves in summer, each with up to three daisylike flowers. Arnica was once used in herbal medicine but is now regarded as toxic and is legally restricted in some countries. *A. cordifolia* grows to 18 inches. Sow arnica seeds in fall or divide mature plants in spring, setting divisions 6 to 8 inches apart. Arnica does not do well in hot, humid sites or where winters are wet. Flower stems become leggy and floppy in rich soils.

Artemisia (ar-tem-IS-ee-a)
WORMWOOD

USDA Hardiness: zones 5-11
AHS Heat: zones 12-8
Height: 6 inches to 5 feet
Plant type: annual, perennial, shrub
Soil: poor, well-drained to dry
Light: full sun

Wormwood (also called mugwort) bears aromatic, feathery silver-gray foliage that is useful as an accent or filler in perennial beds. Forms range from woody evergreen shrubs, 4 to 5 feet high, to feathery

Artemisia stellerana 'Silver Brocade'

mounds scarcely 6 inches high, suitable for edging and ground cover. *A. stellerana* (dusty-miller) grows to 2 ½ feet and has finely divided felty-white leaves up to 4 inches long. Most species thrive in poor, dry soil and may become unkempt in moist, fertile soil. Wormwood does poorly in heat and humidity. It tolerates very light shade, although it much prefers full sun. Cut back frequently to keep plants shapely and in bounds. Propagate by seed or by division.

Aronia melanocarpa

Aronia (a-RO-nee-a)
CHOKEBERRY

USDA Hardiness: zones 5-9
AHS Heat: zones 9-4
Height: 6 to 10 feet
Plant type: shrub
Soil: well-drained
Light: full sun to partial shade

Chokeberry bears a profusion of tiny flowers that produce glossy red berries in hanging clusters that persist into winter. The glossy, dark green, oval leaves turn bright scarlet in fall. The upright colonies of suckers look best when massed for display. Plant chokeberries in almost any garden soil. Flowering, foliage color, and fruiting all occur best in full sun. It is adaptable to dry or moist soil.

Arum (A-rum)
ARUM

USDA Hardiness: zones 7-9
AHS Heat: zones 9-3
Height: 12 to 18 inches
Plant type: tuber
Soil: moist, acid
Light: partial shade

Italian arum is noteworthy for its attractively marbled, arrow-shaped leaves, which appear in fall and persist through the winter. Most gardeners grow arum for the

Arum italicum

plump cluster of glossy, brightly colored berries that follow the flowers in summer. *A. italicum* 'Marmoratum' [also called 'Pictum'] has brilliant orange berries. Arum is easily grown; given a slightly acid loam and protection from afternoon sun, it may spread quickly. Top-dress lightly with organic material in fall. Caution: Both the foliage and berries of Italian arum are poisonous and must be kept out of the reach of children.

Aruncus (a-RUNK-us)
GOATSBEARD

USDA Hardiness: zones 3-9
AHS Heat: zones 10-1
Height: 1 to 6 feet
Plant type: perennial
Soil: moist, rich loam
Light: partial shade

Aruncus dioicus

Goatsbeard carries dramatic, long-lasting 6- to 10-inch plumes of tiny cream-colored blossoms on tall stalks of light green ferny foliage. *A. aethusifolius* (miniature goatsbeard) has dark green 12-inch foliage and long, creamy white flower spires lasting 6 weeks; USDA zones 3-8. *A. dioicus* has handsome shrubby foliage that grows up to 4 feet tall, with flower stalks up to 6 feet; 'Kneiffii' is more compact, with finely divided leaves to 3 feet tall; USDA zones 4-9. Goatsbeard thrives in full sun where summers are cool.

Asclepias (as-KLEE-pee-as)
MILKWEED

USDA Hardiness: zones 3-9
AHS Heat: zones 10-2
Height: 2 to 4 feet
Plant type: perennial, tender
    perennial
Soil: well-drained sandy,
    or moist and deep
Light: full sun

Asclepias tuberosa

Milkweed's flower stalks bear brilliantly colored flower clusters followed by canoe-shaped pods, which burst to release silky seeds. The flowers are excellent for cutting, and the decorative pods dry well. Some species may be weedy. *A. incarnata* (swamp milkweed) bears clusters of fragrant, pink to rose flowers. *A. tuberosa* (butterfly weed) has showy, vibrant orange flower clusters; the leaves and stems are poisonous. Swamp milkweed prefers moist conditions; butterfly weed does best in dry soils, where its long taproot makes plants extremely drought tolerant. Plants thrive in warm weather and can be grown as perennials from USDA zone 8 south.

Asarum (a-SAR-um)
WILD GINGER

USDA Hardiness: zones 4-9
AHS Heat: zones 9-3
Height: 2 to 12 inches
Plant type: perennial
Soil: moist, acid, fertile
Light: shade

Asarum canadense

The rich green, handsomely textured leaves of these ground-hugging perennials make beautiful carpets for the woodland garden. The dusky 1- to 2-inch spring flowers are often hidden by the leaves. *A. arifolium* (wild ginger) has triangular evergreen leaves mottled with paler green; USDA zones 6-10. *A. canadense* (wild ginger, snakeroot) has hairy, deciduous leaves on arching leafstalks; USDA zones 3-8. *A. caudatum* (British Columbia wild ginger) has glossy evergreen leaves; USDA zones 4-8. Wild gingers require shade and ample moisture. They benefit from the addition of organic matter to soil.

Aster (AS-ter)
ASTER

USDA Hardiness: zones 3-9
AHS Heat: zones 9-1
Height: 6 inches to 8 feet
Plant type: perennial
Soil: moist, well-drained, fertile
Light: full sun

Aster novi-belgii

Asters are prized for their daisylike flowers that appear over weeks and even months. Most varieties are subject to mildew in humid climates. Among the better forms are *A. novae-angliae* (New England aster) 'Alma Potschke', with vivid rose-colored blossoms, and 'Harrington Pink', with large salmon pink flowers. *A. novi-belgii* 'Professor Kippenburg' has large clusters of bright lavender flowers with yellow centers from late summer to frost. Good air circulation is essential; well-drained soils deter rot. Asters will not tolerate soil moisture during the winter, and *A. x frikartii* must be winter-mulched in USDA zone 5 or colder. *A. tataricus* (Tartarian aster) is somewhat drought tolerant and can be invasive.

Astilbe arendsii 'Rheinlans'

Astilbe (a-STIL-bee)
SPIREA

USDA Hardiness: zones 3-8
AHS Heat: zones 8-2
Height: 8 inches to 4 feet
Plant type: perennial
Soil: moist, well-drained, fertile
Light: full shade to full sun

Feathery plumes in many colors along with a handsome habit make astilbe one of the treasures of a shade garden. Depending on variety, blooms appear through summer and into early fall; some varieties are nearly as ornamental in seed as they are in flower. Astilbes require shade where the soil does not dry out; in cooler climates, partial or full sun is acceptable if the soil is moisture retentive. Select an area that has good drainage, and enrich the soil with compost, peat moss, or leaf mold. Astilbe is a heavy feeder, so take care not to plant under shallow-rooted trees. Allow soil to dry out in the winter.

Atriplex (AT-ri-plex)
ORACH

USDA Hardiness: zone 0
AHS Heat: zones 12-5
Height: 3 to 5 feet
Plant type: annual
Soil: well-drained, fertile
Light: full sun

Orach is easy to grow and makes an effective summer hedge or screen or a backdrop for shorter annuals. Orach tolerates exposed sites and wind as well as alkaline soil and seaside conditions. Sow seed directly outside after all danger of frost has passed. *A. hortensis* (orach) grows to 6 feet tall and bears 5- to 8-inch-long leaves that mature to green, yellow, or red, and terminal clusters of tiny, purplish red flowers in summer.

Atriplex hortensis

Athyrium nipponicum

Athyrium (a-THER-ee-um)
ATHYRIUM

USDA Hardiness: zones 3-8
AHS Heat: zones 8-1
Height: 1 to 3 feet
Plant type: perennial
Soil: moist, well-drained
Light: full shade

Athyriums are deciduous woodland ferns that thrive in even the deepest shade. Arising in clumps, the delicate light green fronds grow upright or gracefully arched. Although *A. filix-femina* (lady fern) performs best in the slightly acid, rich loam of its native woodland settings, it accepts a wide range of soil types and is among the easiest of all ferns to grow. Locate them out of windy areas, as the fronds are easily broken. *A. nipponicum* [also classified as *A. goeringianum*] 'Pictum' (painted lady fern) needs less light than almost any other fern.

Aucuba (aw-KEW-ba)
AUCUBA

USDA Hardiness: zones 7-10
AHS Heat: zones 12-6
Height: 6 to 10 feet
Plant type: shrub
Soil: moist, well-drained, fertile
Light: partial to deep shade

Aucuba's leathery leaves, often marked with gold or yellow, brighten shady areas. If a male plant is nearby, female aucubas produce scarlet berries that last all winter. *A. japonica* has lustrous medium to dark green leaves up to 8 inches long and up to 3 inches wide that dominate its tiny purple early-spring flowers and bright red berries. Aucuba prefers slightly acid loam but will tolerate other soils. Once established, it withstands moderate drought. Full shade is best to maintain leaf color; direct sun—particularly in warmer climates—tends to blacken the foliage.

Aucuba japonica 'Picturata'

Aurinia saxatilis 'Sunny Border'

Aurinia (o-RIN-ee-a)
BASKET-OF-GOLD

USDA Hardiness: zones 4-10
AHS Heat: zones 9-2
Height: 6 to 12 inches
Plant type: perennial
Soil: well-drained, sandy
Light: full sun

One of the most widely used rock garden plants, basket-of-gold's tiny flowers mass in frothy clusters on low-growing mats of silver-gray foliage. *A. saxatilis* [formerly listed as *Alyssum saxatile*] bears golden yellow flowers in open clusters; 'Citrina' has pale yellow flowers and gray-green, hairy foliage; 'Compacta' is dense and slow spreading, with vivid yellow blossoms; 'Dudley Neville' grows light apricot blooms. Aurinia plants grow and bloom best in full sun and require good drainage; they do not tolerate moist soil or high heat and humidity.

Baptisia (bap-TIZ-ee-a)
WILD INDIGO

USDA Hardiness: zones 3-9
AHS Heat: zones 9-2
Height: 3 to 4 feet
Plant type: perennial
Soil: well-drained to dry, sandy
Light: full sun

Baptisia australis

Wild (false) indigo produces dainty blue pealike flowers from midspring to early summer. Its blue-green leaves are an attractive foil for both its own blooms and those of surrounding plants. The leaves remain handsome throughout the growing season. *B. australis* has indigo blue flowers in long, terminal racemes, good for cutting. *B. alba* is tall with white flowers. Wild indigo adapts to almost any well-drained soil and is dependably drought tolerant. It is slow growing, long-lived, and noninvasive.

Balsamorhiza sagittata

Balsamorhiza (bawl-sa-mo-RI-za)
BALSAMROOT

USDA Hardiness: zones 3-10
AHS Heat: zones 6-1
Height: 24 to 32 inches
Plant type: perennial
Soil: sandy or gravelly, moderately dry
Light: full sun

A perennial native to mountain grasslands and prairies of the West, balsamroot produces bright sunflower-like blossoms in late spring and early summer. *B. sagittata* (balsamroot, Oregon sunflower) forms a low clump of heart-shaped leaves covered with silvery hairs; leaves may be undivided or deeply divided into fernlike segments; flower stems bear a single yellow flower. Balsamroot thrives in full sun and deep, sandy soil, but it will tolerate poor, infertile soil. Because of its deep woody taproot, it does not transplant well.

Begonia (be-GO-nee-a)
WAX BEGONIA

USDA Hardiness: zone 11
AHS Heat: zones 12-1
Height: 5 to 16 inches
Plant type: tender perennial
Soil: moist, fertile
Light: partial shade to shade

Begonia x *semperflorens-cultorum*

Wax begonias add color to the shady garden with both their perpetual clusters of delicate flowers and their glossy rounded leaves. Flowers range from white to pink to red, and leaves may be green, bronze, or variegated green and white. *B.* x *semperflorens-cultorum* (bedding begonia) has a mounding habit and produces flowers nonstop from spring until frost. Selections vary in both flower and leaf color, flower size, and height. Begonias are tolerant of heat, air pollution, and drought. Although the ideal site is filtered shade, plants will tolerate full sun if given sufficient water, especially in cooler regions.

Berberis buxifolia 'Nana'

Berberis (BER-ber-is)
BARBERRY

USDA Hardiness: zones 4-9
AHS Heat: zones 9-4
Height: 18 inches to 8 feet
Plant type: shrub
Soil: well-drained
Light: full sun to light shade

Barberries are dense, some-what stiff-limbed shrubs that produce bright yellow flowers in spring and red, blue, or black fruit. Deciduous forms exhibit bright fall foliage and colorful berries that persist through winter. Barberries are useful as hedges, barriers, foundation plants, or specimens. Evergreen barberries grow best in moist, slightly acid soil in sites that are protected from drying winds and strong sun. Deciduous barberries adapt to almost any soil and are tolerant of drought, humidity, and urban pollution. They show their best fall color in full sun.

Betula (BET-u-la)
BIRCH

USDA Hardiness: zones 4-9
AHS Heat: zones 9-3
Height: 40 to 100 feet
Plant type: tree
Soil: moist, acid
Light: full sun

Betula jacquemontii 'Whitespire'

Birches grace the landscape with trunks of decorative bark and airy canopies of medium to dark green finely toothed leaves. Give birches optimum growing conditions and keep a sharp eye out for insects or disease. Although *B. nigra* (river birch) can thrive in periodic flooding as well as dry spells, most species need good drainage and grow best in loose, rich, acid loams. Amend soil with peat moss, leaf mold, or finished compost. Add sand if the soil is heavy. Mulch to retain moisture and to protect from lawn mower damage.

Bergenia 'Evening Glow'

Bergenia (ber-JEN-ee-a)
BERGENIA

USDA Hardiness: zones 4-9
AHS Heat: zones 9-2
Height: 12 to 18 inches
Plant type: perennial
Soil: moist, well-drained
Light: full sun to partial shade

Striking foliage and flowers often make bergenia a standout in perennial beds and edgings. Slowly creeping by rhizomes, it is effective when used to cover small areas or planted in masses along the edge of a stream. The cabbage-like leaves are evergreen in warmer climates and may turn burgundy in winter. Bergenia tolerates any well-drained soil but maintains the best foliage color in poor soil. Provide afternoon shade in hot climates, and mulch to control weeds. After several years, divide plants in early spring to rejuvenate.

Bletilla (ble-TIL-a)
BLETILLA

USDA Hardiness: zones 5-9
AHS Heat: zones 8-2
Height: 8 to 20 inches
Plant type: bulb
Soil: moist, well-drained, fertile
Light: full shade

Bletilla striata

One of the few orchids that can be grown outdoors, bletilla produces sprays of flowers in late spring or early summer above broad, pointed, papery, veined leaves. *B. striata* (Chinese orchid, Chinese ground orchid, hyacinth orchid, hardy orchid) has nodding deep pink or rosy purple flowers; 'Alba' has creamy white flowers; 'Albostriata' has white-striped leaves and purple to rosy purple flowers. Full shade and rich moist loam are best for bletilla. Plant in a site that is protected from wind. Water during dry periods; drought can result in diminished or no bloom the following spring.

Boltonia asteroides 'Pink Beauty'

Boltonia (bowl-TO-nee-a)
BOLTONIA

USDA Hardiness: zones 4-8
AHS Heat: zones 9-2
Height: 3 to 6 feet
Plant type: perennial
Soil: moist, well-drained loam
Light: full sun

Willowy stems burst with sprays of small daisylike blossoms for a month or longer; good for fall bouquets. *B. asteroides* (white boltonia) has abundant white or lilac to purple flowers up to 1 inch wide on branched stems to 6 feet tall; 'Pink Beauty' grows to 4 feet tall with pink blossoms; 'Snowbank', to 4 feet tall with graceful white flowers. Plant in full sun for compact foliage; partial shade produces lanky growth. Tall boltonias may require staking. Boltonia stands up well to summer heat and humidity.

Bouteloua (boo-te-LOO-a)
GRAMA

USDA Hardiness: zones 5-9
AHS Heat: zones 12-4
Height: 1 to 2 feet
Plant type: ornamental grass
Soil: well-drained to dry
Light: full sun

Bouteloua curtipendula

These clump-forming drought-tolerant grasses are found in prairies and open woodlands and on rocky slopes throughout much of the United States. They are useful for meadow plantings or as accents in a rock garden. *B. curtipendula* (sideoats grama, mesquite grass) forms wiry clumps with small flowers in summer; in fall the seed heads bleach to a tan color and foliage often turns red or purple. *B. gracilis* (blue grama) has narrow, fine-textured foliage and forms a dense sod when mowed, making it a good turf grass for dry climates. Grama grasses require full sun and a well-drained to dry soil. Both are excellent plants for low-maintenance gardens.

Borago officinalis

Borago (bor-RAY-go)
BORAGE

USDA Hardiness: zones 0
AHS Heat: zones 10-3
Height: 2 to 3 feet
Plant type: annual
Soil: well-drained
Light: full sun to light shade

Both the leaves and flowers of borage are edible, with a refreshing cucumber-like flavor. *B. officinalis* (talewort, cool-tankard) is a hardy annual with a rounded, sprawling habit, bristly gray-green foliage, and succulent stems. Flowers are arranged in drooping clusters. Each is ¾ inch across and star-shaped, with five petals. Once established, plants will self-seed and may become a nuisance. Allow 12 to 18 inches between plants. Where summers are very hot, afternoon shade is recommended. Borage tolerates drought.

Brachycome (bra-KIK-o-me)
BRACHYCOME

USDA Hardiness: zones 5-8
AHS Heat: zones 9-3
Height: 9 to 14 inches
Plant type: annual, perennial
Soil: moist, well-drained, fertile
Light: full sun

Brachycome iberidifolia

The daisylike flowers of the brachycomes are produced in masses, making this plant a good choice for rock gardens, edgings, and containers, including hanging baskets. *B. iberidifolia* has a compact habit and a 12-inch spread, with flowers that are about 1 inch across and appear for 4 to 6 weeks in the summer, in white, pink, lavender, and blue. Start seed indoors 5 to 6 weeks prior to the last frost, or sow directly in the garden when the soil has warmed. Successive plantings will lengthen the flowering season. Water during dry spells.

Brodiaea elegans

Brodiaea (bro-di-EE-a)
WILD HYACINTH

USDA Hardiness: zones 5-11
AHS Heat: zones 12-6
Height: 4 to 36 inches
Plant type: bulb
Soil: poor, dry to moist, heavy
Light: full sun to partial shade

Brodiaeas are cormous plants from grasslands and plains in the West. They have grasslike foliage and terminal clusters of tubular flowers on wiry stems. *B. californica* has lilac to violet flowers and is found in the wooded hills and open plains of central California. *B. elegans* (harvest brodiaea) has violet to purple flowers that open in late spring to early summer. *B. pulchella* [also called *Dichelostemma pulchella*] (wild hyacinth) has pinkish violet flowers in spring; USDA zones 5-10. *B. elegans* adapts to full sun or partial shade and to heavy soils ranging from dry to moist. *B. pulchella* prefers full sun and poor, dry soils; it tolerates drought.

Brunnera (BRUN-er-a)
BRUNNERA

USDA Hardiness: zones 3-7
AHS Heat: zones 9-3
Height: 1 to 2 feet
Plant type: perennial
Soil: moist, well-drained loam
Light: full sun to light shade

A genus of only 3 species, *Brunnera* produces airy sprays of dainty azure blue flowers resembling forget-me-nots above large dark green, heart-shaped foliage

Brunnera macrophylla

that grows in loose, spreading mounds. The plant's stems are slightly hairy. *B. macrophylla* (Siberian bugloss) has boldly textured leaves up to 8 inches across and dainty bright blue flowers; 'Hadspen Cream' has light green leaves edged in cream; 'Langtrees', spots of silvery gray in the center of the leaves; 'Variegata', striking creamy white leaf variegations. Propagate from seed, by transplanting the self-sown seedlings, or by division in spring. Useful as a low-maintenance ground cover.

Browallia speciosa

Browallia (bro-WALL-ee-a)
BUSH VIOLET

USDA Hardiness: zones 10-11
AHS Heat: zones 8-1
Height: 8 to 16 inches
Plant type: tender perennial
Soil: moist, well-drained
Light: partial to full shade

A good choice for the shady border, an edging, window boxes, or hanging baskets, bush violet bears flower clusters from early to late summer. *B. speciosa* 'Blue Bells' bears blue-violet flowers with prominent white centers; 'Jingle Bells' bears flowers in a mixture of colors including shades of blue, white, and lavender; 'Silver Bells' bears large white blooms. Start seed indoors about 8 weeks prior to the last frost. Plant in the garden after all danger of frost is past, spacing plants 8 inches apart. Avoid overwatering and overfertilizing.

Buddleia (BUD-lee-a)
BUTTERFLY BUSH

USDA Hardiness: zones 5-9
AHS Heat: zones 10-4
Height: 6 to 20 feet
Plant type: shrub
Soil: well-drained, fertile
Light: full sun

Its arching stems lined with narrow, gray-green leaves, the butterfly bush bears elongated clusters of fragrant flowers with contrasting centers in spring and summer. *B.*

Buddleia davidii 'Black Knight'

alternifolia 'Argentea' bears soft purple flowers on plants to 20 feet tall. *B. davidii* (summer lilac) grows up to 10 feet tall; 'Black Knight' has deep purple blooms; 'Dubonnet', long sprays of dark purple flowers; 'Empire Blue', violet flowers; 'Royal Red', red-purple flower clusters. In northern zones, grow *B. davidii* as a perennial, cutting to the ground in fall for flowers on new shoots in spring. Buddleia tolerates heat and humidity.

Buxus (BUK-sus)
BOXWOOD

USDA Hardiness: zones 5-9
AHS Heat: zones 10-4
Height: 2 to 20 feet
Plant type: shrub
Soil: well-drained
Light: full sun to light shade

Buxus 'Green Velvet'

Boxwood is an elegant long-lived evergreen shrub whose tiny leaves impart a fine texture to any planting. It is well suited for use as a hedge, an edging, or a foundation planting. *B. microphylla koreana* 'Wintergreen' retains bright green leaf color throughout winter; hardy to USDA zone 6. *B. sempervirens* grows to 20 feet, is hardy to USDA zone 5 or 6, and has fine cultivars. *B.* 'Green Velvet' is a dense shrub that grows 3 to 4 feet tall and wide; hardy to USDA zone 5. Plant boxwood in well-drained soil amended with organic matter in a site protected from drying winds. Mulch to help retain moisture. In warm climates, partial shade is beneficial.

Calamagrostis (kal-a-ma-GROS-tis)
REED GRASS

USDA Hardiness: zones 6-9
AHS Heat: zones 9-3
Height: 5 to 7 feet
Plant type: ornamental grass
Soil: adaptable
Light: full sun

Calamagrostis x acutifolia

This dense clump of narrow, arching leaves and feathery flower plumes on tall, upright stems supplies a striking vertical accent to the garden. One of the first ornamental grasses to bloom, reed grass is a multiseasonal specimen, singly or grouped, for perennial beds, borders, or streamside plantings. *C. x acutifolia* (feather reed grass) grows in upright clumps of rich green foliage 18 to 24 inches tall with flower spikes that are reddish brown in spring and golden yellow to buff in winter. Undemanding and drought tolerant, reed grass grows well in heavy, wet soils and poor, dry soils. Little attention is required. Cut to within 6 inches of the ground before new growth begins in spring.

Calamintha (kal-a-MIN-tha)
CALAMINT

USDA Hardiness: zones 6-11
AHS Heat: zones 10-1
Height: 12 to 24 inches
Plant type: perennial
Soil: average, well-drained, neutral to alkaline
Light: full sun to light shade

Calamintha nepeta

Calamint forms neat spreading clumps of erect stems lined with mint-scented oval leaves and tipped with spikes of tiny tubular flowers in summer. Fresh or dried leaves are used for herbal tea. *C. grandiflora* (mountain balm, ornamental savory) has brown-fringed deep green leaves and pink flowers; 'Variegata' has a bushy habit and leaves flecked off-white. *C. nepeta* [also classified as *Satureja calamintha*] (lesser calamint) has shiny green leaves and pale lilac to white flowers. Cut calamint stems back in fall and provide winter mulch in cooler climates.

Calendula (ka-LEN-dew-la)
POT MARIGOLD

USDA Hardiness: zone 0
AHS Heat: zones 8-4
Height: 12 to 24 inches
Plant type: annual
Soil: moist, well-drained
Light: full sun

Calendula officinalis

The long-lasting blooms of pot marigolds are daisylike with flattened, wide-spreading rays ranging in color from deep orange to yellow or cream. *C. officinalis* has a neat, mounding habit; 'Bon-Bon' grows 12 inches tall with a compact, early-blooming habit and a mixture of flower colors. Start seed indoors 6 to 8 weeks prior to the last frost, for transplanting to the garden after the last hard frost. In areas with mild winters it can be sown directly outdoors in fall or early spring. Calendulas thrive in cool conditions and tolerate poor soils if they have adequate water.

Callicarpa (kal-i-CAR-pa)
BEAUTYBERRY

USDA Hardiness: zones 5-10
AHS Heat: zones 12-3
Height: 3 to 8 feet
Plant type: shrub
Soil: well-drained
Light: full sun to light shade

Callicarpa dichotoma

Tiny colorful berries dangle from the tips of beautyberry's arching stems for weeks after the leaves have fallen in autumn. The leaves turn yellowish, sometimes pinkish, before dropping. *C. americana* (American beautyberry) has lavender summer flowers followed by magenta fruit clusters; var. *lactea* produces white berries; USDA zones 7-10. *C. dichotoma* has pink flowers followed by lilac-violet berries and is somewhat naturalized in USDA zone 5. *C. japonica* has violet to metallic purple berries; 'Leucocarpa' grows white berries after inconspicuous pink or white summer flowers; USDA zones 5-8. Prune to within 4 to 6 inches of the ground in early spring to create new shoots; only these produce flowers and fruit.

Callirhoe (ka-LEER-o-ee)
POPPY MALLOW

USDA Hardiness: zones 3-10
AHS Heat: zones 7-1
Height: 6 inches to 4 feet
Plant type: annual, perennial
Soil: sandy, rocky, well-drained
       to dry
Light: full sun

Callirhoe involucrata

This genus includes annuals and long-blooming perennials native to open woods and dry plains over much of the United States, with showy, cup-shaped flowers on slender stems. *C. digitata* (fringed poppy mallow) is an annual with rosy red to violet flowers beginning in spring. *C. involucrata* (purple poppy mallow, winecup) is a short trailing plant with magenta flowers in spring and summer, opening during the day and closing in the evening; USDA zones 4-6. *C. papaver* (poppy mallow) has solitary magenta flowers; USDA zones 5-8. All species thrive in full sun and dry soil, and survive drought well.

Calluna (ka-LOO-na)
HEATHER, LING

USDA Hardiness: zones 5-7
AHS Heat: zones 7-4
Height: 24 inches
Plant type: shrub
Soil: moist, well-drained, acid, sandy
Light: full sun to partial shade

Calluna vulgaris 'Corbetts Red'

C. vulgaris (Scotch heather) produces a sea of wavy blooms when its tiny spikes of flowers begin blooming in midsummer. Minute, scale-like evergreen leaves may turn bronze in winter. Scotch heather can grow to 2 feet, spreading 2 feet or more, and bears purplish pink flower clusters up to 1 foot long until fall; 'Else Frye' has double white flowers and reaches 18 inches. Heathers grow best in loam of low fertility. Good drainage is critical. Plant in full sun with northern exposure for best flowering and protect from drying winds. Mulch to conserve moisture, and water during dry spells.

Caltha (KAL-tha)
MARSH MARIGOLD

USDA Hardiness: zones 5-7
AHS Heat: zones 7-3
Height: 10 to 24 inches
Plant type: perennial
Soil: rich, moist to wet
Light: full sun to partial shade

Caltha palustris 'Flore Plena'

Marsh marigold is a perennial for wet soils, where its clusters of brightly hued 2-inch flowers provide an impressive display in spring. The flowers form on long stems that are held above a clump of lush, dark green foliage. *C. palustris* (marsh marigold, kingcup) has showy flowers in midspring; 'Alba' bears single white flowers with bold yellow stamens. While marsh marigold will grow in moist soil, it performs best in a wet location, especially in the spring. Plants go dormant in late summer, after which some drying out of the soil can be tolerated.

Calycanthus
(kal-i-KAN-thus)
SWEET SHRUB

USDA Hardiness: zones 4-9
AHS Heat: zones 8-4
Height: 6 to 9 feet
Plant type: shrub
Soil: moist, well-drained
Light: full sun to partial shade

Calycanthus floridus

Sweet shrub is an adaptable plant that blends well with other shrubs in many garden settings. Its summer flowers are unusual looking and produce a delightfully fruity fragrance. *C. floridus* has long, dark green aromatic leaves that are deciduous but persist late into fall; rounded, fragrant, dark burgundy flowers with spreading, straplike petals blooming from late spring through early summer; and urn-shaped fruit persisting into winter; 'Athens' is a cultivar with highly fragrant yellow flowers. Although it prefers moist, deep, well-drained soil, sweet shrub tolerates other soil conditions.

Camassia *(ka-MA-see-a)*
CAMASS, QUAMASH

USDA Hardiness: zones 5-9
AHS Heat: zones 12-2
Height: 1 to 4 feet
Plant type: bulb
Soil: moist, well-drained, sandy
Light: full sun to light shade

Camassia quamash

Camass's spires of inch-wide star-shaped flowers open from bottom to top over several weeks. *C. quamash* (common camass) has foot-long spires on 2-foot stems; 'Orion' is very deep blue. Naturalize camass in damp wildflower gardens, alongside streams or ponds, or among other spring-blooming bulbs. Plant camass bulbs in fall, setting them 4 inches deep and 6 to 9 inches apart. Provide shade where summers are dry. Bulbs can be lifted to remove offsets but are best left undisturbed unless flowering declines.

Camellia *(kah-MEEL-ee-a)*
CAMELLIA

USDA Hardiness: zones 7-11
AHS Heat: zones 10-3
Height: 6 to 25 feet
Plant type: shrub, small tree
Soil: moist, well-drained, acid
Light: light shade

Camellia japonica

Camellias are outstanding garden accents from fall through spring, when they are covered with flowers whose fluffy yellow centers are rimmed by single or double rows of ruffled petals. *C. japonica* (Japanese camellia) grows 10 to 25 feet tall with 5-inch blossoms. *C. sasanqua* (sasanqua camellia) is a 6- to 10-foot-tall shrub with 2- to 3-inch flowers. *C.* hybrids include 'Polar Ice', with white flowers; 'Winter's Charm', with double lavender-pink blooms; and 'Winter's Star', with reddish pink flowers. Choose light conditions carefully; excessive sun or shade will cause reduced flowering. Protect from winter winds and mulch heavily. Camellias are tolerant of heat and humidity.

Campanula
(cam-PAN-ew-la)
BELLFLOWER

USDA Hardiness: zones 3-9
AHS Heat: zones 9-1
Height: 6 inches to 5 feet
Plant type: biennial, perennial
Soil: well-drained loam
Light: full sun to light shade

Campanula carpatica

A large genus of nearly 300 species, *Campanula* produces spikes or clusters of showy, bell- or star-shaped flowers on stems rising from deep green foliage and offers a long season of bloom. Dwarf and trailing varieties enhance a rock garden, wall, or border edge. Taller species form neat tufts or clumps in a perennial border or cutting garden. *C. carpatica* (Carpathian harebell) has 2-inch-wide upturned blue flowers on plants up to 1 foot tall. *C. glomerata* 'Superba' and *C. poscharskyana* (Serbian bellflower) are heat tolerant. Dig up and divide every 3 or 4 years to maintain plant vigor.

Canna (KAN-ah)
CANNA

USDA Hardiness: zones 7-11 or
    tender
AHS Heat: zones 12-1
Height: 18 inches to 6 feet
Plant type: rhizome, tender perennial
Soil: moist, well-drained
Light: full sun

Cannas produce a continuous show of bold flowers with a tousled arrangement of petal-like stamens in strong colors from summer through frost.

Canna 'Miss Oklahoma'

The broad leaves line the stems to provide a dramatic back-drop to the flowers. In USDA zones 9 and 10, set cannas out as bedding plants in spring, planting the rhizomes 4 to 6 inches deep. Provide ample moisture and high humidity during the growing season. Cannas can remain in the ground year round in frost-free areas; in USDA zone 8, provide a protective winter mulch.

Carex (KAY-reks)
SEDGE

USDA Hardiness: zones 5-9
AHS Heat: zones 12-1
Height: 6 to 18 inches
Plant type: ornamental grass
Soil: moist, well-drained
Light: full sun to full shade

Sedge is a clump-forming plant with grasslike leaves. Unlike most ornamental grasses, it can grow in the shade, making it a good choice for massing in the

Carex morrowii

front of a shady border or edging a shady walk. Its leaves are arching and often unusually colored; the flowers are in-significant. *C. morrowii* 'Variegata' grows 12 to 18 inches tall; the semi-evergreen leaves have a white stripe down the center. Although sedge thrives in shade, it adapts to full sun as long as it receives sufficient water. It produces such dense mounds of growth that few weeds are able to penetrate.

Capsicum (KAP-si-kum)
PEPPER

USDA Hardiness: zones 10-11
AHS Heat: zones 12-3
Height: 6 to 20 inches
Plant type: annual, tender perennial
Soil: moist, well-drained, fertile
Light: full sun

Bushy, rounded pepper plants produce brightly colored fruit against dark green leaves. *C. annuum* (ornamental pepper) has a bushy, compact habit with evergreen leaves, and

Capsicum annuum

fruit may be red, purple, yellow, green, black, cream, or var-iegated; 'Holiday Cheer' grows to 8 inches with round 1-inch fruit that turns from cream to red; 'Treasure Red' grows 8 inches tall with conical fruit that turns from white to bright red. Start seed indoors in late winter to transplant to the garden after all danger of frost has passed; wear gloves to handle fruit. Perennial in USDA zones 10 and 11.

Carpinus (car-PY-nis)
HORNBEAM

USDA Hardiness: zones 5-8
AHS Heat: zones 8-3
Height: 30 to 60 feet, slow grower
Plant type: tree
Soil: well-drained, moist roots
Light: full sun to partial shade

A dense, easily pruned decid-uous tree with crisp summer foliage, smooth gray bark, and a well-contoured winter silhouette, hornbeam makes a handsome specimen tree,

Carpinus betulus 'Fastigiata'

hedge, or screen. *C. betulus* (European hornbeam) is py-ramidal when young, maturing to a rounded crown, 40 to 60 feet tall, and is a highly adaptable pest- and trouble-free plant, tolerating drought, smoke, dust, heat, and a wide range of soil conditions. 'Columnaris' has a densely branched, steeple-shaped outline; 'Fastigiata' grows 30 to 40 feet tall with a spread of 20 to 30 feet, an oval to vaselike shape, and a forked trunk.

Carthamus *(KAR-tha-mus)*
SAFFLOWER

USDA Hardiness: zones 0
AHS Heat: zones 12-3
Height: 1 to 3 feet
Plant type: annual
Soil: well-drained to dry
Light: full sun

Carthamus tinctorius

Both safflower's stiff stems lined with spiny leaves and its thistlelike summer flowers add texture and color to seasonal borders. Surrounded by a cuff of spiny bracts, the blossoms make excellent cut flowers. Dried flower petals are ground and used as a substitute for saffron in cooking. *C. tinctorius* (safflower, saffron thistle, false saffron, bastard saffron) has yellow to yellow-orange tousled flowers followed by white seeds (which yield polyunsaturated oil for cooking). Safflowers grow best under dry conditions and are subject to disease in rainy or humid areas.

Catharanthus *(kath-ah-RAN-thus)*
PERIWINKLE

USDA Hardiness: zones 9-11
AHS Heat: zones 12-1
Height: 3 to 18 inches
Plant type: annual, tender perennial
Soil: moist, well-drained
Light: sun to partial shade

Catharanthus roseus

Periwinkle provides summer-to-fall ground cover color for temperate gardens. Its flowers resemble those of *Vinca*, and it is available in both creeping and upright varieties. *C. roseus* [sometimes listed as *Vinca rosea*] (Madagascar periwinkle) has creeping varieties growing 3 inches tall, and spreading 18 to 24 inches across. Flowers range in color from shades of pink or mauve to white; 'Parasol' produces large white flowers with pink eyes. Periwinkles thrive in warm, humid, and urban conditions, tolerate pollution, and are perennial in USDA zones 9 to 11.

Caryopteris *(kar-i-OP-ter-is)*
BLUEBEARD

USDA Hardiness: zones 6-9
AHS Heat: zones 9-2
Height: 1½ to 5 feet
Plant type: shrub
Soil: light, well-drained
Light: full sun

Bluebeard is a small deciduous shrub with pleasantly aromatic flowers, stems, and leaves. The rounded mound of gray-green foliage is topped with blue flowers from mid- to late summer. *C. incana* grows to 5 feet and produces violet-blue flowers. Bluebeard requires occasional watering during droughts. Although it produces woody stems, it is best treated as a herbaceous perennial; cut it back to the ground in the winter.

Caryopteris incana

Ceanothus *(see-a-NO-thus)*
WILD LILAC, REDROOT

USDA Hardiness: zones 7-11
AHS Heat: zones 10-3
Height: 18 inches to 25 feet
Plant type: shrub, tree
Soil: well-drained to dry
Light: full sun

Ceanothus thyrsiflorus 'Victoria'

Wild lilacs are widely used on slopes and in masses in West Coast gardens. They improve the soil by fixing nitrogen. Evergreen forms bloom in spring. Wild lilacs thrive on rocky slopes that usually stay dry all summer. Troubled by summer rains and high relative humidity, wild lilacs are generally unsuited for East Coast gardens. *C. thyrsiflorus* (blueblossom) is an evergreen shrub that grows to 8 feet or a tree to 25 feet with finely toothed, glossy green leaves. Plant wild lilacs in light, sandy soil, and water only during their first season. Fast drainage is a must.

Cedrus (SEE-drus)
CEDAR

USDA Hardiness: zones 4-9
AHS Heat: zones 7-2
Height: 100 to 150 feet
Plant type: tree
Soil: well-drained
Light: full sun

Cedrus deodara

Cedars grow into magnificent specimen trees, their sweeping branches and great height best displayed on broad lawns. Prolonged cold or heat will cause a paling of the top of the trees, and ice storms will damage cedars. Give cedars ample room to develop in a site protected from strong winds. *C. deodara* (deodar cedar) grows to 70 feet tall with a nearly equal spread, with light blue to grayish green needles and a gracefully drooping habit. A moderately dry site is best for deodar cedar.

Centaurea (sen-TOR-ee-a)
KNAPWEED

USDA Hardiness: zones 3-9
AHS Heat: zones 9-1
Height: 1 to 6 feet
Plant type: annual, biennial, perennial
Soil: well-drained loam
Light: full sun

Centaurea montana

This large genus includes approximately 500 species of annuals, biennials, and perennials. The tufted blooms of of knapweed come in pink, blue, lavender, yellow, and white. *C. americana* (basket flower) is 6 feet tall with 4- to 5-inch fringed pink flowers with cream centers. *C. cyanus* (bachelor's-button, cornflower) produces 1-inch flowers from early summer until frost and is available in many colors. *C. montana* (mountain bluet) produces 2-inch deep blue-violet flowers on 1- to 2-foot stems; 'Alba' has white flowers. Sow seed in place in late winter or early spring; in areas with mild winters it can also be sown in fall.

Celosia (sel-OH-see-a)
CELOSIA

USDA Hardiness: zones 10-11
AHS Heat: zones 9-2
Height: 6 to 24 inches
Plant type: annual, perennial
Soil: moist to dry, well-drained
Light: full sun

Celosia cristata

This genus includes almost 60 species of annuals and perennials. Their crested or plumed flowers are extremely long-lasting, making them ideal for bedding and cutting for both fresh and dried arrangements. *C. cristata* displays a range of heights and flower types. Flowers are usually in deep shades of red, orange, yellow, or gold. The species is divided according to flower type: Childsii group (crested cockscomb) has crested or convoluted flower heads; Plumosa group (feather amaranth) has feathery flower heads; Spicata group bears flowers in slender spikes; 'Pink Tassels' bears pale pink spikes with bright pink tips. In warm areas, sow directly outside. Celosias thrive in warm weather and tolerate dry soils.

Centranthus (sen-TRAN-thus)
RED VALERIAN

USDA Hardiness: zones 4-9
AHS Heat: zones 9-2
Height: 1 to 3 feet
Plant type: perennial
Soil: well-drained, neutral to slightly alkaline loam
Light: full sun

Centranthus ruber

Dense, round flower clusters that make excellent cut flowers top each of red valerian's erect stems, which grow in vigorous clumps. *C. ruber* (Jupiter's-beard) is a bushy plant to 3 feet tall with fragrant ½-inch spurred flowers in rounded terminal clusters above paired blue-green leaves; 'Atrococcineus' has deep red flowers; 'Coccineus', scarlet flowers; 'Albus', white flowers. Red valerian can thrive in sterile limestone soil and is drought tolerant.

Ceratostigma
(ser-at-o-STIG-ma)

PLUMBAGO, LEADWORT

USDA Hardiness: zones 5-10
AHS Heat: zones 8-1
Height: 8 inches to 4 feet
Plant type: perennial, shrub
Soil: well-drained
Light: full sun to partial shade

Ceratostigma plumbaginoides

Plumbago develops shiny leaves and blue flowers that bloom late in the season. Short *C. plumbaginoides'* foliage turns bronze in fall in cool climates; its summer to late fall flowers are dark blue and saucer shaped; hardy to USDA zone 6. *C. willmottianum* is deciduous, bearing 1-inch bright blue flowers continuously from midsummer through fall; hardy to USDA zone 8. Plumbago requires good drainage but is otherwise tolerant of most soils. It will die out in soils that remain wet over the winter, and it does not compete well with tree roots.

Cercis *(SER-sis)*
REDBUD

USDA Hardiness: zones 4-10
AHS Heat: zones 12-9
Height: 10 to 35 feet
Plant type: shrub, tree
Soil: moist, well-drained
Light: full sun to light shade

Cercis canadensis 'Alba'

The redbud's early-season flowers signal the start of spring. Trees begin blooming when they are very young. *C. canadensis* (Eastern redbud) grows to 20 to 30 feet tall with a 25- to 35-foot spread, heart-shaped leaves and pink flowers in early spring; in USDA zones 4-9; 'Forest Pansy' has purple foliage; *C. occidentalis* (California redbud) grows to 10 to 15 feet; in USDA zones 8-10. Redbuds tolerate most soils as long as they are well drained. They thrive in full sun or as understory trees in a woodland garden. They are short-lived, often surviving no longer than 10 to 15 years.

Chaenomeles
(kee-NOM-e-lees)

FLOWERING QUINCE

USDA Hardiness: zones 5-9
AHS Heat: zones 10-2
Height: 3 to 10 feet
Plant type: shrub
Soil: moist to dry, acid
Light: full sun

Chaenomeles x *superba*

A thorny, rounded spreading shrub, flowering quince bears a showy profusion of early-spring flowers before the foliage appears. The small, yellowish green quincelike fruits that ripen in fall can be used for jams and jellies but cannot be eaten raw. The shrub's dense, twiggy branching makes a coarse winter silhouette. Budded stems can be used for late-winter arrangements. Flowering quince adapts to most soils except the very alkaline. Full sun produces the best bloom. Restore vigor and improve flowering by cutting out older branches. Leaf spot and too much spring rain can cause a loss of foliage, but some leaf drop by midsummer is normal.

Chamaecyparis
(kam-ee-SIP-a-ris)

FALSE CYPRESS

USDA Hardiness: zones 4-8
AHS Heat: zones 8-3
Height: 4 to 75 feet
Plant type: shrub, tree
Soil: well-drained, fertile, acid to neutral
Light: full sun to partial shade

Chamaecyparis pisifera

False cypresses are coniferous evergreen specimen trees with fan-shaped, flattened branch tips and scalelike foliage. Although *C. obtusa* (hinoki) is moderately tolerant of light shade and drier climates, most false cypress—among them *C. lawsoniana* (Lawson false cypress, Lawson cypress, Port Orford cedar), 'Allumii', 'Crippsii', 'Gracilis', and 'Nana Gracilis'—prefer full sun in cool, moist climates. *C. pisifera* (Sawara cypress) grows to 120 feet; 'Aurea' has golden-yellow leaves; 'Nana' is a spreading, dwarf shrub. Provide partial shade in hot regions and protect from drying winds. Amend soil with peat moss or leaf mold to hold moisture.

Chamaemelum
(ka-mee-MAY-lum)
ROMAN CHAMOMILE

USDA Hardiness: zones 6-9
AHS Heat: zones 12-1
Height: 1 to 6 inches
Plant type: perennial
Soil: dry, well-drained
Light: full sun to light shade

Chamaemelum nobile

Roman chamomile's leaves release an apple scent when crushed. The roots spread quickly into dense mats ideal as informal ground covers or as fillers among paving stones. The flowers that bloom from late spring through early fall can be dried and steeped for a tea. *C. nobile* (Roman chamomile) has lacy, ferny bright green leaves and white flowers with golden centers; 'Flore Pleno' has double-petaled cream flowers. Sow Roman chamomile seeds in spring or fall or plant divisions in spring; the species self-sows freely, but cultivars only come true from division. For lawns, space plants 4 to 6 inches apart and allow to spread before mowing.

Chasmanthium
(kaz-MAN-thee-um)
WILD OATS

USDA Hardiness: zones 5-10
AHS Heat: zones 12-1
Height: 2 to 4 feet
Plant type: ornamental grass
Soil: moist, well-drained
Light: full sun to partial shade

The genus *Chasmanthium* offers landscape interest during three seasons of the year. Its green flowers appear in drooping panicles in summer.

Chasmanthium latifolium

In autumn the leaves turn bright yellow-gold. The panicles turn bronze and persist throughout winter, providing color and graceful movement. *C. latifolium* (wild oats) has blue-green, bamboolike leaves and oatlike spikelets of flowers in summer. Unlike most ornamental grasses, chasmanthium adapts well to partial shade, where it has darker green foliage and tends to grow taller than it does in full sun. Fall foliage is most intense in full sun, however.

Cheiranthus *(ky-RAN-thus)*
WALLFLOWER

USDA Hardiness: zones 7-8
AHS Heat: zones 9-2
Height: 6 to 24 inches
Plant type: biennial, perennial
Soil: well-drained, fertile
Light: full sun

Bridging the flowering season between early bulbs and bedding plants, wallflower's fragrant flowers are borne in clusters in deep shades of yellow, orange, red, purple, and brown. *C. cheiri* (English wallflower) has a low, erect habit; dwarf varieties grow 6 to 9 inches, while tall varieties may reach 2 feet. Most varieties are treated as biennials; 'Bowles' Mauve' produces large clusters of deep pink flowers. Sow seed outdoors in spring or fall for bloom the following season. Provide winter protection in areas with severe winters. Wallflowers thrive in cool climates and do well in coastal and mountainous areas such as the Pacific Northwest.

Cheiranthus cheiri 'Bowles' Mauve'

Chelone *(kee-LO-nee)*
TURTLEHEAD

USDA Hardiness: zones 3-9
AHS Heat: zones 9-3
Height: 1 to 4 feet
Plant type: perennial
Soil: moist, rich
Light: partial shade to full sun

Turtleheads are perennials native to marshes, stream banks, low meadows, and moist woodlands in much of eastern North America. Their flowers, which somewhat resemble a turtle's head, appear in terminal racemes on erect stems. *C. glabra* (white turtlehead) bears clusters of white or pale pink flowers; USDA zones 3-8. *C. lyonii* (pink turtlehead) has dark green foliage and clusters of pinkish purple flowers beginning in late summer; USDA zones 3-9. Turtleheads thrive in moist soils in partial shade but will tolerate a sunny location if abundant water is supplied.

Chelone lyonii

Chilopsis linearis 'Regal'

Chilopsis (kill-OP-sis)
DESERT WILLOW

USDA Hardiness: zones 8-10
AHS Heat: zones 11-7
Height: 10 to 25 feet
Plant type: tree
Soil: dry, sandy
Light: full sun

Showy, trumpet-shaped spring flowers resembling snapdragons bloom in clusters at the tips of desert willow's branches in spring and often sporadically until fall. Its open, branching and willowlike leaves, evergreen in milder climates, lend an airy appearance. A heavy crop of thin, foot-long pods persists through winter. Desert willow can be trained into a graceful specimen for dry gardens. Native to arid lands of the Southwest, desert willow enjoys hot temperatures and light soil that is very well drained. Prune to develop a tree form or to eliminate shagginess.

Chrysogonum (kris-AHG-o-num)
GOLDENSTAR

USDA Hardiness: zones 5-9
AHS Heat: zones 9-2
Height: 4 to 9 inches
Plant type: perennial
Soil: well-drained
Light: full sun to full shade

Chrysogonum virginianum

The deep green foliage of goldenstar provides a lush background for its bright yellow, star-shaped flowers, which appear from late spring into summer. Its low-growing, spreading habit makes it useful as a ground cover, for edging at the front of a border, or in a rock garden. *C. virginianum* var. *virginianum* has upright spreading stems and flowers that bloom throughout the spring in warm areas, well into summer in cooler zones; var. *australe* is similar to var. *virginianum* but more prostrate. Goldenstar grows well in most soils with average fertility.

Chrysanthemum parthenium

Chrysanthemum (kri-SAN-the-mum)
CHRYSANTHEMUM

USDA Hardiness: zones 4-10
AHS Heat: zones 12-1
Height: 1 to 3 feet
Plant type: annual, perennial
Soil: well-drained, fertile loam
Light: full sun to partial shade

Reliable performers in the garden, chrysanthemums often bloom throughout summer and are also valued as cut flowers. *C. coccineum* (painted daisy) has white, pink, lilac, crimson, and dark red single flowers, 2 to 4 inches wide, from late spring to early summer; *C. frutescens* (marguerite) bears single or double daisylike flowers in pink, white, or pale yellow and is perennial in USDA zones 9 and 10, annual elsewhere; *C. parthenium* (feverfew) bears pungently scented tiny white flower buttons with yellow centers from early summer through fall. Each species has many cultivars. Chrysanthemums need frequent watering and fertilizing.

Chrysopsis (kri-SOP-sis)
GOLDEN ASTER

USDA Hardiness: zones 4-10
AHS Heat: zones 9-2
Height: 6 inches to 5 feet
Plant type: perennial
Soil: wet to dry, sandy
Light: full sun

Chrysopsis mariana

Golden asters are tough, vigorous plants that punctuate the landscape with long-lasting clusters of bright daisy-like blossoms. *C. graminifolia* [also called *Pityopsis graminifolia*] (grass-leaved golden aster) is evergreen with clusters of bright yellow flowers; USDA zones 5-10. *C. mariana* (Maryland golden aster) bears showy flower clusters; USDA zones 4-9. *C. villosa* (golden aster) ranges in size from 6 inches to 5 feet in height; USDA zones 4-9. *C. graminifolia* and *C. villosa* are easy to grow on sunny, dry sites; they may do poorly in too rich a soil. *C. mariana* requires wet to moist soil.

Cimicifuga simplex 'Brunelle'

Cimicifuga
(si-mi-SIFF-yew-ga)
BUGBANE

USDA Hardiness: zones 3-8
AHS Heat: zones 12-1
Height: 3 to 7 feet
Plant type: perennial
Soil: moist, well-drained, fertile
Light: full sun to partial shade

Bugbane's lacy leaflets create airy columns of foliage topped by long wands of tiny, frilled flowers. Use bugbane as an accent specimen, naturalized in a woodland garden, or massed at the edge of a stream or pond. *C. americana* (American bugbane) has creamy blossoms in late summer to fall; *C. ramosa* (branched bugbane) bears long wands of fragrant white flowers in fall; *C. simplex* 'White Pearl' has wands of white flowers followed by round, lime green fruits. Plant bugbane in cooler areas of the garden in soil enriched with organic matter. Propagate by division in spring.

Citrus aurantiifolia

Citrus (SIT-rus)
LIME, LEMON, ORANGE

USDA Hardiness: zones 9-11
AHS Heat: zones 12-1
Height: 8 to 30 feet
Plant type: shrub, tree
Soil: rich, moist, well-drained
Light: full sun

Glossy evergreen foliage, fragrant white flowers, and juicy fruits with aromatic skins all recommend *Citrus* species as specimen trees. Space them closely for hedges or grow them in containers. *C. aurantiifolia* (lime) is a spiny shrub or small tree with white flowers and greenish yellow fruit. *C. aurantium* (bitter orange) trees grow to 30 feet tall with bright orange fruits. *C. limon* (lemon) 'Eureka' is a nearly thornless spreading tree; 'Meyer' is a cold-resistant tall dwarf with sweet yellow fruits. Choose sites protected from wind and frost. Keep plants constantly moist but ensure good drainage; mulch to conserve moisture.

Cistus corbariensis

Cistus (SIS-tus)
ROCK ROSE

USDA Hardiness: zones 8-10
AHS Heat: zones 12-1
Height: 3 to 5 feet
Plant type: shrub
Soil: dry to well-drained
Light: full sun

Rock roses provide long-lasting color for desert areas or seaside gardens. Useful in rock gardens or mixed borders, massed, or as a ground cover on banks, these mounding shrubs with aromatic leaves bear flowers resembling single roses that last only a day but bloom sporadically for several weeks. Because the downy, mostly evergreen foliage is resistant to burning, rock roses are often planted in fire-hazard areas. Rock roses grow well in poor, dry soil and accept heat, ocean spray, and alkaline or even slightly acid soils.

Cladrastis kentukea

Cladrastis (cla-DRAS-tis)
YELLOWWOOD

USDA Hardiness: zones 4-8
AHS Heat: zones 9-3
Height: 30 to 50 feet
Plant type: tree
Soil: well-drained
Light: full sun

An excellent deciduous shade tree for small landscapes, yellowwood produces long, pendulous clusters of fragrant flowers in mid- to late spring and a broad canopy of bright green foliage that turns yellow in fall. The bark is smooth and gray. Open, delicate, zigzag branching creates an airy form. The color of the interior wood gives the tree its name. Flowering is best every second or third year. Although it occurs naturally on rich, limestone soils, American yellowwood adapts to a wide range of soil types, from acid to alkaline, and is remarkably pest free. Once established, it is heat and drought tolerant. Prune only in summer to prevent heavy sap bleeding.

Clarkia (KLAR-kee-a)
GODETIA

USDA Hardiness: zone 0
AHS Heat: zones 9-1
Height: 1 to 3 feet
Plant type: annual
Soil: dry, sandy
Light: full sun to partial shade

Clarkia rubicunda

Clarkias are free-flowering annuals from the coastal ranges of the western United States. Petals are pink to lavender with a bright red or pink splash at the base; the sepals are red. New cultivated dwarf forms are highly heat tolerant. Sow seed outdoors in fall where winters are mild, and elsewhere in spring as soon as the soil can be worked. Sow fairly heavily since crowding will encourage flowering. Plants perform best where nights are cool.

Clematis (KLEM-a-tis)
VIRGIN'S-BOWER

USDA Hardiness: zones 5-9
AHS Heat: zones 9-1
Height: 4 to 30 feet
Plant type: vine
Soil: moist, well-drained, fertile
Light: partial shade to full sun

Clematis armandi

Gracefully twining stems and showy flowers in white, pink, or purple make clematis an excellent choice for covering trellises, fences, arbors, and even unsightly rock piles. There are more than 230 species of *Clematis;* the small-flowered types are hardy, prolific bloomers. A vine from one of the perfumed varieties can scent a room. Clematis performs best when its roots remain cool and moist but its top is in the sun. Plant against a north-facing wall or in the shade of low shrubs, allowing it to clamber up to the sun. Although fairly adaptable, clematis prefers neutral or slightly alkaline conditions. Mulch well or underplant with a surface-rooting ground cover.

Claytonia (klay-TOH-nee-a)
SPRING BEAUTY

USDA Hardiness: zones 4-9
AHS Heat: zones 6-1
Height: 4 to 12 inches
Plant type: perennial
Soil: moist, rich
Light: shade to partial shade

Claytonia virginica

Spring beauties are low-growing perennials found in rich woodlands throughout much of the eastern and central United States. Their dainty flowers are pink or white with darker pink stripes on the petals and dark pink stamens. The plants disappear shortly after flowering. *C. caroliniana* (broad-leaved spring beauty) produces loose clusters of flowers along the upper portion of 4- to 12-inch stems. *C. virginica* (narrow-leaved spring beauty) has slender, grasslike leaves. Claytonias will thrive and spread rapidly in a moist soil with high humus content. Incorporate generous amounts of organic matter into the soil prior to planting.

Cleome (klee-O-me)
SPIDER FLOWER

USDA Hardiness: zone 0
AHS Heat: zones 12-1
Height: 3 to 4 feet
Plant type: annual
Soil: moist, well-drained
Light: full sun to light shade

Cleome hasslerana 'Purple Queen'

Enormous clusters of pink, lavender, or white 1-inch flowers top the stems of cleome continuously from summer until frost, creating a spiderlike effect further enhanced by the slender, conspicuous seedpods that follow the flowers. *C. hasslerana* [also known as *C. spinosa*] has airy, ball-shaped flower heads; 'Cherry Queen' bears rose red flowers; 'Helen Campbell' has white blooms; 'Pink Queen' bears clear pink blossoms. Start seed indoors 4 to 6 weeks prior to the last frost, or plant directly in the garden in early spring. Cleome thrives in warm, humid weather and responds well to abundant moisture.

97

Clethra barbinervis

Clethra (KLETH-ra)
SUMMERSWEET

USDA Hardiness: zones 3-9
AHS Heat: zones 10-1
Height: 3 to 20 feet
Plant type: shrub
Soil: moist, acid
Light: full sun to full shade

Summersweet is well named; its pink or white flowers appear in midsummer and are delightfully fragrant. With its wide tolerance for growing conditions, this deciduous shrub can easily be sited in any mixed border or moist woodland garden. *C. alnifolia* produces deep green leaves that turn gold in fall and very fragrant white flower clusters; 'Pink Spires' has deep pink buds that open to soft pink flowers. Tall *C. barbinervis* bears fragrant white late-summer flower clusters and smooth, exfoliating bark; USDA zones 5-8. Summer-sweet tolerates most soil types as well as coastal conditions. It thrives in both sun and shade.

Coix (KO-ix)
JOB'S-TEARS

USDA Hardiness: zones 0
AHS Heat: zones 12-1
Height: 3 to 4 feet
Plant type: ornamental grass
Soil: average, moist
Light: full sun to light shade

Job's-tears produces long, narrow leaves clasping tall, jointed stems that create a lacy vertical accent as a border backdrop or temporary screen. It also does well as a container plant. In summer, arching flower spikes rise like froth above the foliage, and female flowers, enclosed in hard, oval husks, hang decoratively in strings like dripping tears. *C. lacryma-jobi* (Job's-tears) has spiky flower clusters, male at the end, female at the base, encased in hard green husks that turn pearly white, gray, or iridescent violet as they ripen. Keep the soil constantly moist for Job's-tears. Potted specimens do best in light shade.

Coix lacryma-jobi

Clintonia andrewsiana

Clintonia (klin-TOH-nee-a)
BEAD LILY

USDA Hardiness: zones 2-9
AHS Heat: zones 8-1
Height: 4 to 20 inches
Plant type: perennial
Soil: moist, rich
Light: shade

Different species of these low-growing perennials are found in eastern and western woodlands. All have broad, glossy leaves, delicate flowers, and marble-sized berries. *C. andrewsiana* (bead lily) has deep rose flowers and steel blue berries; USDA zones 8-9. *C. borealis* (blue bead lily) has greenish yellow flowers and bright blue berries; USDA zones 2-7. *C. umbellulata* (speckled wood lily, white bead lily) has speckled white flowers and black berries. *C. uniflora* (bride's bonnet) is 4 to 8 inches tall with white flowers and amethyst-blue berries; USDA zones 4-8. Clintonias require cool, damp, shady locations. Mulch in winter.

Colchicum (KOL-chi-kum)
AUTUMN CROCUS

USDA Hardiness: zones 4-9
AHS Heat: zones 9-1
Height: 1 foot
Plant type: bulb
Soil: moist, well-drained
Light: full sun to light shade

The broad, straplike spring leaves of *C. autumnale* (meadow saffron) fade away by midsummer, but in early fall, clusters of stemless flowers from white to pink-lavender or deep purple, with prominent yellow anthers, rise to brighten the landscape. All parts of meadow saffron are extremely poisonous. *C. autumnale* has deep green leaves and stemless flowers composed of petal-like pointed tepals; 'Plenum' has double lilac-pink blooms.

Colchicum autumnale

Collinsia (ko-LIN-see-a)
COLLINSIA

USDA Hardiness: zones 10-11
AHS Heat: zones 11-1
Height: 8 to 24 inches
Plant type: annual
Soil: moist, well-drained to dry
Light: full sun to full shade

Collinsia heterophylla

Found in the western United States, collinsias are annuals with flowers resembling snapdragons. They are suited to rock gardens, woodland gardens, meadows, and borders. *C. grandiflora* (blue lips) has bicolored two-lipped flowers, with one lip in white or purple and the other in blue or violet. With *C. heterophylla* (Chinese houses), the upper lip of the flower is lilac or white and the lower lip is rose-purple or violet. Grow *C. grandiflora* in full sun to partial shade. It does not tolerate high temperatures and requires cool nights. *C. heterophylla* thrives in partial to full shade.

Consolida (kon-SO-li-da)
LARKSPUR

USDA Hardiness: zone 0
AHS Heat: zones 9-1
Height: 1 to 4 feet
Plant type: annual
Soil: well-drained, fertile
Light: full sun to light shade

Consolida ambigua

Dense clusters of long-lasting flowers, in shades of blue, lilac, pink, red, purple, to white, bloom on stately, erect spikes. *C. ambigua* (rocket larkspur) has spurred flowers in many pastel shades; tall cultivars include 'Imperial Blue Bell', with double blue flowers; 'Imperial White King' has double white flowers. Start seed indoors in peat pots 6 to 8 weeks prior to the last frost. Seed can be sown directly outdoors in fall from USDA zone 7 south and or in early spring elsewhere. Plants thrive in cool conditions, and where summers are warm they will benefit from light shade. Keep soil evenly moist throughout the growing season.

Comptonia (komp-TONE-ee-a)
SWEET FERN

USDA Hardiness: zones 2-8
AHS Heat: zones 8-3
Height: 3 to 5 feet
Plant type: shrub
Soil: well-drained, sandy, acid
Light: full sun to light shade

Comptonia peregrina

Sweet fern perfumes the air in the wildflower garden or perennial border, where it makes an ideal specimen planting. Sweet fern's lacy deciduous leaves, covered with rusty brown hairs, form mounds almost as wide as they are tall. *C. peregrina* has fans of narrow, pointed leaves with red-brown dangling male catkins and smaller, round female flowers in summer followed by shiny conical brown nutlets in fall. Sow ripe sweet fern seeds in fall, and overwinter in cold frames to transplant in spring. Otherwise, remove and transplant rooted suckers in spring or layer branches to develop rooted cuttings. Sweet fern grows best in loose, open soils and tolerates dry conditions.

Convallaria (kon-va-LAIR-ee-a)
LILY OF THE VALLEY

USDA Hardiness: zones 4-9
AHS Heat: zones 9-1
Height: 9 to 12 inches
Plant type: rhizome
Soil: rich, moist
Light: light to full shade

Convallaria majalis

Lily of the valley's fragrant white flower bells are a welcome sight in spring planted beneath deciduous trees in shade or wildflower gardens. The tiny blossoms lining arching, square stems clasped by a pair of broad green leaves add fragrance to nosegays or small bouquets. *C. majalis* has deeply veined leaves and 5 to 13 small flower bells followed by orange to red fall berries. Lily of the valley can be forced for indoor enjoyment. Plant lily of the valley pips in late fall, setting them 1 inch deep and 6 to 12 inches apart. Propagate by division in fall.

Coreopsis (ko-ree-OP-sis)
TICKSEED

USDA Hardiness: zones 4-9
AHS Heat: zones 12-1
Height: 6 inches to 3 feet
Plant type: annual, perennial
Soil: well-drained to dry
Light: full sun

This easy-to-grow plant is native to the eastern United States and is a common component of wildflower mixtures. Daisylike flowers in yellow, orange, red, ma-

Coreopsis verticillata 'Zagreb'

hogany, and bicolors appear throughout the summer to early fall. *C. tinctoria* (calliopsis) produces notched and often banded ray flowers surrounding a dark red or purple center. *C. verticillata* (threadleaf coreopsis) bears yellow flowers 1 to 2 inches across from late spring to late summer atop stems lined with finely cut, delicate leaves; 'Moonbeam' is a warm-climate variety that grows 18 to 24 inches tall with a prolific output of creamy yellow flowers. Plants tolerate hot weather and drought.

Cornus (KOR-nus)
DOGWOOD

USDA Hardiness: zones 3-9
AHS Heat: zones 9-1
Height: 15 to 30 feet
Plant type: shrub, tree
Soil: well-drained
Light: bright shade to full sun

Dogwoods can turn the spring landscape into a fairyland and in fall provide bright red fruit for birds. They may also offer red to reddish purple fall foliage,

Cornus kousa 'Satomi'

colorful bark, and low, layered branching for an attractive winter silhouette. Give dogwoods a moist, acid soil enriched with leaf mold, peat moss, or compost. Partial shade is best in hotter areas. Mulch to keep soil cool. *C. kousa* (Kousa dogwood) is more drought tolerant than *C. florida* (flowering dogwood). For colder climates, the best bud hardiness in flowering dogwoods occurs in trees native to those regions.

Coriandrum (kor-ri-AND-rum)
CORIANDER

USDA Hardiness: zone 0
AHS Heat: zones 10-1
Height: 1 to 3 feet
Plant type: annual
Soil: rich, well-drained
Light: full sun to light shade

Coriander's pungent young leaves, commonly known as cilantro or Chinese parsley, are a staple in East Asian, Mexican, and Indian cuisines.

Coriandrum sativum

The seeds are used in cooking as well. *C. sativum*'s young leaves grow in small, scalloped fans resembling parsley; older leaves look ferny and threadlike, with flat, loose clusters of tiny white to mauve summer flowers; 'Long Standing' is a slow-to-bolt cultivar. Sow coriander seed in spring and thin seedlings to stand 8 inches apart.

Corydalis (ko-RID-a-lis)
FUMEWORT

USDA Hardiness: zones 5-8
AHS Heat: zones 8-3
Height: 8 to 15 inches
Plant type: perennial
Soil: moist, well-drained
Light: dappled to full shade

Fumewort is useful for edgings, rock gardens, and perennial beds. Spikes of small trumpet-shaped flowers bloom from midspring through summer. The fern-

Corydalis lutea

like foliage remains attractive throughout the growing season. *C. flexuosa* 'Blue Panda' bears bright blue flower spikes from late spring until frost. *C. lutea* (yellow corydalis, yellow bleeding heart) is bushy, with yellow flowers flaring out from spikes above the foliage. Fumewort grows best in light or dappled shade but will tolerate deep shade. Good drainage is essential.

Corylopsis
(kor-ee-LOP-sis)
WINTER HAZEL

USDA Hardiness: zones 5-9
AHS Heat: zones 9-2
Height: 4 to 15 feet
Plant type: shrub
Soil: moist, well-drained, acid
Light: full shade to full sun

One of the first shrubs to flower in spring and one of the best for thick summer foliage, winter hazel is useful against bare walls or in infor-

Corylopsis pauciflora

mal shrub borders. Drooping panicles of fragrant yellow bell-shaped flowers appear before the leaves in April. Selected species include *C. glabrescens* (fragrant winter hazel), *C. pauciflora* (buttercup winter hazel), and *C. sinensis* (Chinese winter hazel). Winter hazels grow best in light shade, but they need some sun in early spring to promote flowering. Protect from winter winds, sudden temperature dips, and spring frosts that can easily kill flower buds.

Cotinus (ko-TYE-nus)
SMOKE TREE

USDA Hardiness: zones 5-9
AHS Heat: zones 9-3
Height: 10 to 15 feet
Plant type: shrub, tree
Soil: well-drained
Light: full sun

For most of the summer and early fall, *C. coggygria* (smokebush) almost explodes with puffy, smoky pink plumes, actually hairs arising from the 6- to 8-inch fruiting

Cotinus coggygria

stalks as the tiny yellowish flowers fade. *C. coggygria* is a loose and open multistemmed deciduous shrub, 10 to 15 feet wide, bearing 1½- to 3-inch-long leaves that unfurl pink-bronze. Tolerant of a wide range of soils, smokebush demands only that a site be well drained. Too-rich or too-moist soil reduces bloom and subdues leaf color. Pollution-tolerant smokebush is excellent for small city gardens.

Cosmos (KOS-mos)
COSMOS

USDA Hardiness: zone 11
AHS Heat: zones 12-1
Height: 10 inches to 6 feet
Plant type: annual, tender perennial
Soil: well-drained to dry
Light: full sun to light shade

Showy, delicate, daisylike blossoms, in many shades, appear on cosmos singly or in long-stalked loose clusters from midsummer until frost. Tall *C. bipinnatus* bears flow-

Cosmos bipinnatus 'Sonata'

ers in shades of red, pink, and white. Sow seed directly in the garden after the last frost in spring. Thin to allow 12 to 18 inches between plants. Do not fertilize. Taller types may need staking. Plants often self-seed. Some *Cosmos* cultivars are perennial in the South.

Cotoneaster
(ko-toe-nee-AS-ter)
COTONEASTER

USDA Hardiness: zones 7-9
AHS Heat: zones 8-3
Height: 1 to 15 feet
Plant type: shrub
Soil: well-drained
Light: full sun to partial shade

Red berries decorate the stiff, spreading branches of cotoneasters in fall and winter, and the tiny, deep green leaves lend a fine texture to the garden in all seasons.

Cotoneaster dammeri 'Canadian Creeper'

White or pink flowers, often quite small, appear in spring. Usually spreading at least as wide as their height, cotoneasters are used as fast-growing ground covers that are ideal for slopes, rock gardens, and walls; in masses; or as shrubs for borders and screens. Cotoneasters can also be trained into espaliers. Mature plants will tolerate drought, seashore conditions, and wind; dry or poor soil often produces the best fruiting.

Crambe (KRAM-bee)
CRAMBE

USDA Hardiness: zones 6-9
AHS Heat: zones 8-1
Height: 2 to 6 feet
Plant type: perennial
Soil: well-drained, slightly alkaline
Light: full sun

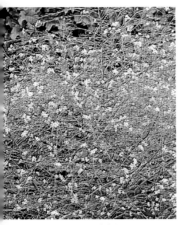

Crambe cordifolia

Crambe forms broad mounds of wrinkly, gray-green, heart-shaped leaves with deep lobes, making it attractive as an edging or filler. In late spring or early summer, stout stems carry an enormous branching cloud of tiny, strongly scented white flowers above the fleshy leaves to create an unusual accent in a border. Crambe thrives in deep, fertile, neutral to slightly alkaline soil with even moisture. Although it prefers full sun, crambe will tolerate some shade in the South.

Crocosmia (kro-KOS-mee-a)
MONTBRETIA

USDA Hardiness: zones 6-9
AHS Heat: zones 9-2
Height: 2 to 4 feet
Plant type: perennial
Soil: moist, well-drained, fertile
Light: full sun

Crocosmia masoniorum

Montbretia's wiry stems are lined with up to 50 or more tightly clasped flower buds that unfurl in succession from bottom to top over a long season of bloom. The vividly colored tubular flowers flare into open stars. In areas with mild winters, crocosmias will slowly spread into large clumps. Elsewhere, they make excellent container plants or can be treated as tender bulbs. Where conditions are favorable, *Crocosmia* can become invasive. In USDA zones 7-8, choose sites sheltered from wind and protect from frost with winter mulch. North of USDA zone 7, lift corms in fall, cutting foliage back to 6 inches and allowing corms to dry slightly before storing at approximately 50°F for replanting in spring.

Crataegus (kra-TEE-gus)
HAWTHORN

USDA Hardiness: zones 5-8
AHS Heat: zones 8-1
Height: 20 to 35 feet
Plant type: tree, shrub
Soil: well-drained
Light: full sun

Crataegus x 'Autumn Glory'

Hawthorns develop round crowns of lobed, triangular leaves with finely toothed edges that give them a delicate texture as a specimen tree or in a shrub border. The foliage has a reddish cast when young, turns green through the summer, then colors attractively in fall. Small white spring flowers produce red berries that persist through winter. Thorns along its branches are a drawback. *C. phaenopyrum* (Washington hawthorn) has foliage that turns scarlet in fall. *C. viridis* 'Winter King' (green hawthorn) is a round to vase-shaped tree to 35 feet tall with lustrous green foliage coloring purple or red in fall. Plant drought tolerant hawthorns in loose, slightly alkaline soil.

Crocus (KRO-kus)
CROCUS

USDA Hardiness: zones 3-8
AHS Heat: zones 10-1
Height: 2 to 8 inches
Plant type: corm
Soil: well-drained
Light: full sun

Crocus chrysanthus

Crocus flowers hug the ground on short stems from late winter through mid-spring. Each flower has six wide petals that open into a deep, oval cup shape, then relax into a round, open bowl. Crocuses are available in a broad range of hues, and are often striped, streaked, or tinged with more than one color. Prominent yellow or orange stigmas decorate the center of each blossom. Mass crocuses for best effect in beds, borders, and rock gardens. Crocuses are not fussy about soil, but good drainage is essential; they can tolerate hot summer sun during their dormancy. Where crocuses have established themselves in lawns, avoid mowing in spring until the foliage of spring-flowering crocuses dies back.

Cupressus
(kew-PRESS-us)
CYPRESS

USDA Hardiness: zones 7-9
AHS Heat: zones 9-3
Height: 30 to 40 feet
Plant type: tree
Soil: dry to well-drained
Light: full sun

Cupressus sempervirens

These graceful, fine-textured trees make handsome speci-mens, screens, or wind-breaks. Their aromatic foliage consists of scalelike leaves closely pressed on braided-cord stems. Cones with shieldlike scales are 1 inch across. *C. sempervirens* (Italian cypress) has a slender columnar shape. Best suited to the West and the Southwest, cypress enjoys mild to hot, dry cli-mates and needs no supplemental water once established. Soil must be perfectly drained. When grown in its natural habitat, cypress is generally insect and disease free. It is short-lived in the Southeast.

Cynara (SIN-ah-ra)
CYNARA

USDA Hardiness: zones 8-11
AHS Heat: zones 12-1
Height: 4 to 6 feet
Plant type: tender perennial
Soil: moist, well-drained, fertile
Light: full sun

Cynara cardunculus

This genus forms clumps of thick stems lined with spiny, lacy silver-gray leaves with woolly undersides that pro-vide a bold accent in a border or form a fast-growing sum-mer hedge. Fuzzy thistlelike purple flower globes tip each stem from summer through fall. Both leaves and flowers are prized by floral designers for fresh and dried arrangements. Start seed indoors in late winter, transplanting to succes-sively larger pots as needed before moving to the garden in midspring. Allow 3 feet between plants.

Cymbopogon
(sim-bo-PO-gon)
OIL GRASS

USDA Hardiness: zones 10-11
AHS Heat: zones 12-1
Height: 2 to 6 feet
Plant type: grass
Soil: well-drained, sandy, slightly acid
Light: full sun to light shade

Cymbopogon citratus

The fragrant leaves of *C. citratus* (lemon grass, fever grass) are a staple in Thai and Vietnamese cuisine. Steep fresh or dried leaves for tea. *C. citratus* has inch-wide aromatic evergreen leaves with sharp edges growing from bulbous stems in clumps to 6 feet tall and 3 feet wide. Apply mulch both to conserve moisture in summer and to protect roots in winter. Where frost is a possibility, pot divisions in fall after cutting back to 3 inch-es and keep indoors over the winter, watering only sparing-ly to prevent root rot.

Cyrtomium
(sir-TOH-mee-um)
HOLLY FERN

USDA Hardiness: zones 8-10
AHS Heat: zones 12-7
Height: 1 to 2 feet
Plant type: fern
Soil: moist, well-drained, acid, organic
Light: partial to full, deep shade

Cyrtomium falcatum

The shiny deep green leath-ery fronds of holly fern rise in a spiral from an erect crown and arch gracefully. This vase-shaped, woody ever-green is ideal for the north side of walls, the foreground of partly shaded foundation plantings, and woodland gardens in dappled light. Holly fern is easier to grow than many ferns and is more tolerant of low humidity, partial sun, salt, and drought. Plant in moist, loose soil well amended with peat moss, leaf mold, or compost. Use sand to improve drainage of heavy clay soil. Holly fern is usually free of in-sects and disease. Propagate by dividing in spring or summer.

Cytisus x *praecox*

Cytisus (SIT-is-us)
BROOM

USDA Hardiness: zones 6-8
AHS Heat: zones 8-4
Height: 6 inches to 6 feet
Plant type: shrub
Soil: well-drained to dry, poor
Light: full sun

Broom is a fast-growing shrub that brightens the spring border with its masses of pealike, often fragrant, pale lemon or bright yellow flowers. Small simple or trifoliate leaves line arching stems that remain green all year, providing welcome interest during winter months. *C.* x *praecox* produces creamy-yellow flowers from mid- to late spring. Broom is adaptable to seaside conditions, but does poorly in damp, humid locations.

Danae (DAY-nah-ee)
ALEXANDRIAN LAUREL

USDA Hardiness: zones 6-9
AHS Heat: zones 9-2
Height: 2 to 4 feet
Plant type: shrub
Soil: moist, well-drained
Light: dappled to bright full shade

The lustrous rich green leaves of Alexandrian laurel and its gracefully arching habit lend elegance and texture throughout the seasons.

Danae racemosa

Orange-red berries appear in the fall. *D. racemosa* has long, pointed, rich green "leaves" that are actually flattened stems, inconspicuous greenish yellow flowers, and showy berries. Alexandrian laurel prefers light, open shade; direct hot sun can discolor leaves or, in winter, produce leaf burn. Supplement the soil with organic matter such as leaf mold or peat moss.

Dahlia pinnata 'All Triumph'

Dahlia (DAH-lee-a)
DAHLIA

USDA Hardiness: zones 9-11 or tender
AHS Heat: zones 9-3
Height: 12 inches to 8 feet
Plant type: tuber, tender perennial
Soil: moist, well-drained, fertile
Light: full sun

Dahlias reliably brighten the flower border over a long season of bloom with highly diverse blossoms varying from flat-faced, single-petaled types to round, dense mounds of petals. Dahlia sizes are variable, with some flowers only a few inches across and others the diameter of a dinner plate. Colors range widely, and some dahlias are bicolored or variegated, with petals tipped, streaked, or backed with contrasting color. To keep plants blooming continuously, give them at least an inch of water weekly while blooming, and mulch with 2 to 3 inches of manure, compost, or peat moss to retain moisture and provide nutrients.

Daphne (DAF-nee)
DAPHNE

USDA Hardiness: zones 7-9
AHS Heat: zones 9-2
Height: 3 to 4 feet
Plant type: shrub
Soil: well-drained, alkaline
Light: full sun to partial shade

Daphne is a small evergreen shrub whose intensely fragrant flowers appear in late winter. *D.* x *burkwoodii* is a partly evergreen, upright shrub to 4 feet; it bears fragrant white flowers, flushed pink. *D. odora* (winter daphne)

Daphne x *burkwoodii*

has a mounded habit, dark green leaves, and extremely fragrant pinkish purple flowers in terminal clusters that bloom from late winter to early spring. Winter daphne is probably the least fussy of its genus. It tolerates most soils, though it prefers soil that is slightly alkaline to neutral. Daphnes often thrive with little or no care, but they sometimes die for no apparent reason.

Datura (da-TOOR-a)
ANGEL'S-TRUMPET

USDA Hardiness: zones 9-11
AHS Heat: zones 12-1
Height: 2 to 5 feet
Plant type: annual, tender perennial
Soil: moist, well-drained
Light: full sun to light shade

Datura's large flower trumpets bloom above coarse, oval leaves on shrubby plants that are useful as fillers or as backdrops in a border. Each

Datura inoxia

summer-blooming flower opens at sunset and lasts only a day. Most plant parts are extremely poisonous. Plant them only in places where they are completely out of the reach of children and pets. Start seed indoors 6 to 8 weeks prior to moving outdoors to warmed soil. Provide shelter from wind. *D. inoxia* may survive as a short-lived perennial in USDA zones 9 and 10.

Delphinium (del-FIN-ee-um)
DELPHINIUM

USDA Hardiness: zones 3-8
AHS Heat: zones 6-1
Height: 2 to 8 feet
Plant type: perennial
Soil: moist, well-drained, fertile
Light: full sun

Enormous showy spikes of 2-inch flowers on stiff stalks bloom above delphinium's clumps of finely cut, lobed leaves. The spurred flowers often have deeply contrasting

Delphinium 'Astolat'

centers. *D.* x *belladonna* (belladonna delphinium) has blue or white flowers on branching 3- to 4-foot-tall stems. *D.* 'Blue Fountains' is a dwarf form with flowers in shades of blue. *D. elatum* 'Pacific Hybrids' have blue, violet, lavender, pink, or white mostly double flowers on stalks usually 4 to 6 feet tall. Plant delphiniums in slightly alkaline soil enriched with organic matter. Stake tall varieties.

Daucus (DAW-kus)
DAUCUS

USDA Hardiness: zone 9
AHS Heat: zones 9-1
Height: 3 to 4 feet
Plant type: biennial
Soil: average to poor, well-drained
Light: full sun

This native of Eurasia has naturalized in the United States along roadsides and in abandoned fields and is known as Queen Anne's lace. It is very closely related to the

Daucus carota var. *carota*

garden carrot but is grown for its dainty 4-inch flower heads, called umbels, which appear in late spring to midsummer. The flat-topped umbels consist of tiny white flowers with, often, a single dark red flower at the center. Sow seed outdoors in late spring for flowers the following year. Once established, plants will vigorously self-seed. To prevent unwanted plants, remove flowers before seeds mature. Plants are easy to grow and thrive in well-drained soil.

Dennstaedtia (den-STET-ee-a)
CUP FERN

USDA Hardiness: zones 3-8
AHS Heat: zones 8-1
Height: 1½ to 3 feet
Plant type: fern
Soil: dry to moist, well-drained,
    slightly acid
Light: bright full shade to full sun

D. punctilobula (hay-scented fern, boulder fern) forms wide-ranging, dense mats of fragrant, finely textured light green fronds. A moderately

Dennstaedtia punctilobula

fast-growing ground cover, it is particularly useful for shady slopes and rocky areas that need filling in but are difficult to manage. Hay-scented fern has very lacy fronds covered with gland-tipped whitish hairs from which the scent emerges. Although hay-scented fern grows best in slightly acid, loamy soils, it tolerates a wide range of soil conditions and, once it is established, can withstand summer drought.

Dentaria diphylla

Dentaria (den-TAR-ee-a)
TOOTHWORT

USDA Hardiness: zones 4-9
AHS Heat: zones 8-2
Height: 6 to 16 inches
Plant type: perennial
Soil: moist, rich
Light: partial to full shade

Toothworts are low-growing perennials native to rich woods and bottom lands in the eastern and central United States. They grow from rhizomes, producing loose clusters of small bell-shaped flowers in the spring. After flowering, the plant disappears. *D. diphylla* (toothwort, crinkleroot) bears loose clusters of white or pale pink four-petaled flowers from early to late spring; USDA zones 4-7. *D. laciniata* (cut-leaved toothwort) bears clusters of pink or white flowers above the foliage in spring; USDA zones 4-9. Toothworts do not tolerate direct sun. Mulch lightly with leaves in winter.

Dianthus (dy-AN-thus)
PINK

USDA Hardiness: zones 5-8
AHS Heat: zones 9-1
Height: 4 inches to 2 feet
Plant type: annual, biennial, tender perennial
Soil: moist, well-drained, slightly alkaline
Light: full sun to partial shade

Dianthus gratianopolitanus

Pinks form mats of grassy foliage with white, pink, red, and bicolored flowers. Low-growing types make delightful edgings or rock-garden or container specimens, while taller selections are useful in the foreground or middle of a border, and as cut flowers. D. *barbatus* (sweet William) is a biennial that self-seeds freely; dwarf varieties grow 4 to 10 inches tall, while tall varieties may reach 2 feet. Flowers are borne from late spring to early summer. D. *gratianopolitanus* 'Bath's Pink' withstands heat and humidity. Sow sweet William seed outdoors in late spring for flowers the following year and provide a winter mulch. In hot climates, pinks prefer afternoon shade.

Deutzia gracilis

Deutzia (DEWT-see-a)
SLENDER DEUTZIA

USDA Hardiness: zones 4-8
AHS Heat: zones 8-4
Height: 2 to 5 feet
Plant type: shrub
Soil: moist, well-drained
Light: full sun to partial shade

Slender deutzia is a graceful deciduous shrub bearing pure white flowers in midspring. Like forsythia, it has a relatively short season of interest but is easy to grow and adaptable to most sites. Deutzia can be effectively used as a hedge, as a background for perennials, or in a mixed-shrub border. *D. gracilis* has slender arching stems in a broad mounding habit, and white flowers in erect clusters in spring that are effective for 2 weeks. Planted in spring, deutzia is easy to transplant and grow and is tolerant of most soils.

Dicentra (dy-SEN-tra)
BLEEDING HEART

USDA Hardiness: zones 3-8
AHS Heat: zones 10-1
Height: 1 to 3 feet
Plant type: perennial
Soil: moist, well-drained loam
Light: partial shade

Dicentra formosa

Bleeding heart's unusual puffy, heart-shaped flowers dangle beneath arched stems above mounds of lacy leaves in their long blooming season. D. *eximia* (fringed bleeding heart) has pink to purple flowers, and requires some afternoon shade in the South; 'Alba' has white flowers. D. *formosa* (Pacific bleeding heart) tolerates heat well and bears deep pink flowers on 12- to 18-inch stems; 'Luxuriant', bears cherry pink flowers; 'Sweetheart' has white flowers; D. *spectabilis* (common bleeding heart) has pink, purple, or white flowers.

Dictamnus albus

Digitalis grandiflora

Dictamnus (dik-TAM-nus)
GAS PLANT

USDA Hardiness: zones 3-9
AHS Heat: zones 8-1
Height: 2 to 3 feet
Plant type: perennial
Soil: moist, well-drained, slightly
    alkaline
Light: full sun to light shade

As a border specimen, gas plant offers open mounds of lemon-scented glossy foliage crowned in late spring to early summer with tall flower spikes, followed by star-shaped seed capsules. All parts of the plant are now considered potentially toxic. *D. albus* (gas plant, fraxinella, white dittany) has leathery oval leaflets with finely toothed edges and spikes of white flowers on erect stems; 'Purpureus' has mauve-purple blossoms veined deeper purple; 'Ruber', rose pink flowers. Sow gas plant seeds in soil amended with organic matter.

Digitalis (di-ji-TAL-us)
FOXGLOVE

USDA Hardiness: zones 5-9
AHS Heat: zones 10-1
Height: 2 to 6 feet
Plant type: biennial, perennial
Soil: moist, well-drained, acid
Light: partial shade

Foxglove's summer-blooming flower trumpets line the tips of stiff stalks above clumps of coarse, hairy leaves. Though most bloom their second season, some varieties flower the first year from seed. The perennial species are propagated by seed or by division. The common species and cultivars are usually treated as biennials. *D. grandiflora* (yellow foxglove) grows to 3 feet and bears yellow flowers marked with brown. *D. purpurea* (common foxglove) bears purple, pink, white, rust, or yellow blooms with spotted throats. Leaves contain digitalis and are poisonous if eaten. Foxgloves thrive in a rich, loose soil and benefit from the addition of compost. Water during dry periods and mulch after the ground freezes in fall.

Diphylleia cymosa

Dodecatheon meadia

Diphylleia (dy-FIL-ee-a)
DIPHYLLEIA

USDA Hardiness: zones 6-9
AHS Heat: zones 9-3
Height: to 3 feet
Plant type: perennial
Soil: moist, well-drained, fertile
Light: deep to bright full shade

Diphylleia is a decorative plant useful for naturalizing in drifts under trees and large shrubs. Mammoth rounded, cleft leaves form the background for the cymes of white flowers with yellow stamens that appear in late spring or early summer. A month later, small powdery blue berries arrive. *D. cymosa* (umbrella leaf) has foliage emerging copper colored before turning light green, flowers that appear over the foliage in flat-topped clusters, followed later by berries. Diphylleia is easily grown in settings that duplicate its native woodlands. Work leaf mold, peat moss, or compost into the soil before planting.

Dodecatheon (doh-de-KATH-ee-on)
SHOOTING STAR

USDA Hardiness: zones 4-8
AHS Heat: zones 8-2
Height: 4 to 20 inches
Plant type: perennial
Soil: moist to dry
Light: partial shade to full sun

Shooting stars grow in moist, open woods, on prairies, and on rocky slopes. These perennials have a basal rosette of leaves and leafless stalks bearing showy flowers with backswept petals. *D. amethystinum* [also called *D. pulchellum*] (amethyst shooting star) bears rose-crimson flowers and requires moist, well-drained, alkaline soil in partial shade to sun; USDA zones 4-7. *D. dentatum* (dwarf shooting star) has a purple spot at the base of its white petals and requires a moist, shaded site; USDA zones 4-8. *D. meadia* (shooting star) has white to deep pink flowers and prefers light, sandy soil with abundant moisture while blooming and drier conditions in fall and winter; USDA zones 5-8.

Dolichos lablab

Dolichos (DO-li-kos)
HYACINTH BEAN

USDA Hardiness: zones 10-11
AHS Heat: zones 12-1
Height: 10 to 20 feet
Plant type: tender perennial
Soil: loose, well-drained
Light: full sun

This lush, tropical twining vine produces purplish stems and purple-veined compound leaves. Attractive clusters of pink, purple, or white pealike flowers appear in summer and are followed by showy red-purple seedpods. The seeds are edible and are an important food source in many parts of the world. Start seed indoors in peat pots 4 to 6 weeks prior to the last frost, or sow directly in the garden after the soil has warmed. Space plants 12 to 24 inches apart and provide support for climbing. Hyacinth bean thrives in warm weather and is perennial in USDA zones 10 and 11.

Dryopteris (dry-OP-te-ris)
WOOD FERN

USDA Hardiness: zones 3-9
AHS Heat: zones 9-3
Height: 1½ to 3½ feet
Plant type: fern
Soil: moist to wet, well-drained, fertile
Light: deep to bright full shade

Dryopteris erythrosora

Native to moist woodlands or swamps but adaptive to the home garden, wood ferns give textural accents to rock gardens, shelter early bulbs, and provide soft backgrounds in perennial beds. *D. cristata* (narrow swamp fern, crested wood fern, crested fern) is evergreen in USDA zones 6-7, and hardy to USDA zone 3. *D. dilatata* (broad wood fern, broad buckler fern) is deciduous. *D. erythrosora* (Japanese shield fern, copper shield fern, autumn fern) is hardy to USDA zone 5. *D. cristata* grows well in moist soil, and it flourishes close to streams and ponds. Once established in soil that has been well amended with organic matter, wood ferns need little care.

Doronicum cordatum

Doronicum (do-RON-i-kum)
LEOPARD'S-BANE

USDA Hardiness: zones 4-8
AHS Heat: zones 12-5
Height: 1½ to 2 feet
Plant type: perennial
Soil: moist loam
Light: full sun to partial shade

The daisylike flowers of leopard's-bane stand brightly above mounds of heart-shaped dark green leaves. *D. cordatum* (Caucasian leopard's-bane) bears large yellow flowers. *D.* 'Spring Beauty' has double-petaled yellow flowers. Space leopard's-bane 1 to 2 feet apart in full sun but in cool locations where its shallow roots will receive constant moisture. In the South it requires partial shade. Foliage dies out after flowers bloom.

Dyssodia (dis-OH-dee-ah)
DAHLBERG DAISY

USDA Hardiness: zone 0
AHS Heat: zones 11-1
Height: 4 to 8 inches
Plant type: annual, tender perennial
Soil: well-drained to dry
Light: full sun

Dyssodia tenuiloba

Dahlberg daisies (also called golden-fleece) constantly flower throughout the summer. *D. tenuiloba* grows to 8 inches tall and 18 inches wide. Flower heads are ½ to 1 inch across with orange-yellow ray flowers surrounding a yellow center. Start seed indoors 6 to 8 weeks prior to the last frost to transplant to the garden after all danger of frost has passed. In warm areas they can be planted directly in the garden and will self-seed. Water sparingly and do not fertilize. Plants thrive in sunny, dry locations and tolerate heat, drought, and coastal conditions.

Echinacea *(ek-i-NAY-see-a)*
PURPLE CONE-FLOWER

USDA Hardiness: zones 3-9
AHS Heat: zones 12-1
Height: 2 to 4 feet
Plant type: perennial
Soil: well-drained loam
Light: full sun to light shade

Echinacea purpurea

Drooping petals surrounding dark brown, cone-shaped centers bloom on purple coneflower's stiff stems over many weeks. *E. pallida* (pale coneflower) has rosy purple or creamy white flowers on 3- to 4-foot stems. *E. purpurea* bears pink, purple, or white flowers on stems 2 to 4 feet tall; 'Bright Star' has rosy pink petals surrounding maroon centers; 'Robert Bloom', reddish purple blooms with orange centers on 2- to 3-foot stems; 'White Lustre', abundant white flowers with bronze centers. Echinacea is heat and drought tolerant.

Echium *(EK-ee-um)*
VIPER'S BUGLOSS

USDA Hardiness: zones 10-11
AHS Heat: zones 9-4
Height: 1 to 10 feet
Plant type: biennial
Soil: dry, poor
Light: full sun

Echium candicans

From early to late summer, these tropical natives provide a striking accent to borders and rock gardens. They are especially useful in sunny, dry locations where the soil is poor. *E. candicans* (pride-of-Madeira) produces erect 20-inch clusters of white or purple flowers held well above the leaves. *E. lycopsis* (viper's bugloss) grows 1 to 3 feet tall with blue, lavender, purple, pink, or white flowers. Start seed indoors 6 to 8 weeks before the last frost or outdoors as soon as soil can be worked in spring. In USDA zone 9 and south, seed can be sown in fall for earlier bloom. Plants thrive in poor soils and will produce few flowers on a fertile site. Water sparingly.

Echinops *(EK-in-ops)*
GLOBE THISTLE

USDA Hardiness: zones 3-9
AHS Heat: zones 12-1
Height: 3 to 4 feet
Plant type: perennial
Soil: well-drained, acid loam
Light: full sun

Echinops ritro

The round, spiny, steel blue flowers of globe thistle are held well above coarse, bristly foliage on stiff, erect stems. Several stout stems emerge from a thick, branching taproot. Flowers are excellent for both cutting and drying. *E. exaltatus* (Russian globe thistle) has spiny flowers that grow on stems up to 5 feet tall above deep green foliage. *E. ritro* (small globe thistle) bears bright blue flower globes up to 2 inches across on stems 3 to 4 feet tall; 'Taplow Blue' has medium blue flowers. Once established, globe thistles are drought tolerant.

Elaeagnus *(e-lee-AG-nus)*
OLEASTER

USDA Hardiness: zones 2-9
AHS Heat: zones 11-7
Height: 12 to 20 feet
Plant type: shrub
Soil: well-drained
Light: full sun

Elaeagnus x *ebbingei*

Several species of *Oleaster* are valued as landscape plants for difficult sites because they are extremely adaptable. Their silvery gray foliage contrasts well with that of green-leaved plants. They produce small but strongly fragrant flowers in late spring to early summer, and mealy fruit that attracts a wide variety of birds to the garden. *E.* x *ebbingei* 'Gilt Edge' is a variegated shrub that grows to 9 feet and is evergreen in mild climates. Oleasters tolerate wind, drought, alkaline soil, and seaside conditions.

Enkianthus
(en-kee-AN-thus)

ENKIANTHUS

USDA Hardiness: zones 4-7
AHS Heat: zones 7-3
Height: 6 to 30 feet
Plant type: shrub, tree
Soil: moist, well-drained, acid, organic
Light: full sun to partial shade

Enkianthus campanulatus

Pendulous clusters of dainty flowers in spring and brilliant fall foliage make this deciduous shrub a stand-alone specimen or a welcome addition to groups of acid-loving rhododendrons and azaleas. In parts of the West where dry shade is accompanied by high heat and low humidity, enkianthus does well. Mix peat moss or leaf mold into the soil before planting. Mulch to retain moisture. Pruning is rarely necessary.

Epimedium
(ep-i-MEE-dee-um)

BARRENWORT

USDA Hardiness: zones 5-8
AHS Heat: zones 8-5
Height: 6 to 12 inches
Plant type: perennial
Soil: moist, well-drained
Light: partial to full shade

Epimedium grandiflorum
'Rose Queen'

The small, heart-shaped leaves of barrenwort are reddish bronze when they first emerge in spring. They soon turn deep green, providing a lush ground cover for shady gardens before turning bronze again in fall. Red, pink, yellow, or white flowers rise above the foliage on delicate, wiry stems in spring. Barrenwort is a rugged plant that grows in a clump and increases in size without becoming invasive. It can withstand dry periods with sufficient shade.

Epilobium *(ep-i-LO-bee-um)*
FIREWEED

USDA Hardiness: zones 2-9
AHS Heat: zones 7-3
Height: 4 inches to 5 feet
Plant type: perennial
Soil: dry to moist, well-drained
Light: full sun

Epilobium angustifolium

These summer-blooming perennials are native to mountain slopes, dry clearings, and stream banks. They are named for their ability to rapidly colonize an area that has been swept by fire. *E. angustifolium* (fireweed, willow herb) produces spikes of lilac-purple, rose, or occasionally white flowers throughout summer. *E. latifolium* (dwarf fireweed) grows 4 to 16 inches tall with clusters of large magenta-pink flowers. Epilobiums require full sun but tolerate moist or dry soils provided they are well drained. Given favorable conditions, the plants spread quickly and may become invasive.

Eranthis *(e-RAN-this)*
WINTER ACONITE

USDA Hardiness: zones 4-9
AHS Heat: zones 9-1
Height: 2 to 4 inches
Plant type: tuber
Soil: moist, well-drained, fertile
Light: full sun to light shade

Eranthis hyemalis

Often blooming before the snow has melted, winter aconites produce cheery buttercup-like flowers composed of waxy, curved petals cradling a loose pompon of frilly stamens. The blossoms close tightly to protect themselves during cold nights, then reopen the next day with the sun's warmth. Plant winter aconite tubers in late summer or very early fall to allow roots time to establish themselves for late-winter blooming. Soak the brittle roots overnight, then set tubers 2 to 3 inches deep and 3 inches apart.

Eremurus *(e-ray-MEW-rus)*
DESERT-CANDLE

USDA Hardiness: zones 7-9
AHS Heat: zones 8-1
Height: 3 to 8 feet
Plant type: bulb
Soil: well-drained, sandy, fertile
Light: full sun

Eremurus stenophyllus

Desert-candles carry hundreds of tiny bell-shaped flowers in enormous, elongated spikes above rosettes of thick, fleshy leaves. Over a period of several weeks, the small flowers open from bottom to top along the stem so that each spike offers a range of textures and tones, from lighter-colored mature flowers with prominent frothy anthers to more deeply colored, tight oval buds. Once established, desert-candles are best left alone unless their crowns lift out of the soil. Support tall species by staking in windy sites, taking care not to disturb the tubers when setting the stakes. Provide winter mulch in colder zones.

Eriobotrya
(air-ee-o-BOT-ree-a)
LOQUAT

USDA Hardiness: zones 8-10
AHS Heat: zones 12-4
Height: 15 to 25 feet
Plant type: shrub
Soil: moist, well-drained
Light: full sun to partial shade

Eriobotrya japonica

Lustrous wrinkled evergreen leaves that are sometimes a foot long bear stiff panicles of fragrant, but not showy, woolly flowers in fall or winter, and by late spring edible yellow-orange fruits are ready to be picked in the Deep South. *E. japonica* (Chinese loquat, Japanese plum, Japanese medlar) is a tree or rounded shrub 15 to 25 feet tall and wide with tiny white flowers borne in 6-inch clusters, and pear-shaped fruit almost 2 inches long in the southern half of its range. Loquat prefers moist loam but tolerates moderately alkaline soils and occasional drought. Provide protection from wind.

Erigeron *(e-RIJ-er-on)*
FLEABANE

USDA Hardiness: zones 3-8
AHS Heat: zones 8-4
Height: 1½ to 2 feet
Plant type: perennial
Soil: well-drained loam
Light: full sun

Erigeron hybrid 'Wayne Roderick'

Fleabane's asterlike blossoms, blooming constantly from early spring to frost in some Pacific coastal areas, grow singly or in branched clusters with a fringe of petal-like ray flowers surrounding a yellow center. *E.* hybrid 'Wayne Roderick' (midsummer aster) has very narrow-petaled daisy-like blooms, purple with yellow centers. *E. pulchellus* (Poor Robin's plantain) has pink, lavender, or white flowers. *E. speciosus* (Oregon fleabane), the most popular species in the genus, bears purple flowers. Fleabanes thrive in dry, windy, coastal areas; they do not tolerate high humidity.

Eriogonum *(er-ee-OG-o-num)*
WILD BUCK-WHEAT

USDA Hardiness: zones 3-10
AHS Heat: zones 12-1
Height: 3 inches to 3 feet
Plant type: perennial
Soil: dry, rocky
Light: full sun

Eriogonum umbellatum

Wild buckwheats are drought-tolerant perennials native to open rocky slopes and plains in the western United States. *E. compositum* (northern buckwheat) bears white or yellow flower clusters in late spring to summer; USDA zones 4-7. *E. umbellatum* (sulfur buckwheat) bears rounded clusters of sulfur yellow to cream summer flowers that fade to orange or red; height varies from 3 inches to 3 feet; USDA zones 3-8. *E. wrightii* (Wright buckwheat) has white flower clusters that turn reddish orange in cool weather; USDA zones 6-10. Grow wild buckwheat species in poor to average well-drained soil in full sun. Propagate by seed.

Eruca vesicaria ssp. *sativa*

Eruca (e-ROO-ka)
ROCKET, ARUGULA

USDA Hardiness: zone 0
AHS Heat: zones 9-3
Height: 2 to 3 feet
Plant type: hardy annual
Soil: rich, moist
Light: full sun to light shade

Arugula's tangy young leaves add biting zest to mixed green salads. *E. vesicaria* ssp. *sativa* (arugula, rocket, Italian cress, roquette) has mustardlike leaves, coarsely toothed along their midrib, and delicate purple-veined creamy late-summer-to-fall flowers followed by slender upright seedpods. Make successive sowings of arugula seed from early spring through early summer. Plants develop their best flavor when they grow quickly in cool, moist soil; mature leaves or those grown in dry ground during hot weather become strong and bitter.

Erythronium 'Kondo'

Erythronium (eh-rith-RONE-ee-um)
DOGTOOTH VIOLET

USDA Hardiness: zones 3-8
AHS Heat: zones 12-7
Height: 6 inches to 2 feet
Plant type: corm
Soil: moist, well-drained, fertile
Light: partial to full shade

Dogtooth violets are native woodland wildflowers producing delicate, nodding lily-like blooms rising from pairs of oval, pointed leaves. Provide adequate moisture in summer after flowers and foliage fade. Most of the numerous species and cultivars are hardy to USDA zone 3. Propagate from seed to bloom in 3 to 4 years, or by removing and immediately replanting the small cormels that develop at the base of mature corms in late summer or fall.

Eryngium giganteum 'Miss Wilmot's Ghost'

Eryngium (e-RIN-jee-um)
RATTLESNAKE MASTER

USDA Hardiness: zones 4-9
AHS Heat: zones 12-1
Height: 2 to 6 feet
Plant type: perennial
Soil: well-drained, moist to dry
Light: full sun

The genus *Eryngium* is a perennial native to the central and eastern United States and can be found growing on prairies and in open woodlands. Its stiff, spiny leaves and thistlelike flowers add interesting texture to sunny borders and meadow gardens. *E. giganteum* grows to 6 feet and has blue or pale green flowers. *E. yuccifolium* (rattlesnake master, button snakeroot) bears greenish white flowers on upright stems in mid- to late summer. The leaves look like small versions of yucca foliage. Eryngium is easy to grow in full sun and a well-drained soil. It tolerates poor, dry soils as well as humidity and can withstand short periods of flooding.

Escallonia organensis

Escallonia (es-ka-LOAN-ee-a)
ESCALLONIA

USDA Hardiness: zones 8-10
AHS Heat: zones 9-2
Height: 3 to 5 feet
Plant type: shrub
Soil: well-drained
Light: full sun

Escallonia produces short clusters of pink, white, or red funnel-shaped flowers amid glossy, often sweetly fragrant foliage over a long blooming season. A good choice for coastal gardens, escallonia is often used for hedges or screens and in masses. A native of Chile, escallonia thrives in salt spray and coastal winds. Escallonia will thrive in average soils and withstands some drought but is intolerant of high alkalinity. Pinch back or prune after flowers fade.

Eschscholzia
(es-SHOL-zee-a)
CALIFORNIA POPPY

USDA Hardiness: zones 8-10
AHS Heat: zones 9-2
Height: 4 to 24 inches
Plant type: annual, tender perennial
Soil: dry
Light: full sun

This genus includes both annuals and tender perennials native to the grasslands of California and the Southwest.

Eschscholzia californica

Flowers open during the day and close at night and in cloudy weather. *E. caespitosa* (tufted California poppy, pastel poppy) is an annual with pale yellow flowers; *E. californica* is a 1- to 2-foot tender perennial from USDA zone 8 south but is grown as an annual elsewhere, with 1- to 3-inch yellow or orange flowers from spring to fall and feathery blue-green foliage. Plant seed outdoors in early spring; seedlings do not transplant well. Once established, plants self-seed freely. Though they tolerate most soils, they prefer a poor, sandy one.

Euonymus (yew-ON-i-mus)
SPINDLE TREE

USDA Hardiness: zones 4-9
AHS Heat: zones 9-5
Height: 4 inches to 70 feet
Plant type: vine, ground cover, shrub
Soil: well-drained
Light: full sun to deep shade

This broad genus includes deciduous shrubs that produce dazzling fall foliage and a cleanly defined winter silhouette, as well as evergreen ground covers, shrubs, and

Euonymus fortunei

clinging vines. Inconspicuous flowers form in spring, and pink to red fruit capsules, which are usually hidden, split to expose orange seeds in fall, attracting birds. *E. fortunei* is an evergreen shrub that climbs by rootlets to 20 feet. *E. japonica* (Japanese euonymus) shows great tolerance for salt spray and seaside conditions. Euonymus does well in all except very wet soils and accepts severe pruning.

Eucalyptus (yew-ka-LIP-tus)
EUCALYPTUS

USDA Hardiness: zones 9-11
AHS Heat: zones 12-7
Height: 60 to 160 feet
Plant type: tree
Soil: rich, organic
Light: full sun

Eucalyptus is best known for its evergreen or lemon-camphor-scented leaves, but the smooth bark on the bare, branching trunks also lends an architectural accent. The

Eucalyptus torquata

oil derived from leaves, roots, and bark is toxic but has many medicinal uses. *E. torquata* (coral gum) grows to 25 feet or more. Eucalyptus prefers light soil, requires good drainage, and tolerates both heat and drought. Sow eucalyptus seeds in spring or fall. Choose planting sites carefully, as roots secrete toxins that inhibit the growth of nearby plants.

Eupatorium
(yew-pa-TOR-ee-um)
BONESET

USDA Hardiness: zones 5-11
AHS Heat: zones 9-1
Height: 1 to 6 feet
Plant type: perennial
Soil: moist, well-drained loam
Light: full sun to partial shade

Boneset produces flat, dense clusters of fluffy, frizzy flowers on erect stems lined with hairy, triangular leaves. The flowers provide a fall foil for

Eupatorium coelestinum

yellow or white flowers such as chrysanthemums. *E. coelestinum* (mist flower, hardy ageratum, blue boneset) has bluish purple to violet flowers crowded in clusters in late summer to fall. *E. fistulosum* (hollow Joe-Pye weed) bears large flat clusters of mauve flowers in late summer through fall. *E. maculatum* (Joe-Pye weed, smokeweed) has large flattened clusters of reddish purple or white flowers. Boneset will tolerate drought with occasional watering.

Euphorbia *(yew-FOR-bee-a)*
EUPHORBIA

USDA Hardiness: zones 6-10
AHS Heat: zones 10-2
Height: 18 inches to 3 feet
Plant type: annual, perennial
Soil: light, well-drained
Light: full sun to partial shade

A large, diverse genus, *Euphorbia* includes many easy-care annuals and perennials. *E. corollata* (flowering spurge) is a perennial that bears clusters of flowers surrounded by small white bracts in mid- to late summer; slender green leaves turn red in the fall. *E. marginata* (snow-on-the-mountain) is a hardy annual native to many parts of the United States and is grown as much for its neatly variegated leaves as for its late-summer tiny green flowers surrounded by white bracts. Sow seed directly in the garden in late fall or early spring. They self-seed easily and may become invasive. The sap may cause skin irritation. Use gloves when handling stems to avoid contact with the sap.

Euphorbia marginata

Fargesia *(far-JEEZ-ee-a)*
BAMBOO

USDA Hardiness: zones 5-9
AHS Heat: zones 9-4
Height: 10 to 15 feet or more
Plant type: ornamental grass
Soil: adaptable
Light: partial shade

Narrow, tapered dark green evergreen leaves flutter from purplish sheaths on slender purplish gray culms, or canes, that arch as they mature and spread to form mounded clumps. Bamboo is adaptable to dry or moist conditions. As clumps begin to develop above soil level, divide and replant. *F. nitida* (clump bamboo) is less invasive than *F. murielae* (umbrella bamboo).

Fargesia murielae

Fagus *(FAY-gus)*
BEECH

USDA Hardiness: zones 3-9
AHS Heat: zones 9-4
Height: 50 to 70 feet or more
Plant type: tree
Soil: moist, well-drained, acid
Light: full sun to dappled shade

Long-lived beeches have massive trunks clad in smooth gray bark and reach 50 to 70 feet in height. In spring, as inconspicuous flowers form, silky leaves unfurl, turning bronze or ochre in the fall. Native to the hardwood forests of southern coastal plains, beeches are shallow rooted, often with branches sweeping the ground. Beeches shouldn't be underplanted and usually inhibit grass. Beeches enjoy acid soil, although *F. sylvatica* (European beech) adapts to most soils. Best growth occurs in full sun.

Fagus sylvatica

Fatsia *(FAT-see-a)*
JAPANESE ARALIA

USDA Hardiness: zones 8-10
AHS Heat: zones 12-2
Height: 6 to 10 feet
Plant type: shrub
Soil: moist, well-drained
Light: shade

A bold, dramatic plant with a tropical effect, Japanese aralia creates a rounded mound of deeply lobed dark leaves up to 14 inches wide. In mid-autumn, round clusters of tiny white flowers form, followed by round black fruit that persists through winter. *F. japonica* (Japanese fatsia, Formosa rice tree) is a moderate to fast grower 6 to 10 feet high and wide, with an open, sparsely branched habit displaying lustrous evergreen leaves on white stalks. Although fatsia tolerates clay and sandy soils, it grows best in light soils high in organic matter. Protect from drying winds and exposure to sun, even in winter. Leaves are easily burned or desiccated. Prune to control legginess.

Fatsia japonica

Ficus carica

Ficus (Fy-kus)
FIG

USDA Hardiness: zones 8-11
AHS Heat: zones 12-1
Height: 20 to 60 feet
Plant type: shrub, tree, vine
Soil: moist, well-drained
Light: full sun to partial shade

This large genus includes both edible and ornamental figs. All bear insignificant clusters of flowers in spring or summer. *F. carica* (common fig) grows to 30 feet and is grown for the fruit. *F. pumila* (creeping fig, climbing fig, creeping rubber plant) has numerous intertwined, slender stems that crisscross to form a dense mat rapidly growing 20 to 60 feet, with evergreen leaves. Figs are tolerant of heat and humidity.

Forsythia (for-SITH-ee-a)
GOLDEN-BELLS

USDA Hardiness: zones 3-8
AHS Heat: zones 8-4
Height: 10 feet
Plant type: shrub
Soil: average
Light: full sun

Forsythia x *intermedia*

Useful in shrub borders, masses, and banks, forsythia produces a burst of yellow bloom in fountainlike sprays in early spring. A showy shrub for only one season and bland for the rest of the year, forsythia is best blended into shrub borders or hedges or in drifts in the lawn. *F.* x *intermedia* 'Spectabilis' bears a profusion of richly hued, bright yellow flowers at the stem axils and is easily the showiest-blooming cultivar. Forsythia tolerates almost any soil but does best in loose loam. Best flowering occurs in full sun.

Filipendula ulmaria

Filipendula (fil-i-PEN-dew-la)
MEADOWSWEET

USDA Hardiness: zones 4-7
AHS Heat: zones 8-1
Height: 3 to 8 feet
Plant type: perennial
Soil: moist, rich
Light: full sun to partial shade

Filipendula is a perennial that grows in the wet woodlands and prairies of the eastern and central United States. Its feathery, long-lasting clusters of pink flowers, held above mounds of fine-textured foliage, provide a lovely show in the summer border. *F. rubra* bears flowers in branched clusters at the tops of stems. They have a fuzzy appearance and resemble astilbes. The leaves of the cultivar 'Venusta Magnifica' emerge mahogany and gradually turn green. The cultivar 'Venusta Alba' bears white flowers. *F. ulmaria* (queen-of-the-meadow) grows to 6 feet and bears creamy-white flowers. Filipendula thrives in full sun or partial shade but requires constant moisture. Mulch in spring.

Fothergilla (faw-ther-GIL-a)
FOTHERGILLA

USDA Hardiness: zones 4-9
AHS Heat: zones 9-2
Height: 3 to 10 feet
Plant type: shrub
Soil: moist, well-drained, sandy, acid
Light: partial shade to full sun

Fothergilla gardenii

Fothergilla works well massed in borders and in foundation plantings. Fragrant white bottle-brush flowers appear in spring. The blue-green leaves turn a brilliant yellow, orange, and scarlet in fall. *F. gardenii* (witch alder, dwarf fothergilla) forms a dense 3-foot mound; 'Blue Mist' has a feathery habit; 'Jane Platt' has narrow leaves and long flower clusters. *F. major* [also classified as *F. monticola*] (large fothergilla) is 6 to 10 feet tall and bears white flower spikes tinged with pink, and brilliant fall foliage colors; USDA zones 4-8. Fothergilla does not tolerate limy soils. Virtually pest free, it requires little care.

Fraxinus *(FRAK-si-nus)*
ASH

USDA Hardiness: zones 4-9
AHS Heat: zones 8-2
Height: 45 to 80 feet
Plant type: tree
Soil: wet to dry
Light: full sun

Ashes are moderate- to fast-growing trees that give light shade. In fall, the leaves may crumble after they drop, requiring little if any raking. Small greenish yellow flowers

Fraxinus griffithii

are borne on separate male and female trees in spring. Paddle-shaped winged seeds on female trees germinate easily and may become a nuisance. Select a male clone or a seedless variety. The deep taproot of the ashes make them suitable for city sidewalks.

Fuchsia *(FEW-sha)*
FUCHSIA

USDA Hardiness: zones 9-11
AHS Heat: zones 9-1
Height: 1½ to 5 feet
Plant type: annual or tender shrub
Soil: moist, well-drained
Light: partial shade

The pendulous, colorful blooms of fuchsia dangle from stems that may reach 3 to 5 feet in length. Plants are grown most often in a hanging basket or container that

Fuchsia x hybrida

can take advantage of their trailing habit. Plant fuchsia in a moisture-retentive, well-drained potting medium. Provide even moisture; it often requires daily watering in warm weather. Plants thrive in good indirect light or partial shade, although in areas with cooler summers they tolerate some direct sun. Protect them from midday sun, which causes flowers to fade.

Fritillaria *(fri-ti-LAH-ree-a)*
FRITILLARY

USDA Hardiness: zones 4-9
AHS Heat: zones 8-2
Height: 6 inches to 2½ feet
Plant type: bulb
Soil: moist, well-drained, sandy
Light: full sun to light shade

From the imposing, musky-scented *Fritillaria imperalis* (crown imperial) bearing a garland of blossoms aloft on stout stalks to small, dainty woodland species with single

Fritillaria meleagris

blooms on wiry stems, fritillaries produce nodding flower bells in unusual colors and patterns in a variety of forms to accent spring gardens. The often glossy leaves are highly variable. Most fritillaries like full sun and very well-drained soil, but *F. camschatcensis*, *F. meleagris*, and *F. pallidiflora* prefer light shade and moist soil. For all fritillaries, avoid sites with cold, wet soils, and reduce watering once foliage dies back.

Gaillardia *(gay-LAR-dee-a)*
BLANKET-FLOWER

USDA Hardiness: zones 3-8
AHS Heat: zones 12-1
Height: 1 to 3 feet
Plant type: annual, biennial, perennial
Soil: well-drained, sandy
Light: full sun

Annual, biennial, and perennial gaillardias grow wild in prairies, meadows, and plains in the central and western United States. *G. aristata* (blanket-flower) is a perennial

Gaillardia aristata

bearing showy yellow flowers with yellow or purple centers, appearing from mid- to late summer; USDA zones 3-8. *G. pulchella* (Indian blanket) is an annual bearing flowers with yellow or yellow and red centers and petals that are solid yellow, solid red, or red at the base and yellow at the tips. Gaillardias are easy to grow in full sun in almost any well-drained soil. Add a generous amount of sand to clayey soil to assure good drainage. All species are drought tolerant.

Galanthus (ga-LANTH-us)

SNOWDROP

USDA Hardiness: zones 3-8
AHS Heat: zones 8-1
Height: 6 to 12 inches
Plant type: bulb
Soil: moist, well-drained, sandy
Light: full sun to light shade

Galanthus nivalis

Snowdrops produce small white flowers that often bloom before the last snow melts. Each winged blossom is composed of three longer petals almost concealing three shorter, inner petals tipped with green. *G. elwesii* (giant snowdrop) has large blossoms above blue-green leaves. *G. nivalis* (common snowdrop) and its cultivars 'Flore Pleno', 'Sam Arnott', and 'Viridi-Apice' are not particularly heat tolerant, preferring cool, moist, shady spots. Plant bulbs 3 inches deep and 3 inches apart in late summer or fall.

Gardenia (gar-DEE-ni-a)

GARDENIA

USDA Hardiness: zones 8-10
AHS Heat: zones 10-2
Height: 1 to 6 feet
Plant type: shrub
Soil: moist, well-drained, acid
Light: full sun to partial shade

Gardenia jasminoides

While hardy only to USDA zone 8, this shrub is worth the effort to grow wherever conditions allow. Where it is not hardy, it can be grown as a container plant. Each intensely fragrant, double, camellialike flower is creamy white, and is attractively displayed against the dark evergreen leaves in spring and summer. *G. jasminoides* is an evergreen shrub that grows to 6 feet tall and wide with a dense, rounded habit, and bears double blooms up to 5 inches across. Plant gardenias in acid soil enriched with organic matter. It thrives in hot, humid weather, and requires monthly fertilizing during the growing season. Propagate by cuttings.

Galium (GAY-lee-um)

SWEET WOODRUFF

USDA Hardiness: zones 4-8
AHS Heat: zones 8-3
Height: 6 to 36 inches
Plant type: perennial
Soil: moist to dry
Light: full shade to full sun

Galium verum

Sweet woodruff spreads into ground-covering mats with small clusters of white spring flowers above leaves that become vanilla scented as they dry. *G. odoratum* (sweet woodruff) has open flower clusters. *G. verum* (yellow bedstraw, Our-Lady's bedstraw) bears plumes of honey-scented yellow flowers from summer to fall. Sweet woodruff enjoys a shady, moist location enriched with organic matter. Bedstraw does best in an average to dry location in sun or light shade; to control spread, set a can with the bottom removed in the soil; plant the seeds or divisions in the can.

Gaultheria (gawl-THER-ee-a)

GAULTHERIA

USDA Hardiness: zones 3-8
AHS Heat: zones 8-3
Height: 3 inches to 4 feet
Plant type: shrub
Soil: moist, well-drained, acid
Light: dappled to bright full shade

Gaultheria procumbens

Gaultheria forms a lustrous evergreen carpet for shady areas. Small bell-shaped flowers appear in spring amid clustered leaves that release their scent when crushed. Mint-flavored bright red berries develop later and remain into spring. *G. procumbens* (wintergreen, checkerberry, teaberry, mountain tea) forms a low carpet of foliage that is red when new, green in summer, and bronze in the fall; *G. shallon* (salal, shallon) has a variable habit, including ground cover to 2 feet tall or shrub to 4 feet tall in normal landscape conditions; hardy to USDA zone 5. Gaultheria thrives in humus-rich soil. Mulch to maintain moisture.

Gaura lindheimeri

Gaura (GAW-ra)
GAURA

USDA Hardiness: zones 4-9
AHS Heat: zones 9-2
Height: I to 5 feet
Plant type: perennial
Soil: dry, sandy to well-drained
Light: full sun to partial shade

Native to prairies, roadsides, and pond edges in the central and western United States, these perennials have an extended bloom season and a tolerance for summer heat and drought that make them valuable in herbaceous borders and meadow gardens. *G. coccinea* (scarlet gaura) bears fragrant flowers that resemble honeysuckle, opening white, fading to pink, and finally turning red. *G. lindheimeri* (white gaura) blooms from early summer until frost; the delicate four-petaled flowers open white and fade to pink as they age. After the first flowering, cut back the flowering stems for reblooming 4 to 6 weeks later.

Gazania rigens

Gazania (ga-ZAY-nee-a)
GAZANIA

USDA Hardiness: zones 8-11
AHS Heat: zones 12-3
Height: 6 to 16 inches
Plant type: tender perennial
Soil: well-drained to dry
Light: full sun

This tender perennial from South Africa produces daisy-like flowers from midsummer to frost. Blossoms open when the sun is out and close at night and on overcast days. They provide a colorful show in beds or containers. Sow seed indoors in early spring to transplant to the garden after all danger of frost has passed. Space plants 12 inches apart. Do not overwater. They thrive in sunny, dry locations and tolerate wind and coastal conditions.

Gelsemium (jel-SEE-mee-um)
CAROLINA JASMINE

USDA Hardiness: zones 7-9
AHS Heat: zones 8-2
Height: 10 to 20 feet
Plant type: perennial vine
Soil: moist, well-drained
Light: full sun to light shade

Gelsemium sempervirens

Carolina jasmine is a twining vine, evergreen in the warmest climates, that produces fragrant yellow funnel-shaped flowers in late winter to early spring. Allow it to cover fences, trellises, or unsightly features, scramble up a tree, or spill over a retaining wall, or use it as a rambling ground cover. Caution: All parts of the plant are poisonous to humans and livestock. Gelsemium grows best in highly organic soils similar to its native woodland loams but tolerates average soils, from acid to slightly alkaline, and mild droughts. Best flowering occurs in full sun. If vine becomes top-heavy, cut back severely.

Gentiana (jen-shee-AH-na)
GENTIAN

USDA Hardiness: zones 3-8
AHS Heat: zones 8-1
Height: 6 to 30 inches
Plant type: perennial
Soil: moist, well-drained, rich
Light: full sun to partial shade

Gentiana saponaria

Several gentians inhabit low woodlands, alpine meadows, and damp prairies over much of eastern North America. Their clustered flowers are generally shades of blue or purple, providing contrast to the predominately yellow flowers of late summer and fall. *G. andrewsii* (bottle gentian, closed gentian) has deep blue bottle-shaped flowers with white bands; USDA zones 3-7. *G. saponaria* (soapwort gentian) has blue-violet flowers; USDA zones 4-7. Gentians require cool temperatures and rich, well-drained soil with ample moisture throughout the growing season.

Geranium *(jer-AY-nee-um)*
CRANESBILL

USDA Hardiness: zones 4-8
AHS Heat: zones 12-2
Height: 4 inches to 4 feet
Plant type: perennial
Soil: moist, well-drained loam
Light: full sun to partial shade

Geranium sanguineum

Geranium is a widely culti-vated genus valued for both its dainty flat, five-petaled flowers and its neat mounds of lobed or toothed leaves that turn red or yellow in the fall. The plants are sometimes called hardy geraniums to distinguish them from annual geraniums, which belong to the genus *Pelargonium. G. sanguineum* (bloody cranesbill) bears solitary magenta flowers 1 inch across in spring and summer on 9- to 12-inch-high spreading mounds of leaves which turn deep red in fall; 'Album' has white flowers. Cranesbill grows in full sun to partial shade in cool areas but needs partial shade in warmer zones.

Geum *(JEE-um)*
GEUM, AVENS

USDA Hardiness: zones 5-9
AHS Heat: zones 9-3
Height: 8 to 30 inches
Plant type: perennial
Soil: well-drained, fertile loam
Light: full sun to light shade

Geum x *borisii*

Geums produce flat-faced flowers in single or double blooms. The flowers, which resemble wild roses with ruf-fled petals surrounding frilly centers, are borne on attrac-tive mounds of foliage ideal for the front of a border or for the rock garden. There are dozens of species. *G.* x *borisii* has orange-scarlet flowers on 12-inch plants. Enrich soil with organic matter. Geums grow best in moist but well-drained sites in cooler climates and will not survive wet winter soil. Most species dislike high temperatures; protect the plants from hot afternoon sun in warmer zones.

Gerbera jamesonii

Gerbera *(GER-be-ra)*
TRANSVAAL DAISY

USDA Hardiness: zones 8-11
AHS Heat: zones 12-2
Height: 12 to 18 inches
Plant type: perennial
Soil: well-drained
Light: full sun to partial shade

Transvaal daisies produce spectacular 4-inch flowers on sturdy stems. Although they are hardy only to USDA zone 8, in cooler areas they can be planted as annuals or dug up in the fall and planted in con-tainers to grow indoors as houseplants. *G. jamesonii* has long gray-green leaves and flowers with strap-shaped petals in yellow, salmon, cream, pink, rose, or red. Incorporate or-ganic matter into the soil before planting Transvaal daisies, and fertilize regularly. Water deeply, allowing soil to dry be-fore watering again. Protect plants over the winter in USDA zone 8 with a nonmatting mulch.

Gilia *(GIL-ee-a)*
BIRD'S-EYES

USDA Hardiness: zone 0
AHS Heat: zones 12-1
Height: 1 to 2½ feet
Plant type: annual
Soil: loose, well-drained
Light: full sun

Gilia tricolor

Gilias are annuals native to coastal areas of California and the nearby mountain ranges. They are vigorous plants well suited to a sunny meadow garden. *G. achilleifo-lia* (showy gilia, yarrow gilia) has late spring, deep blue fun-nel-shaped flowers in dense terminal clusters. *G. capitata* (globe gilia) has powder blue globe-shaped flower heads ap-pearing in late spring and early summer. *G. tricolor* (bird's-eyes) flowers are blue with a yellow throat and a dark purple ring at the top. Gilias are adaptable to most well-drained soils.

Gillenia trifoliata

Gillenia *(gil-LEE-nee-a)*
BOWMAN'S ROOT

USDA Hardiness: zones 4-9
AHS Heat: zones 9-2
Height: 2 to 4 feet
Plant type: perennial
Soil: moist, well-drained loam
Light: light to moderate shade

Gillenia is a tall, delicate, woodland perennial with white, star-shaped flowers, often blushed with pink. The flowers emerge from wine-colored sepals, which remain as ornament after the petals drop. Gillenia is native to the eastern U.S. *G. trifoliata* [formerly *Porteranthus trifoliata*] (bowman's root) has five-petaled flowers growing in loose, airy clusters above lacy leaves with toothed edges. Space gillenia 2 to 3 feet apart in sites with abundant moisture and light to moderate shade. Incorporate organic matter into soil to help retain water.

Gleditsia *(gle-DIT-see-a)*
HONEY LOCUST

USDA Hardiness: zones 5-9
AHS Heat: zones 9-4
Height: to 70 feet
Plant type: tree
Soil: well-drained
Light: full sun

Leafing late in spring on a wide-spreading canopy of arching branches, honey locust produces bright green ferny foliage, then inconspicuous fragrant flowers, followed by strap-shaped pods, usually viewed as a nuisance.

Gleditsia triacanthos

Honey locusts grow best in moist, rich loam but tolerate acid and alkaline soils, drought, and salt. Under average conditions, they grow 2 feet per year or more but may be insect and disease prone.

Gladiolus communis ssp. *byzantinus*

Gladiolus *(glad-ee-O-lus)*
CORN FLAG

USDA Hardiness: zones 5-11 or tender
AHS Heat: zones 9-3
Height: 1 to 7 feet
Plant type: bulb
Soil: well-drained, fertile
Light: full sun

Gladiolus produces spikes of 1½- to 5½-inch flowers above fans of stiff, sword-shaped leaves. Abundant, sometimes fragrant, flowers open one at a time to provide several weeks of bloom. Use tall gladiolus in groups at the back of a border, shorter species in rock gardens or mixed in borders with spring bulbs. *G. communis* spp. *byzantinus* (Byzantine gladiolus) has white-streaked burgundy flowers on 2-foot stems in spring to summer; USDA zones 5-11. North of USDA zone 8, plant hardy gladiolus in fall; plant tender ones in spring and dig them up in fall for replanting in spring.

Gomphrena *(gom-FREE-na)*
GLOBE AMARANTH

USDA Hardiness: zone 0
AHS Heat: zones 9-2
Height: 8 to 24 inches
Plant type: annual
Soil: well-drained
Light: full sun

Colorful cloverlike flower heads of this half-hardy annual top upright stems from summer to frost. *G. globosa* produces erect, branched

Gomphrena globosa

stems and somewhat coarse, hairy leaves. The globular flower heads are 1 inch long and may be pink, white, magenta, orange, or red. Start seed indoors 8 to 10 weeks before the last frost and transplant outdoors after all danger of frost has passed. Seed can be sown directly outside in late spring. Though slow to start, plants are easy to grow once established, and they thrive in warm weather. To use in dried arrangements, cut before the flowers are fully open and hang them upside down in an airy room.

Grevillea hybrid 'Bronze Rambler'

Grevillea (gre-VIL-ee-a)
GREVILLEA

USDA Hardiness: zones 10-11
AHS Heat: zones 12-3
Height: 4 to 150 feet
Plant type: shrub, tree
Soil: well-drained, acid
Light: full sun

This large genus includes a wide range of tender broadleaf evergreen trees and shrubs. *G.* hybrid 'Bronze Rambler' has gracefully weeping branches and can be used as a ground cover or trained to climb; it bears reddish purple blooms in the spring; new growth is bronzy red. *G. robusta* grows to 150 feet, bears golden-orange flowers in early spring and is grown as an ornamental tree in warm regions.

Haemanthus (heem-ANTH-us)
BLOOD LILIES

USDA Hardiness: zones 9-11
AHS Heat: zones 9-2
Height: 12 to 18 inches
Plant type: bulb
Soil: moist, well-drained
Light: full sun to light shade

Haemanthus katherinae

Blood lilies produce frothy clusters of tubular flowers with colorful protruding stamens cradled within broad, petal-like bracts or in spherical clusters atop stout, leafless stems. While sometimes grown outdoors in warm zones, they bloom best as rootbound container specimens. *H. katherinae* (Catherine-wheel) bears over 200 small pink-red flowers in 9-inch globes on 18-inch stems. Plant 6 to 8 inches apart outdoors or in pots, with the tip of the bulb at the soil surface. Start potted lilies in spring, then dry off and store over winter. Propagate from seed or from bulb offsets.

Gypsophila elegans

Gypsophila (jip-SOFF-il-a)
BABY'S-BREATH

USDA Hardiness: zones 3-9
AHS Heat: zones 9-3
Height: 8 inches to 4 feet
Plant type: annual, perennial
Soil: well-drained, alkaline
Light: full sun

Clouds of tiny flowers on branched stems from midspring to early fall characterize this hardy plant. *G. elegans* has a mounded habit with thin, multibranched stems bearing pairs of narrow gray-green leaves and airy clusters of white, pink, red, or purple flowers. *G. paniculata* (perennial baby's-breath) has stems to 4 feet tall; 'Bristol Fairy' has double white flowers. Propagate from seed. Sow seed directly in the garden in midspring. Supplement acid soils with limestone. Plants are short-lived, so make successive sowings every 2 to 3 weeks for continuous bloom. Thin plants to 9 to 12 inches apart. Taller varieties may need staking. In USDA zone 9 and south, provide afternoon shade.

Hakonechloa (hah-kon-eh-KLO-a)
HAKONECHLOA

USDA Hardiness: zones 5-9
AHS Heat: zones 9-2
Height: 12 to 18 inches
Plant type: ornamental grass
Soil: moist, well-drained, fertile
Light: partial to bright full shade

Hakonechloa macra (in winter)

A slow-spreading deciduous ground cover, hakonechloa can also be used as an accent alone, in masses along walkways, or in borders and rock gardens. *H. macra* 'Aureola' (golden variegated hakonechloa) has tapering, cream-colored, bronzy-green-edged leaves that usually spill over in the same direction and become buff colored in fall, as well as inconspicuous open panicles of yellowish green flowers that appear in late summer or early fall. Hakonechloa needs shelter from hot afternoon sun. Amend the soil liberally with organic matter such as compost, leaf mold, or peat moss before planting.

Halesia monticola

Halesia (ha-LEE-zhi-a)
SILVER BELL

USDA Hardiness: zones 4-8
AHS Heat: zones 8-1
Height: 25 to 80 feet
Plant type: tree
Soil: moist, well-drained, acid, fertile
Light: bright full shade to full sun

Silver bell's dangling clusters of white or rose-colored bell-shaped flowers in spring appear before or with the dark yellow-green leaves, which hold their color until they turn yellow early in the fall. Green to brown four-winged fruits remain after the leaves have fallen. The furrowed and plated bark is gray, brown, and black. Silver bell serves well as an understory tree but can also be used to create shade for other plants. Silver bells do best in soil supplemented with organic matter. They are tolerant of full sun, are pest resistant, and require little maintenance.

Hebe (HEE-bee)
HEBE

USDA Hardiness: zones 8-10
AHS Heat: zones 9-3
Height: 2 to 5 feet
Plant type: shrub
Soil: well-drained
Light: full sun to partial shade

Native to New Zealand, hebes are rounded, leathery-leaved evergreen shrubs that produce spikes of white, pink, red, lavender, or purple flowers 2 to 4 inches long at

Hebe buxifolia

the ends of the branches, making them good candidates for shrub borders, hedges, edgings, rock gardens, and perennial beds. Hebes need good drainage and prefer either acid or alkaline soil of average fertility. They thrive in cool coastal gardens and need partial shade where summers are hot. They are tolerant of salt spray.

Hamamelis mollis

Hamamelis (ha-ma-MEL-lis)
WITCH HAZEL

USDA Hardiness: zones 5-8
AHS Heat: zones 9-3
Height: 15 to 20 feet
Plant type: shrub, tree
Soil: moist, well-drained
Light: partial shade to full sun

Witch hazel brightens and perfumes the winter landscape with yellow to red ribbonlike flowers, then dazzles the fall garden with colorful foliage. Best located where their scent and bright flowers can be appreciated at close range, witch hazels are underused in American gardens. Witch hazel grows best in slightly acid soil enriched with organic matter. If the plant becomes open, prune to encourage dense growth. Propagate by layering if a shrub, with cuttings if a tree.

Hedeoma (hed-ee-O-ma)
AMERICAN PENNYROYAL

USDA Hardiness: zone 0
AHS Heat: zones 12-2
Height: 4 to 12 inches
Plant type: hardy annual
Soil: rich, sandy
Light: full sun to light shade

With mint-scented leaves growing along erect, branching stems, American pennyroyal develops into low, bushy mounds. Tiny, insignificant

Hedeoma pulegioides

flower clusters grow where leaves meet stems, emerging from summer through fall. Use American pennyroyal as an edging, ground cover, or filler plant in informal borders. *H. pulegioides* (American pennyroyal) has hairy oval leaves along square stems and blue to lavender flowers. Sow it into lawns for fragrance. Hedeoma seeds are widely used as an herbal repellent for fleas and weevils. Although it figures in herbal medicine, its oil can be toxic. Start American pennyroyal seed indoors 6 weeks before the last frost or sow directly outdoors.

Helenium autumnale

Helenium (hel-EE-nee-um)
SNEEZEWEED

USDA Hardiness: zones 4-8
AHS Heat: zones 8-1
Height: 2½ to 6 feet
Plant type: perennial
Soil: moist, well-drained
Light: full sun

Sneezeweed's clumps of erect stems lined with willowy leaves bear daisylike flowers with fan-shaped petals and prominent centers in summer. *H. autumnale* (common sneezeweed) bears flowers up to 2 inches wide that bloom in summer and persist through frost on 5- to 6-foot-tall stems; 'Brilliant' has profuse bronze blossoms; 'Bruno', mahogany flowers on 4-foot plants; 'Butterpat', clear yellow petals surrounding bronze centers on 4- to 5-foot plants; 'Moerheim Beauty', reddish bronze blossoms on 4-foot stems. Heleniums require adequate moisture, full sun, and rich soil.

Helianthus (hee-lee-AN-thus)
SUNFLOWER

USDA Hardiness: zones 4-9
AHS Heat: zones 11-3
Height: 2 to 10 feet
Plant type: annual, perennial
Soil: moist, well-drained
Light: full sun

This large genus includes over 150 species of heat-loving annuals and perennials. Sunflowers in yellow, cream, mahogany, crimson, and assorted blends appear from

Helianthus maximiliana

midsummer to frost on erect stalks. *H. annuus* (common sunflower) produces flowers composed of yellow rays surrounding brown or purple disk flowers. *H. angustifolius* (swamp sunflower) has flowers 2 to 3 inches across with brown to purple centers on stems to 7 feet tall. *H. maximiliana* (Maximilian's sunflower) has 3-inch, yellow blooms from August to late fall on stems 7 to 10 feet tall. Sow annual sunflower seed outdoors after frost. Propagate perennial sunflowers by division in spring. Plants thrive in hot, dry weather conditions.

Helianthemum nummularium

Helianthemum (hee-lee-AN-the-mum)
SUN ROSE, ROCK ROSE

USDA Hardiness: zones 6-8
AHS Heat: zones 10-3
Height: 6 to 12 inches
Plant type: shrub
Soil: dry, poor, well-drained, alkaline
Light: full sun

Sun roses provide a colorful cover for dry, sunny slopes, look good tumbling out of a crevice in a rock wall, and brighten rock gardens. From late spring to early summer, flowers resembling wild roses with five crepe-paper-like petals cover a low-growing mound with trailing stems. Varieties come in yellow, orange, red, rose, pink, apricot, salmon, peach, white, bicolors, and in double flowers. Sun roses like dry, poor, gravelly or sandy soils and do not grow well in fertile soils. Good drainage is essential. Prune in early spring to encourage dense growth, and prune again after flowering. Protect with mulch over the winter.

Helichrysum (hel-i-KRY-sum)
EVERLASTING

USDA Hardiness: zones 7-11
AHS Heat: zones 9-3
Height: 1 to 3 feet
Plant type: tender perennial, perennial
Soil: light, well-drained
Light: full sun

This Australian native, also known as immortelle, produces papery-textured flowers in shades of white, yellow, orange, salmon, red, and pink. What appear to be the

Helichrysum hybrid June Bride™ 'Monse'

flower's petals are actually colorful bracts; the true flowers are at the center of the flower head. Flowers retain their colors very well when dried. *H.* hybrid June Bride™ 'Monse' bears warm rose-pink flower heads on erect stems 2 to 3 feet tall. Start seed indoors 6 to 8 weeks prior to the last frost. In warm climates, seed can be sown directly in the garden. Once established, plants thrive in dry soil and often self-seed. They do not perform well in areas with very high humidity.

Helictotrichon
(he-lik-toh-TRY-kon)

BLUE OAT GRASS

USDA Hardiness: zones 4-8
AHS Heat: zones 9-1
Height: 2 to 3 feet
Plant type: ornamental grass
Soil: well-drained
Light: full sun

Blue oat grass produces a dense clump of stiff, steel blue foliage and is a valuable addition to a rock garden or a

Helictotrichon sempervirens

herbaceous border for both color and form. The flowers are buff-colored and appear in graceful sprays above the leaves. *H. sempervirens* forms a dense mound with light blue-gray leaves and flowers arrayed in drooping, one-sided clusters on slender stems held above the foliage. Blue oat grass is easy to grow in most soils, including dry, infertile ones. It requires good air circulation to prevent disease.

Heliotropium
(hee-lee-oh-TRO-pee-um)

HELIOTROPE

USDA Hardiness: zones 10-11
AHS Heat: zones 12-1
Height: 1 to 3 feet
Plant type: tender perennial
Soil: well-drained, fertile
Light: full sun to partial shade

Heliotrope is a tender perennial from Peru grown as an annual in temperate zones. Large clusters of summer flowers range from deep pur-

Heliotropium arborescens

ple to white and bear a lovely vanilla fragrance. *H. arborescens* (cherry pie) bears five-petaled flowers occurring in clusters as large as a foot across; 'Marine', a compact variety reaching 2 feet, has large deep purple flowers and is excellent for bedding, although it lacks intense fragrance. Start seed indoors 10 to 12 weeks prior to the last frost, or buy young plants in spring. Plants can also be started from cuttings. Do not transplant to the garden until soil has warmed, as plants are very frost sensitive. Keep heliotropes well watered.

Heliopsis *(hee-li-OP-sis)*

FALSE SUNFLOWER

USDA Hardiness: zones 4-9
AHS Heat: zones 9-1
Height: 3 to 5 feet
Plant type: perennial
Soil: moist, well-drained loam
Light: full sun

False sunflower bears bright flowers in shades of yellow and gold with single or double rows of petals surrounding prominent centers on

Heliopsis helianthoides

bushy plants. They make excellent cut flowers. *H. helianthoides* var. *scabra* bears single, semidouble, or double flowers 2 to 3 inches across on plants 3 to 5 feet tall; 'Golden Plume' grows double yellow flowers; 'Incomparabilis', semidouble yellow flowers with dark centers; 'Summer Sun', semidouble golden yellow flowers; 'Karat', large single yellow flowers. Heliopsis is vigorous in full sun but requires watering in dry spells.

Helleborus *(hell-e-BOR-us)*

HELLEBORE

USDA Hardiness: zones 4-9
AHS Heat: zones 8-1
Height: 15 to 24 inches
Plant type: perennial
Soil: moist, well-drained, organic
Light: bright full shade

Cup-shaped flowers in subtle hues and evergreen foliage are hellebore's trademarks. Plant in borders and along paths where its quiet, sometimes off-season beauty can

Helleborus orientalis

be enjoyed. *H. orientalis* (Lenten rose) bears cream, pink, plum, brownish purple, chocolate brown or nearly black flowers 2 inches wide in clusters of 2 to 6 in early to midspring. Cover loosely with mulch in severe winters. Propagation by division is difficult; roots are brittle, and older plants may fail to bloom for a year after being disturbed.

Hemerocallis hybrid 'Yellow Lollipop'

Hemerocallis
(hem-er-o-KAL-is)
DAYLILY

USDA Hardiness: zones 3-9
AHS Heat: zones 12-1
Height: 12 inches to 4 feet
Plant type: perennial
Soil: average, well-drained
Light: full sun to partial shade

Trumpet-shaped, lilylike flowers rise above dense mounds of arching, grasslike leaves on naked branched stems. Each bloom lasts only a day, but flowering can last for weeks or even months. Of the hundreds of cultivated varieties, the large hybrids are useful for naturalized areas, ground covers, banks, and borders. Smaller varieties are ideal for border fronts and rock gardens. Some pale varieties, which fade in the hot sun, are night-bloomers. Daylilies tolerate a range of soil types, but a too-rich soil will produce much foliage and few flowers; partial shade is preferable in the South.

Heuchera (HEW-ker-a)
ALUMROOT

USDA Hardiness: zones 3-8
AHS Heat: zones 8-2
Height: 12 to 30 inches
Plant type: perennial
Soil: moist, well-drained, fertile
Light: partial shade to full sun

Heuchera micrantha

Mounds of handsome lobed leaves make alumroot useful for rock gardens, edgings, and perennial beds. Delicate bell-shaped flowers bloom in late spring and summer. *H. micrantha* 'Palace Purple' (small-flowered alumroot) is primarily a foliage plant with wrinkled leaves that are deep purple-red in spring and fall, fading to purplish bronze-green in hot weather. *H. sanguinea* (coral bells) has pink, white, or red flowers. Alumroot grows best in shade in warmer climates. Supplement soil with peat moss, leaf mold, or finished compost.

Heteromeles arbutifolia

Heteromeles
(het-er-oh-MEE-leez)
TOYON, CALIFORNIA HOLLY

USDA Hardiness: zones 8-10
AHS Heat: zones 12-8
Height: 12 to 25 feet
Plant type: small tree, shrub
Soil: well-drained
Light: full sun to partial shade

The California holly has glossy, dark, evergreen leaves. In late summer it produces large clusters of orange-to-red berries that attract birds and other wildlife to the garden. *H. arbutifolia* has leathery, sharply toothed leaves and inconspicuous white flowers that bloom in spring and are followed by showy clusters of fruit. Although California holly prefers a fertile, well-drained soil and full sun, it tolerates a wide range of conditions, including drought and partial shade.

Hibiscus (hy-BIS-kus)
MALLOW, ROSE MALLOW

USDA Hardiness: zones 9-11
AHS Heat: zones 12-1
Height: 18 inches to 8 feet
Plant type: shrub
Soil: moist, well-drained
Light: full sun to light shade

Hibiscus rosa-sinensis

These shrubby tender perennials are attractively grown as annuals in many temperate gardens. Some are grown for their ornamental foliage, while others produce large funnel-shaped five-petaled flowers in burgundy, purple, red, rose, white, or bicolors, with prominent stamens that add a tropical flavor to a border. *H. rosa-sinensis* (tropical hibiscus, Chinese hibiscus) produces a profusion of blooms and vigorous growth when placed in full sun. These showy shrubs are useful as screening, in containers, and in the back of a border. Plants tolerate heat as long as abundant moisture is supplied.

Hierochloë odorata

Hierochloë (hi-er-OK-low-ee)
SWEET GRASS

USDA Hardiness: zones 4-9
AHS Heat: zones 10-3
Height: 10 to 24 inches
Plant type: grass
Soil: moist, well-drained
Light: full sun to light shade

Sweet grass forms dense tufts of bright green leaves that gradually spread into wide mats. In spring, tall flowering stalks bear loose clusters of brown spikelets above the leaves. Use sweet grass as an informal edging or allow tufts to spread in a meadow garden. Its creeping runners form mats of roots that help hold soil in steep or difficult locations. Leaves develop a long-lasting aroma of vanilla or new-mown hay when dried. Sweet grass runners can be invasive; confine plants in pots with the bottoms removed to contain their spread.

Humulus (HEW-mew-lus)
HOP

USDA Hardiness: zones 6-9
AHS Heat: zones 9-1
Height: 10 to 25 feet
Plant type: perennial
Soil: rich, moist, well-drained
Light: full sun to light shade

Humulus lupulus

Twining deciduous vines with coarse foliage like that of grapevines, hops quickly clamber over trellises. In summer, female and male flowers appear on separate plants. Dried female flowers, young leaves, and young side shoots are used as a bitter fragrance and flavoring. Because female plants are more desirable than male ones and the gender of plants grown from seed is unknown for 3 years, it is best to grow hops from tip cuttings taken from female plants, divide their roots, or remove their rooted suckers in spring.

Hosta fluctans

Hosta (HOS-ta)
PLANTAIN LILY

USDA Hardiness: zones 4-9
AHS Heat: zones 9-2
Height: 15 inches to 4 feet
Plant type: perennial
Soil: moist, well-drained, slightly acid
Light: partial to bright full shade

The many forms of plantain lilies are prized mainly for their spreading clumps of attractive foliage, making them ideal for textural and color accents in perennial beds and borders. Trumpet-shaped flowers appear in summer. Good drainage is essential, especially in winter. Although most hostas thrive in deep shade, variegated and blue forms need bright shade to hold their color. Hosta tolerates sun in cooler areas with abundant moisture. Hostas for hot, muggy climates include *H. fortuneii* 'Albomarginata'.

Hyacinthoides (hy-a-sin-THOY-deez)
BLUEBELL

USDA Hardiness: zones 4-10
AHS Heat: zones 9-1
Height: to 20 inches
Plant type: bulb
Soil: moist, well-drained, fertile
Light: bright full shade to full sun

Hyacinthoides hispanica

Dainty bell-shaped flowers nod from stems above clumps of foliage in spring. Excellent for naturalizing beneath trees, in mass plantings, and in borders with other bulbs, bluebells also make good container plants and are useful as cut flowers. *H. hispanica* (Spanish bluebell) has 20-inch stems producing up to 15 flowers ranging from white to pink to violet. Bluebells are vigorous growers and successfully compete with tree roots. Amend soil with organic matter and plant 3 to 4 inches deep in the fall. Water regularly during dry periods, except in summer. Bluebells spread quickly by self-seeding and can often become weedy. Propagate by division.

Hydrangea *(hy-DRANE-jee-a)*
HYDRANGEA

USDA Hardiness: zones 6-9
AHS Heat: zones 9-3
Height: 3 to 80 feet
Plant type: shrub, vine
Soil: moist, well-drained
Light: bright full shade to full sun

Hydrangea macrophylla

Hydrangeas produce flowers that change color through their bloom period, usually from white to purplish pink, then to brown. Most are shrubs, but the climbing hydrangea is a vine with twining stems. The flower clusters consist of small, starlike, fertile flowers surrounded by larger, showier, sterile flowers. The long-lasting blossoms are valued for fresh and dried arrangements and wreaths. All hydrangeas are coarse in texture, and some offer colorful fall foliage and attractive exfoliating bark. Hydrangeas are intolerant of drought at any time of year and wilt under hot afternoon sun in warmer climates. They can be grown as herbaceous perennials in colder climates.

Hydrastis *(hy-DRAS-tis)*
ORANGEROOT

USDA Hardiness: zones 4-9
AHS Heat: zones 8-4
Height: 6 to 12 inches
Plant type: perennial
Soil: organic, moist, well-drained
Light: full to light shade

Hydrastis canadensis

H. canadensis (goldenseal, turmeric) sends up solitary stems, each with a few broad, coarse leaves, and very slowly spreads into mats in woodland gardens. Tiny spring flowers develop into inedible fruits resembling raspberries in fall. Goldenseal has been used in various herbal medicines, however modern herbalists now consider it toxic, especially in large doses. In the past, inflated claims for its medicinal powers led to overcollecting in the wild, and goldenseal is now endangered in many places. Protect hydrastis with a winter mulch.

Hymenocallis *(hy-men-o-KAL-is)*
SPIDER LILY

USDA Hardiness: zones 6-10
AHS Heat: zones 12-8
Height: 18 to 30 inches
Plant type: bulb
Soil: sandy, wet
Light: full sun to partial shade

Hymenocallis occidentalis

Spider lilies grow from bulbs and are found in low woodlands, swamps, and moist fields. Their large, fragrant flowers are composed of six straplike petals surrounding a funnel-shaped cup. They are excellent additions to a bog garden. *H. occidentalis* [also listed as *H. caroliniana*] (spider lily) bears white flowers appearing in spring in the South and in summer in cooler regions. Plant *H. occidentalis* bulbs in full sun to partial shade in fall, in a location where they will receive abundant moisture. North of USDA zone 6, where spider lilies are not hardy, the bulbs can be planted in spring and lifted and brought indoors for winter.

Hypericum *(hy-PER-i-kum)*
ST.-JOHN'S-WORT

USDA Hardiness: zones 5-9
AHS Heat: zones 9-2
Height: 1 to 3 feet
Plant type: perennial
Soil: average to poor
Light: full sun to partial shade

Hypericum x moseranum

St.-John's-wort bears brilliant yellow five-petaled flowers. *H. calycinum* (creeping St.-John's-wort) spreads by stolons and rooting stems to create a thick carpet of dark green semi-evergreen leaves and is useful for covering difficult hillsides. *H.* x *moseranum* (gold flower) grows to 2 feet with bowl-shaped flowers; 'Tricolor' has variegated leaves edged in red. Shrubbier forms are suited for borders and edgings. St.-John's-wort grows well in poor, sandy, or gravelly soils and requires little care. Cold winters often kill plant tops, but subsequent flowering is not affected.

Hyssopus (hiss-O-pus)
HYSSOP

USDA Hardiness: zones 6-8
AHS Heat: zones 9-2
Height: 18 to 36 inches
Plant type: perennial
Soil: well-drained to dry
Light: full sun to light shade

Hyssopus officinalis

Hyssop's square stems are lined with camphor-scented narrow leaves and tipped with thick spikes of tubular flowers having flared lips favored by bees and hummingbirds. Grow them as bushy specimens or plant them closely for low hedges. Hyssop is used in cooking, herbal teas, and potpourri. *H. officinalis* (common hyssop, European hyssop) has willowlike leaves and blue-violet flowers; 'Albus' [also called 'Alb'] (white hyssop) has white flowers; ssp. *aristatus* (rock hyssop) produces fine leaves on 18- to 24-inch plants. Hyssop is sometimes evergreen in milder climates.

Ilex (EYE-lex)
HOLLY

USDA Hardiness: zones 4-10
AHS Heat: zones 9-3
Height: 2 to 50 feet
Plant type: shrub, tree
Soil: moist, well-drained
Light: full sun to partial shade

Ilex aquifolium

The genus produces a broad range of mostly evergreen plants. Hollies are ideal foundation plants, hedges, and background plants. The taller hollies make lovely specimen plants and effective screens. Although hollies tolerate partial shade, they prefer full sun. Most evergreen hollies do not endure hot, windy, or dry climates. For best results, provide a loose, well-drained loam. Long-stalked holly tolerates heavy soils and drying wind.

Iberis (eye-BEER-is)
CANDYTUFT

USDA Hardiness: zones 5-9
AHS Heat: zones 9-1
Height: 6 to 18 inches
Plant type: annual, perennial
Soil: well-drained
Light: full sun

Iberis umbellata

These European wildflowers are easy to grow and free flowering. Like the perennial species *[I. sempervirens]*, annual candytuft produces clusters of tiny four-petaled flowers in white, pink, red, lilac, or violet above dark green leaves. Plants flower throughout the summer and are effective in rock gardens and borders, as an edging, or in a planter, where their sweet fragrance will be noticed. Sow annual seed in the garden in fall or as soon as soil can be worked in the spring, thinning to allow 6 to 9 inches between seedlings. Propagate perennial candytuft from stem cuttings taken after flowering or by division in spring or fall. Plants thrive in city conditions.

Impatiens (im-PAY-shens)
BALSAM, JEWELWEED

USDA Hardiness: zone 11
AHS Heat: zones 10-11
Height: 6 inches to 8 feet
Plant type: annual
Soil: moist, well-drained
Light: full sun to full shade

Impatiens wallerana

Massed as edgings or ground covers, impatiens brighten a shady garden with flowers in jeweled hues from summer through frost. Low-growing types such as *I. wallerana* (busy Lizzie) are ideal for planters and hanging baskets. Start impatiens indoors 3 to 4 months prior to the last frost, or purchase bedding plants to transplant to the garden after all danger of frost has passed. Plant 8-foot-tall *I. glandulifera* seed outdoors in fall. Space *I. glandulifera* 2 feet apart, others 12 to 18 inches apart. Most species prefer some shade and abundant water.

Imperata *(im-per-AY-ta)*
JAPANESE BLOOD GRASS

USDA Hardiness: zones 6-9
AHS Heat: zones 9-4
Height: 12 to 18 inches
Plant type: ornamental grass
Soil: well-drained
Light: full sun to partial shade

Imperata cylindrica rubra

Japanese blood grass produces clumps of leaves whose top half turns a rich blood red. The flowers of this grass are ornamentally insignificant, but its vivid foliage, which provides color from summer through fall, makes it well worth including in a garden. *I. cylindrica rubra* 'Red Baron' is outstanding for long-season color contrast. Japanese blood grass grows in sun or partial shade in nearly any well-drained soil. *Note:* If any part of 'Red Baron' reverts to green, it should be removed at once. The green form is highly aggressive and is listed in the United States as a noxious weed.

Inula *(IN-yew-la)*
INULA

USDA Hardiness: zones 4-9
AHS Heat: zones 8-1
Height: 6 to 12 inches
Plant type: perennial
Soil: well-drained, average fertility
Light: full sun to partial shade

Inula ensifolia

Inula produces cheerful, bright yellow, daisylike flowers at the tips of wiry stems that form mounds. *I. acaulis* (stemless inula) has single yellow flowers over tufts of spatulate leaves in midsummer. The dense blooms of *I. ensifolia* (swordleaf inula) last 2 to 3 weeks in warmer zones, up to 6 weeks in cooler areas. Propagate inulas from seed or by division in spring or fall.

Ipomoea *(eye-po-MEE-a)*
MORNING GLORY

USDA Hardiness: zones 10-11
AHS Heat: zones 12-1
Height: 15 to 20 feet
Plant type: vine
Soil: moist, well-drained, sandy
Light: full sun

Ipomoea tricolor

This large genus of over 500 species includes many ornamentals that are particularly useful for covering fences, trellises, and banks. *I. tricolor* includes the popular 'Heavenly Blue', with dark, sky-blue flowers on a twining vine. *I. alba* (moonflower) has large, white fragrant flowers that open at night. Amend heavy soils with sand, and add only a modest amount of organic matter; too-rich soil will produce lush foliage but few flowers. Plant seeds 12 to 18 inches apart in a sunny location after all danger of frost has passed, or start seeds indoors in individual pots 4 to 6 weeks before the last frost date and then transplant gently. Most species are drought tolerant.

Iris *(EYE-ris)*
FLAG, FLEUR-DE-LIS

USDA Hardiness: zones 4-11
AHS Heat: zones 8-4
Height: 18 inches to 5 feet
Plant type: rhizome
Soil: moist, well-drained, fertile
Light: partial shade to full sun

Iris sibirica

Irises bloom in a rainbow of colors on zigzag stems rising from sword-shaped leaves that remain attractive even when plants are not in bloom. With over 200 species and thousands of varieties, irises vary widely in their appearance, season, and cultural requirements. *I. sibirica* (Siberian iris) grows to 4 feet tall and has violet to blue flowers 3 to 4 inches wide above slender arhcing leaves in early summer. Iris enjoys moisture-retentive soil rich in organic matter.

Itea virginica

Itea (IT-ee-a)
SWEETSPIRE

USDA Hardiness: zones 5-9
AHS Heat: zones 10-7
Height: 2 to 5 feet
Plant type: shrub
Soil: fertile, moist
Light: full sun to partial shade

Sweetspire flowers appear in midsummer, well after most shrubs have finished blooming. In fall its leaves turn reddish purple to scarlet and persist for several weeks. *I. japonica* 'Beppu' leaves are rich green in summer and red in fall, and its flowers are white and fragrant; it is useful as a ground cover. *I. virginica* 'Henry's Garnet' has green leaves turning purple-red in fall, with fragrant white flower clusters. Sweetspire is easily transplanted, and new plants can be obtained by dividing an existing specimen. It prefers a rich, moist to wet site. In mild climates it is semi-evergreen.

Juniperus (joo-NIP-er-us)
JUNIPER

USDA Hardiness: zones 2-9
AHS Heat: zones 9-1
Height: 6 inches to 60 feet
Plant type: shrub, tree, ground cover
Soil: light, well-drained
Light: full sun

Juniperus horizontalis

Junipers vary from wide, flat mats that hug the ground to tall, thin spires good for accents or corner plantings. Their scalelike evergreen foliage ranges in color from green to silvery blue to yellow and sometimes assumes a different shade in winter. Tall forms make good screens and windbreaks. Tolerant of almost any soil as long as it is well drained, junipers do best in moist, light soils. Loosen heavy soils with sand. Most junipers tolerate drought and pollution. *J. conferta* (shore juniper) grows well in seaside gardens. *J. horizontalis* (creeping juniper) grows 1 to 2 feet high by 4 to 8 feet wide with trailing branches and foliage turning plum-purple in winter.

Jasminum floridum

Jasminum (JAZ-min-um)
JASMINE, JESSAMINE

USDA Hardiness: zones 6-10
AHS Heat: zones 10-2
Height: 3 to 15 feet
Plant type: shrub, vine
Soil: well-drained, average to poor
Light: full sun to partial shade

A perfect solution for slopes with poor soil, jasmine forms a wide-spreading mound of arching stems that bear bright yellow trumpetlike flowers and triplets of dark green leaflets. Evergreen only in the Deep South, the branches root wherever they contact the soil and can soon cover a large area. Jasmine can also be trained to climb a support, where it may reach 15 feet. In winter, the naked green stems are effective, especially when allowed to trail over a wall. In the Deep South, cut back almost to the ground every 3 to 5 years to restore vigor. Best bloom occurs in full sun.

Kalmia (KAL-mee-a)
MOUNTAIN LAUREL

USDA Hardiness: zones 4-9
AHS Heat: zones 8-3
Height: 7 to 15 feet
Plant type: shrub
Soil: moist, well-drained, acid
Light: full sun to full shade

Kalmia latifolia

In early summer, mountain laurel bears white, pink, or rose-colored blossoms, set off by a background of dark, leathery leaves. It is equally at home as a foundation plant, within a mixed-shrub border, or in a naturalized, woodland garden. Mountain laurel is easy to grow and virtually maintenance free as long as its cultural conditions are met. While it adapts to sun or shade, it requires a moist, acid soil to which generous amounts of organic matter have been added. Mulch to maintain moisture.

Kerria japonica

Kerria *(KER-ee-a)*
JAPANESE KERRIA

USDA Hardiness: zones 4-9
AHS Heat: zones 8-3
Height: 3 to 8 feet
Plant type: shrub
Soil: fertile, loamy, well-drained
Light: partial to full shade

Japanese kerria produces masses of bright yellow spring flowers on arched, lime green stems. Its green stems add color to the winter landscape. *K. japonica* is deciduous, with bright green leaves and bright yellow flowers; 'Picta' leaves have an attractive white margin; 'Pleniflora' flowers are double, rounded, and golden yellow. Japanese kerria performs better with some shade; too much sun causes flowers to fade quickly. Prune to remove dead branches whenever they appear, and remove green shoots that arise among the variegated foliage of 'Picta'.

Kochia *(KOE-kee-a)*
BURNING BUSH

USDA Hardiness: zone 11
AHS Heat: zones 9-2
Height: 2 to 4 feet
Plant type: annual
Soil: moist, well-drained
Light: full sun

Kochia scoparia f. trichophylla

Its fine-textured foliage and neat, symmetrical form make burning bush an attractive summer hedge, screen, or background for a flower border. *K. scoparia f. trichophylla* (summer cypress, firebush) has dense, feathery foliage that is light green in summer, turning bright red in fall; 'Acapulco Silver' produces variegated silver-tipped leaves. Start seed indoors in individual peat pots 6 to 8 weeks prior to the last frost or plant directly in the garden after all danger of frost has passed. Do not cover the seed; it needs light for germination. Plants can be sheared to maintain their shape or size, and they tolerate heat. Avoid overwatering. In windy locations, plants may require staking.

Kniphofia uvaria

Kniphofia *(ny-FO-fee-a)*
TORCH LILY, TRITOMA

USDA Hardiness: zones 5-9
AHS Heat: zones 9-1
Height: 2 to 4 feet
Plant type: perennial
Soil: well-drained, sandy loam
Light: full sun

Torch lily's stiff clusters of tubular flowers on bare stems held above tufts of stiff, gray-green leaves are a bold accent in a mixed border and a favorite visiting place of hummingbirds. *K. uvaria* (red-hot poker) bears individual flowers clustered along the top several inches of stem like a bristly bottle brush; these open a bright red, then turn yellow as they mature. Plant torch lilies 1½ to 2 feet apart in locations protected from strong winds. They are heat tolerant.

Koelreuteria *(kol-roo-TEER-ee-a)*
GOLDEN RAIN TREE

USDA Hardiness: zones 5-9
AHS Heat: zones 8-5
Height: 30 to 40 feet
Plant type: tree
Soil: well-drained
Light: partial shade to full sun

Koelreuteria paniculata

A delightful small tree to shade a garden bench or patio, the golden rain tree produces airy sprays of yellow flowers in early summer on wide-spreading branches. The dense canopy consists of large compound leaves that are medium bright green, changing to yellow before dropping in fall. Golden rain tree tolerates a wide variety of conditions, including drought. Easily grown from seed, it grows best in soil well amended with peat moss or leaf mold. Provide shelter from wind.

Lagerstroemia
(la-gur-STREE-mee-a)
CRAPE MYRTLE

USDA Hardiness: zones 7-9
AHS Heat: zones 10-2
Height: 7 to 25 feet
Plant type: tree
Soil: moist, well-drained
Light: full sun

Lagerstroemia indica

Crape myrtle's large trusses of crinkly flowers in pink, white, rose, or purple come in late summer at a time when little else may be in bloom. In fall, the dark green leaves turn red, orange, and yellow, all on the same plant. As the light gray bark ages, it exfoliates, revealing dark gray and brown underbark. Crape myrtle enjoys summer heat. *L. indica* will tolerate drought with occasional deep watering. At its northern limits, it is grown as a herbaceous perennial; when severe cold kills the plant to the ground, it returns the next spring with abundant, lush new growth and flowers late in the growing season.

Lamium *(LAY-mee-um)*
DEAD NETTLE

USDA Hardiness: zones 4-8
AHS Heat: zones 8-1
Height: 8 to 12 inches
Plant type: perennial
Soil: well-drained
Light: partial to full shade

Lamium maculatum

The spreading, trailing habit of dead nettle makes it useful as a ground cover among shrubs or trees or in the front of a shady border. It is well suited for cascading over a stone wall or from a container. *L. maculatum* 'Beacon Silver' has silver leaves with narrow green margins, and whorls of pink flowers in late spring; 'Chequers' has green leaves with a wide stripe down the center, and pink flowers in late spring through summer. Dead nettle tolerates a wide range of soils as long as they are well drained. Bare patches may appear if the plant is allowed to dry out too often. It prefers shade but will tolerate sun if sufficient moisture is supplied.

Lathyrus *(LATH-er-us)*
LATHYRUS

USDA Hardiness: zones 9-10
AHS Heat: zones 8-1
Height: 6 inches to 9 feet
Plant type: annual, perennial
Soil: moist, well-drained
Light: full sun to partial shade

L. odoratus (sweet pea) is a hardy annual that bears puffy flowers on branching flowering stalks. It can be used as a trailing ground cover, a climbing vine for a

Lathyrus odoratus

screen or backdrop, or a bushy accent among bulbs. The sweet pea produces deep rose, blue, purple, scarlet, white, cream, salmon, pink, and bicolored flowers; 'Bijou Mixed' is a bush type that grows to 12 inches with a full range of colors; 'Royal Family' is a vining type that comes in a wide range of colors, grows to 6 feet, and is heat resistant. Provide climbing types with support. Perennial species such as *L. latifolius* (perennial pea) are propagated by seeds and cuttings. Mulch to keep soil cool, and provide abundant water.

Laurus *(LAR-us)*
LAUREL, SWEET BAY

USDA Hardiness: zones 8-11
AHS Heat: zones 12-7
Height: 4 to 40 feet
Plant type: shrub, tree
Soil: well-drained
Light: full sun to light shade

In warm climates, evergreen *L. nobilis* (bay laurel) grows as a multistemmed shrub or tree to 40 feet; in colder climates, it reaches 4 to 6 feet as

Laurus nobilis

a container-grown standard. The intensely flavored leaves are used in cooking and bouquets garnis. Bay laurel is a traditional medicinal and insect-repellent herb. *L. nobilis* (bay laurel, bay, bay tree, true laurel) has narrow, gray-green leaves; 'Angustifolia' (willow-leaved bay) has extremely narrow leaves; 'Aurea', tapered golden yellow leaves. Choose sites protected from winds for laurel.

Lavandula (lav-AN-dew-la)

LAVENDER

USDA Hardiness: zones 5-10
AHS Heat: zones 12-7
Height: 1 to 4 feet
Plant type: perennial, small shrub
Soil: well-drained to dry, neutral to alkaline
Light: full sun

The gray-green woolly foliage of lavender, prized for its fragrance, contrasts well with both dark green and blue plants in the landscape.

Lavandula stoechas

Dainty flower spikes top tightly packed upright stems in late spring to summer. Lavender is used in edgings, rock gardens, and perennial beds, and its fine-textured evergreen foliage softens the landscape. The species can also be trimmed into a low hedge. *L. stoechas* (Spanish lavender) grows to 3 feet tall with short dark purple spikes. Good in hot, dry areas, fast drainage is essential for lavender; loosen heavy soils with sand, and do not fertilize.

Leptospermum
(lep-toh-SPER-mum)

NEW ZEALAND TEA TREE

USDA Hardiness: zones 9-10
AHS Heat: zones 12-3
Height: 6 to 10 feet
Plant type: shrub
Soil: fertile, moist, well-drained, acid
Light: full sun to light shade

The New Zealand tea tree is a fine-textured evergreen shrub with a dense branching habit and small leaves. Its flowers

Leptospermum scoparium

are borne in winter, spring, or summer, and though blossoms of the species are white, varieties are available with pink or red flowers. The New Zealand tea tree is easy to grow in mild climates in a well-drained acid to neutral soil. It prefers full sun, except in hot dry areas, where it benefits from partial shade, and thrives under humid, coastal conditions. Although it is somewhat drought tolerant, supplemental water should be supplied moderately, especially where the climate is hot.

Lavatera (lav-a-TEER-a)

TREE MALLOW

USDA Hardiness: zone 0
AHS Heat: zones 12-1
Height: 2 to 6 feet
Plant type: annual
Soil: well-drained
Light: full sun

Lavatera is a hardy annual with a bushy habit and long-blooming cup-shaped summer flowers that resemble hollyhocks. *L. trimestris* pro-

Lavatera trimestris

duces solitary flowers, each with five wide petals, borne in great numbers throughout the summer in shades of pink, red, and white; 'Mont Blanc' bears pure white flowers; 'Silver Cup' bears salmon pink flowers with darker veins. Sow seed outdoors in midspring. Young plants require abundant water and should be mulched. Once established, plants are drought resistant. Deadhead to prolong flowering.

Leucojum (loo-KO-jum)

SNOWFLAKE

USDA Hardiness: zones 3-9
AHS Heat: zones 9-1
Height: 6 to 18 inches
Plant type: bulb
Soil: moist, well-drained
Light: dappled shade to full sun

A native of woodlands, the snowflake is at home in the dappled light of the shade garden. Dainty, bell-shaped white flowers bloom above dark green straplike leaves.

Leucojum aestivum

Snowflakes look best when planted in masses and left undisturbed. *L. aestivum* (summer snowflake, Loddon lily) blooms in the spring and early summer in the East but in the late fall and winter in warm areas of the West; *L. vernum* (spring snowflake) blooms in late winter or spring. Although they grow in average garden soil, snowflakes prefer sandy loam to which leaf mold, peat moss, or dried compost has been added.

Lewisia (loo-ISS-ee-a)
BITTERROOT, LEWISIA

USDA Hardiness: zones 3-8
AHS Heat: zones 8-3
Height: 4 to 12 inches
Plant type: perennial
Soil: dry, rocky
Light: partial shade

Lewisia cotyledon

Lewisias are low-growing perennials that inhabit rocky slopes and open woods of the western United States. They are excellent choices for rock gardens. *L. columbiana* (bitterroot) has clusters of pink-veined white or pink flowers in spring; USDA zones 4-8. *L. cotyledon* (broadleaf lewisia) bears white or pink striped flower clusters in early summer; USDA zones 6-8. *L. rediviva* (bitterroot) produces rosettes of cylindrical leaves in late summer and remains green over winter. In early spring showy rose-colored flowers are borne on short stems; USDA zones 4-8. Lewisias prefer partial shade and must have excellent drainage.

Ligularia (lig-yew-LAY-ree-a)
GOLDEN-RAY

USDA Hardiness: zones 4-10
AHS Heat: zones 8-1
Height: 2 to 6 feet
Plant type: perennial
Soil: moist loam or bog
Light: bright full shade

Ligularia dentata

Large, often colorful leaves decorate clumps 4 to 6 feet tall topped with bold yellow to orange flowers in summer. *L. dentata* (bigleaf golden-ray) has huge saucerlike leaves and daisylike flowers; 'Desdemona' has reddish orange flowers; 'Othello' has yellow-orange blooms; USDA zones 4-8. *L. stenocephala* [also listed as *L. przewalskii*] 'The Rocket' has yellow flower spikes on black stems that emerge in summer and last longer than most blooms of the genus; USDA zones 5-8. Because its enormous leaves lose large amounts of water, golden-ray does best in a cool spot where a continuous supply of moisture is assured.

Liatris (ly-AY-tris)
GAY-FEATHER

USDA Hardiness: zones 3-9
AHS Heat: zones 9-2
Height: 18 inches to 6 feet
Plant type: perennial
Soil: sandy, well-drained
Light: full sun to light shade

Liatris spicata

This genus includes 40 species of hardy North American perennials that grow from 1 to 6 feet tall. The flowers of gay-feather are borne on erect stems, and unlike most spike flowers the top buds open first and proceed downward. The effect is that of a feathery bottle brush. Tall *L. pycnostachya* (Kansas gay-feather) has bright purple flower spikes. *L. spicata* (spike gay-feather) is shorter, with purple or rose flowers in mid- to late summer; 'Kobold' is a dwarf form with bright purple flowers. Most species are extremely tolerant of heat, cold, drought, and poor soil.

Ligustrum (li-GUS-trum)
PRIVET, HEDGE PLANT

USDA Hardiness: zones 6-10
AHS Heat: zones 9-1
Height: 6 to 15 feet
Plant type: shrub
Soil: adaptable
Light: full sun or shade

Ligustrum japonicum

Privet is usually used for hedges, screens, and foundation plants and can also be tailored into topiary specimens. White flowers bloom in late spring or early summer, followed by black or blue-black berries. *L. japonicum* (Japanese privet, waxleaf privet) is an upright, dense evergreen shrub; *L. ovalifolium* 'Aureum' (California privet) has yellow leaves with a green spot in the center when planted in sun, and is semi-evergreen to evergreen in warmer climates. Easily grown and undisturbed by insects or disease, privet adapts to almost any soil except those that are constantly wet.

Lilium (LIL-ee-um)
LILY

USDA Hardiness: zones 3-9
AHS Heat: zones 8-4
Height: 2 to 8 feet
Plant type: bulb
Soil: moist, well-drained, fertile
Light: full sun to light shade

Lilium hybrid 'Orange Pixie'

The dramatic funnel-shaped flowers of the huge genus *Lilium* are varied in color, height, and season of bloom. The wide range of choices allows fanciers to plant lilies for continuous bloom throughout the summer. Lilies attract attention when planted in borders, where they quickly develop into spreading clumps. *L.* hybrid 'Orange Pixie' has bright orange, upward-facing flowers in early summer on 16- to 18-inch stems. Mulch lilies to keep roots cool and moist in summer and protected from frost in winter. Good air circulation is essential, as lilies are susceptible to leaf fungus. Amend soil with organic matter.

Lindera (lin-DER-a)
SPICEBUSH

USDA Hardiness: zones 4-9
AHS Heat: zones 8-1
Height: 6 to 15 feet
Plant type: shrub
Soil: moist, acid
Light: light shade

Lindera benzoin

A round, dense deciduous shrub with erect branches, *L. benzoin* (spicebush, Benjamin bush) offers three-season interest, fragrance, and flavor as a specimen or in a shrub border. Flowers bloom along bare branches of both male and female plants in early spring, followed by spicy-scented leaves. On female plants, leaves color and drop in fall to reveal bright red fruits. The leaves are used in herbal tea, the berries can be ground and used as allspice, and both leaves and berries add to woodsy potpourris. Spicebush is a woodland native, and thrives in moist, shady spots.

Limonium (ly-MO-nee-um)
STATICE

USDA Hardiness: zones 4-11
AHS Heat: zones 12-3
Height: 10 to 24 inches
Plant type: annual, biennial, perennial
Soil: well-drained, sandy, slightly
    alkaline
Light: full sun

Limonium latifolium

Statice, also called sea lavender, bears clusters of brightly colored flowers surrounded by a papery calyx that remains after the rest of the flower drops in a long-lasting display. *L. latifolium* bears branching flower stems carrying an airy, rounded crown of lavender-blue blossoms above a tuft of leathery, oblong evergreen leaves. *L. sinuatum* (notchleaf statice) has pink, blue, lavender, yellow, and white flowers. Start seed indoors in individual peat pots 8 weeks prior to the last frost, or sow directly outdoors in midspring in warm climates. Plants tolerate drought and seaside conditions but will rot in soil that remains wet.

Linum (LY-num)
FLAX

USDA Hardiness: zones 7-9
AHS Heat: zones 8-2
Height: 12 to 24 inches
Plant type: perennial
Soil: well-drained, sandy loam
Light: full sun to light shade

Linum perenne

Delicate flax blooms prolifically with inch-wide, cup-shaped flowers held aloft on soft stems. Though blossoms last only one day, new buds open continuously for 6 weeks or more. *L. flavum* (golden flax) has bright yellow flowers. *L. perenne* (perennial flax) has sky blue, saucer-shaped flowers; 'Diamant White' has abundant white blossoms. Flax is a short-lived perennial but often reseeds itself. It is dependably drought tolerant. It may not survive soil moisture in winter.

Lippia graveolens

Lippia (LIP-ee-a)
MEXICAN OREGANO

USDA Hardiness: zones 10-11
AHS Heat: zones 12-3
Height: 3 to 6 feet
Plant type: tender perennial, shrub
Soil: organic, sandy, well-drained
Light: full sun

Mexican oregano's upright branches are lined with intensely aromatic wrinkled leaves that are widely used in cooking. In frost-free areas, Mexican oregano can be grown as a specimen plant or pruned into a hedge. Elsewhere, grow it as a container plant to move indoors for the winter. *L. graveolens* (Mexican oregano) has pointed, oval, downy leaves and tiny yellow to white winter-to-spring flowers growing where leaves meet stems. Keep Mexican oregano plants slightly on the dry side.

Liriodendron tulipifera

Liriodendron (lir-ee-o-DEN-dron)
TULIP TREE

USDA Hardiness: zones 4-9
AHS Heat: zones 8-2
Height: 70 to 100 feet or more
Plant type: tree
Soil: moist, well-drained, slightly acid
Light: full sun

A giant suitable only for large areas, the deciduous tulip tree has distinctive bright green foliage that turns golden yellow in fall. In mid- to late spring, tuliplike orange and greenish white flowers appear high on the tree after the foliage unfurls. *L. tulipifera* (yellow poplar, tulip magnolia, tulip poplar, whitewood) is a fast-growing species potentially topping 100 feet tall, bearing lobed leaves and cup-shaped flowers 2½ inches wide with six petals. Give tulip trees a moist, deep loam with plenty of room to grow, and lots of water during droughts. They prefer slightly acid soils but will tolerate neutral to slightly alkaline soils.

Liquidambar (li-kwid-AM-bar)
SWEET GUM

USDA Hardiness: zones 6-9
AHS Heat: zones 8-1
Height: 60 to 120 feet
Plant type: tree
Soil: moist, slightly acid
Light: full sun

The sweet gum is a neatly conical tree whose star-shaped leaves linger till late fall and turn lovely shades of yellow, purple, and scarlet.

Liquidambar styraciflua

The bark is deeply furrowed and resembles cork. *L. styraciflua* (American sweet gum, red gum, bilsted) is narrow-pyramidal in youth, maturing into a semirounded crown, bearing glossy rich medium green leaves. Although native to rich, moist bottom lands, sweet gum is tolerant of poor soils if they are neutral to slightly acid and reasonably moist. Plant in spring in soil amended with organic matter.

Liriope (li-RYE-o-pee)
LILYTURF

USDA Hardiness: zones 5-11
AHS Heat: zones 8-3
Height: 12 to 18 inches
Plant type: perennial
Soil: moist to dry, fertile
Light: full shade to full sun

Lilyturf's foliage forms fountainlike tufts that spread into clumps. Flowers resembling grape hyacinths, 6 to 8 inches long, bloom for several weeks in summer and are re-

Liriope muscari

placed by black berries in fall. Although lilyturf tolerates deep shade, full sun, and periodic drought, it grows best in dappled shade and rooted in moist loam. Evergreen in the South, the foliage usually turns brown and disheveled in winter in colder regions.

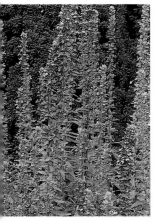

Lobelia (lo-BEE-lee-a)

LOBELIA

USDA Hardiness: zones 3-9
AHS Heat: zones 9-2
Height: 4 inches to 6 feet
Plant type: annual, perennial
Soil: moist, well-drained to wet
Light: full sun to partial shade

Lobelias range from compact annuals to moisture-loving perennials that may grow as tall as 6 feet and provide outstanding color. *L. cardinalis* (cardinal flower) is a perenni-

Lobelia siphilitica

al that bears bright red flowers on 8-inch spikes in summer or fall; *L. siphilitica* (great blue lobelia) is a perennial with blue tubular flowers on erect, 2- to 3-foot leafy stems from late summer to early fall; USDA zones 4-7. Grow annual lobelia from seed; plant perennial types in moist areas. Propagate by seed or division.

Lonicera (lon-ISS-er-a)

HONEYSUCKLE

USDA Hardiness: zones 4-1
AHS Heat: zones 9-3
Height: 4 to 20 feet
Plant type: woody vine, shrub
Soil: moist to dry, average
Light: partial shade to full sun

Honeysuckles produce abundant medium green foliage studded with fragrant flowers and berries often liked by birds. *L. japonica* (Japanese honeysuckle) is a climbing

Lonicera japonica

vine with white or purplish, fragrant flowers; it is naturalized in North America and can be a serious woodland invasive in the Mid-Atlantic states. *L. pileata* (privet honeysuckle) is an evergreen or semi-evergreen spreading shrub. Honeysuckles are easy to grow in almost any soil. Provide vines with a support. Privet honeysuckle does well in seashore conditions.

Lobularia (lob-yew-LAIR-ee-a)

SWEET ALYSSUM

USDA Hardiness: zone 0
AHS Heat: zones 9-1
Height: 4 to 12 inches
Plant type: tender perennial
Soil: well-drained
Light: full sun to partial shade

Sweet alyssum spreads to nearly twice its height, producing tiny fragrant flowers from late spring to frost. In

Lobularia maritima

the front of a mixed border, it neatly covers the dying foliage of spring-flowering bulbs. *L. maritima* is a fine-textured plant with a low-branching and spreading habit and four-petaled flowers borne in clusters; colors include white, lilac, pink, and purple. Start seed indoors 6 to 8 weeks prior to the last frost, or sow directly in the garden in early spring. Avoid overwatering seedlings. In warm areas, they will self-seed. They thrive in cool weather; flowering may stop in hot temperatures.

Lunaria (loo-NAY-ree-a)

HONESTY, MONEY PLANT

USDA Hardiness: zones 6-9
AHS Heat: zones 8-1
Height: 2 to 3 feet
Plant type: annual, biennial
Soil: well-drained
Light: full sun to partial shade

Honesty is grown primarily for its fruit, a flat, oval, translucent seedpod. *L. annua* (silver-dollar, bolbonac) has pink or purple flower

Lunaria annua

clusters in late spring, followed by the seedpods; 'Alba' produces white flowers well displayed when grown against a dark background. Lunaria can be grown as an annual or a biennial. For flowers and seedpods the first year, sow seed outdoors in very early spring, or plant in midsummer to early fall for flowers and seedpods the following year. They tolerate wet and dry conditions and are not fussy about soil quality, as long as it is well drained.

Lupinus 'Russell Hybrids'

Lupinus (loo-PY-nus)
LUPINE

USDA Hardiness: zones 3-10
AHS Heat: zones 9-1
Height: 4 inches to 4 feet
Plant type: perennial
Soil: moist to dry
Light: full sun to partial shade

Lupines inhabit prairies, open woodlands, and dry mountain slopes and bear dense, showy terminal clusters of flowers in spring or summer. *L. perennis* (wild lupine) has late-spring to early-summer flowers that are purplish blue, white, or pink from Maine to Florida; USDA zones 4-8. *L.* 'Russell Hybrids' includes plants to 4 feet tall with showy 18- to 24-inch-long summer-blooming flower spires that open from the bottom up in a multitude of colors and combinations; dwarf strains reach only 18 inches. Most lupines need full sun and dry soils with excellent drainage. *L. sericeus* also thrives in partial shade and is tolerant of both moist and dry soils.

Lysimachia (ly-sim-MAK-ee-a)
LOOSESTRIFE

USDA Hardiness: zones 4-10
AHS Heat: zones 9-3
Height: 1 to 3 feet
Plant type: perennial
Soil: moist, organic, rich
Light: full sun to partial shade

Perennial loosestrifes are native to moist prairies and stream banks throughout the eastern and central United States. Their yellow summer flowers create an attractive display on the banks of a pond or in a moist border. *L. ciliata* (fringed loosestrife) has willowlike pale green leaves. *L. clethroides* (gooseneck loosestrife) grows to 3 feet and has whorls of white flowers. *L. quadrifolia* (prairie loosestrife) has whorls of yellow flowers marked with red, and very narrow, stiff leaves. Loosestrifes thrive in rich soil with ample moisture. Propagate by division.

Lysimachia clethroides

Lychnis coronaria

Lychnis (LIK-nis)
CATCHFLY, CAMPION

USDA Hardiness: zones 4-9
AHS Heat: zones 7-1
Height: 1 to 3 feet
Plant type: perennial
Soil: moist, well-drained, fertile loam
Light: full sun to partial shade

Lychnis bears intensely colored flowers singly or in clusters on slender stems with airy foliage. *L.* x *arkwrightii* (Arkwright campion) has orange-red flowers with nicely contrasting bronze foliage. *L. chalcedonica* (Maltese cross) has 4-inch clusters of scarlet flowers. *L. coronaria* (rose campion) bears cerise flowers amid woolly gray-green leaves. *L. viscaria* (German catchfly) has magenta flowers above tufts of grasslike leaves. Lychnis does best in full sun and dry soil, but will tolerate shade and excess moisture as long as it has good drainage.

Machaeranthera (mak-e-RAN-ther-a)
MACHAERAN-THERA

USDA Hardiness: zones 7-9
AHS Heat: zones 9-5
Height: 6 to 12 inches
Plant type: annual, biennial, perennial
Soil: well-drained, sandy to rocky
Light: full sun

Native to the sunny, open spaces from southern Canada through the Great Plains to the southwestern United States, *M. tanacetifolia* (Tahoka daisy) bears clusters of 2-inch asterlike lavender flowers with yellow centers and dense mounds of deeply cut, sharply pointed foliage 6 to 12 inches tall. Plants readily seed themselves and will make a pretty and colorful ground cover on a favorable site. Tahoka daisy requires full sun and is tolerant of most soils as long as they have excellent drainage. *M. tortifolia* (Mojave aster) is a drought-tolerant perennial that bears blue-violet to lavender flowers; it is found on the desert slopes of the Southwest.

Machaeranthera tanacetifolia

Macleaya cordata

Macleaya (mak-LAY-a)
PLUME POPPY

USDA Hardiness: zones 3-8
AHS Heat: zones 12-7
Height: 6 to 10 feet
Plant type: perennial
Soil: moist, well-drained
Light: full sun

Plume poppy's large clumps of foliage, growing almost as wide as high, develop into imposing, shrubby specimens. Feathery clusters of tiny flowers bloom at the tips of erect stems lined with broad, deeply lobed leaves that cover the plants, producing a frothy effect. Best when used at the back of a border, as temporary screens, or as an anchor in the center of an island bed. Shady conditions and fertile soils will accentuate plume poppy's invasive tendencies.

Mahonia (ma-HO-nee-a)
OREGON GRAPE

USDA Hardiness: zones 5-8
AHS Heat: zones 8-2
Height: 10 inches to 12 feet
Plant type: shrub
Soil: moist, well-drained, acid, fertile
Light: full to dappled shade

Mahonia bealei

Mahonia's yellow flowers in earliest spring can perfume a shady garden. The grapelike berries, maturing in summer, are covered with a blue bloom and are relished by birds. Stiff and formal in habit, mahonia has leathery, hollylike, compound leaves that are blue-green in summer and purplish in winter. Mahonia needs a deep, loamy soil in a site protected from wind. Dry soils or too much sun will yellow leaves. Keep well watered, and mulch to retain moisture. *M. aquifolium* (Oregon grape) tolerates drought. *M. bealei* (leatherleaf mahonia) has very fragrant flowers and berries that turn from robin's-egg blue to blue-black on a 10- to 12-foot-tall shrub.

Magnolia stellata

Magnolia (mag-NO-lee-a)
MAGNOLIA

USDA Hardiness: zones 4-9
AHS Heat: zones 9-1
Height: 10 to 80 feet
Plant type: shrub, tree
Soil: moist to wet, acid, fertile
Light: partial shade to full sun

Large or small, the various forms of magnolia make outstanding accent or specimen plants, their showy flowers sweet with fragrance in spring or summer, and their fat, conelike fruit capsules splitting open to expose red seeds in fall. *M. virginiana* (sweet bay) grows well in wet soils; the other magnolias need moist, well-drained loam. Mulch to conserve moisture and keep the roots cool. *M. stellata* (star magnolia) buds are easily killed by late winter freezes; provide a sheltered spot, and avoid southern exposure that would encourage buds to swell early. Magnolias are surface rooters; do not underplant.

Malus (MAY-lus)
CRAB APPLE

USDA Hardiness: zones 4-8
AHS Heat: zones 8-2
Height: 15 to 25 feet
Plant type: shrub, tree
Soil: moist, well-drained, acid
   to nearly neutral
Light: full sun

Malus 'Radiant'

In spring, scented blossoms 1 to 2 inches wide cloak the entire length of the crab apple's branches, followed by small fruit that may linger into fall if birds allow. There are many species, varieties, and cultivars available, with single and double flowers in white, pink, coral, and reddish purple. Although easy to grow in average soil, crab apples do best in heavy loam. Any pruning should be done before summer, when buds are formed for the next year. Crab apples are susceptible to a number of diseases, including fire blight.

Mandevilla sanderi

Mandevilla
(man-div-ILL-a)
MANDEVILLA

USDA Hardiness: zones 10-11
AHS Heat: zones 12-1
Height: 10 to 20 feet
Plant type: vine
Soil: rich, moist, well-drained
Light: partial shade

Mandevilla can be grown north of its hardiness zone as an annual or as a pot plant kept indoors over winter. The twining vine can be trained to a trellis, post, or arbor, where its pink or white trumpet-shaped flowers produce an elegant summer display set off by lush foliage. Some species bear flowers that are extremely fragrant. Keep mandevilla evenly moist throughout the growing season. Where it is hardy, mulch in fall.

Marshallia *(mar-SHAL-ee-a)*
MARSHALLIA

USDA Hardiness: zones 5-9
AHS Heat: zones 8-2
Height: 8 to 24 inches
Plant type: perennial
Soil: moist, well-drained to dry, sandy
Light: full sun to partial shade

Marshallia grandiflora

These clump-forming perennials grow wild in the eastern and central United States. Their buttonlike flowers and tidy form suit them to planting at the front of a mixed border, along a garden walk, or among stones in a rock garden or terrace. *M. caespitosa* var. *caespitosa* (Barbara's buttons) has ball-shaped clusters of dainty, fragrant white flowers. *M. grandiflora* (large-flowered marshallia) has large, densely packed balls of rose pink flowers with purple stamens. Marshallias will grow well in either moist or dry soils as long as drainage is excellent.

Marrubium supinum

Marrubium
(ma-ROO-bee-um)
HOREHOUND

USDA Hardiness: zones 4-9
AHS Heat: zones 10-2
Height: 18 to 24 inches
Plant type: perennial
Soil: poor, sandy, well-drained to dry
Light: full sun

Horehound's deeply puckered, aromatic gray-green leaves, woolly with white hairs, add texture and soft color as fillers or edgings. Horehound can also be pruned into container specimens. Flowers attract bees. The foliage is a fine filler in fresh or dried bouquets; fresh or dried leaves, which taste slightly of thyme and menthol, are used in teas. Horehound is a staple for cough remedies in herbal medicine. *M. vulgare* (common horehound, white horehound) has heart-shaped leaves with deeply scalloped edges and whorls of tiny white spring-to-summer flowers.

Matricaria
(mat-ri-KAY-ree-a)
GERMAN CHAMOMILE

USDA Hardiness: zones 8-11
AHS Heat: zones 12-1
Height: 24 to 30 inches
Plant type: annual
Soil: average to poor, well-drained
Light: full sun

Matricaria recutita

The erect stems of *M. recutita* (German chamomile, sweet false chamomile, wild chamomile), lined with feathery, finely divided leaves, are crowned with numerous daisy-like, honey-scented flowers from late spring to early summer. The soft foliage is excellent as a filler, especially among plants reaching their maximum size in late summer, as German chamomile tends to disappear after flowering and setting seed. Used in fresh or dried bouquets, its flowers make a soothing tea. Plants self-sow freely. Hang stems in bundles to dry.

Matteuccia (ma-TOO-chee-a)
OSTRICH FERN

USDA Hardiness: zones 2-8
AHS Heat: zones 8-1
Height: 2 to 6 feet
Plant type: fern
Soil: very moist, well-drained, fertile
Light: partial to bright full shade

Under average garden conditions, these magnificently feathery, medium green, deciduous ferns easily tower to 4 feet—and even more in wet soil—making them excellent

Matteuccia struthiopteris

background plants. Vase-shaped, they spread vigorously by way of stolons and can soon cover large areas. Fertile fronds are useful in dried flower arrangements. *M. struthiopteris* (shuttlecock fern) bears upright plumelike fronds with 30 to 50 pairs of feathery leaflets surrounding fertile fronds, which are olive green at first, then change to light brown. Ostrich ferns appreciate consistently moist locations and can tolerate full sun only in moisture-retentive soil in cool climates. They also grow in wet, but not waterlogged, soil.

Melissa (mel-ISS-a)
BALM

USDA Hardiness: zones 4-9
AHS Heat: zones 12-1
Height: 12 to 24 inches
Plant type: perennial
Soil: moist, well-drained
Light: full sun to light shade

The highly aromatic foliage and small flowers of *M. officinalis* (lemon balm, bee balm, sweet balm) attract bees and perfume the garden. Cultivars with colorful foliage are

Melissa officinalis

often sheared and used as ground covers. The plant's fresh leaves are used in cooking, and dried leaves and stems scent potpourri. Sow lemon balm seeds or divide mature plants in spring or fall, spacing them 1 to 2 feet apart. Lemon balm self-sows readily.

Melampodium (mel-am-PO-dee-um)
BLACKFOOT DAISY

USDA Hardiness: zones 4-9
AHS Heat: zones 12-3
Height: 6 to 12 inches
Plant type: annual, perennial
Soil: dry, rocky, well-drained
Light: full sun

The genus includes annuals and perennials that inhabit the dry Southwest. A deep taproot ensures excellent toler-

Melampodium divaricatum

ance for drought. The long-blooming, daisy-like flowers of this genus can be used to brighten meadows, beds and borders. *M. leucanthum* (blackfoot daisy) has 1-inch white daisy-like flowers with yellow centers borne profusely throughout spring and summer. This low-growing evergreen perennial is a good selection for rock gardens and can be massed on a sunny bank to help control erosion. Gray-green leaves form a neat evergreen mound. While sensitive to overwatering, plants will thrive with neglect.

Mentha (MEN-tha)
MINT

USDA Hardiness: zones 4-9
AHS Heat: zones 9-1
Height: 1 to 3 feet
Plant type: perennial
Soil: moist
Light: full sun to partial shade

Mints produce attractive foliage that is valued for its delightful fragrance and intense flavor. In mid- to late summer, mints produce spikes of pink, lavender, or violet flow-

Mentha x piperita

ers. Because they develop a wide-ranging, deep root system, mints spread rapidly and often become invasive. *M. x piperita* (peppermint) has pointed oval leaves, dark green above and often purple-green below, on reddish stems to 3 feet tall, with dense spikes of violet flowers in late summer.

Mertensia virginica

Mertensia (mer-TENZ-ee-a)
BLUEBELLS, LUNGWORT

USDA Hardiness: zones 3-8
AHS Heat: zones 7-1
Height: 18 to 24 inches
Plant type: bulb
Soil: moist, well-drained, fertile
Light: light shade to full sun

Mertensia produces loose clusters of pink buds opening to nodding blue flower bells over several weeks. The blossoms dangle near the top of stems lined with oval, pointed, soft green leaves. Bluebells will slowly grow into large clumps in woodland borders, rock gardens, and wildflower gardens, and provide textural contrast when interplanted with spring bulbs such as narcissus and tulip.

Mirabilis (mi-RAB-i-lis)
FOUR-O'CLOCK

USDA Hardiness: zones 9-11
AHS Heat: zones 12-1
Height: 18 to 36 inches
Plant type: tender perennial
Soil: well-drained to dry, sandy
Light: full sun to partial shade

This native of the American tropics produces a fresh crop of fragrant blossoms in a wide range of colors each evening throughout the summer and into fall. Plants fit well into beds and borders and provide a dense, shrubby edging for walkways and vegetable gardens. M. jalapa (marvel-of-Peru, beauty-of-the-night) has a bushy habit with deep green leaves that provide a perfect foil for colorful trumpet-shaped flowers; colors include white, red, yellow, pink, violet, and bicolors. Once established, these plants often self-seed. They grow equally well in sun or partial shade, and are tolerant of heat and pollution.

Mirabilis jalapa

Mimulus x hybridus

Mimulus (MIM-yew-lus)
MONKEY FLOWER

USDA Hardiness: zone 11
AHS Heat: zones 8-1
Height: 10 to 14 inches
Plant type: tender perennial
Soil: moist, well-drained, fertile
Light: partial to full shade

Blooming from midsummer to fall, monkey flower adds bright color to shady beds and borders. M. x hybridus has tubular flowers in shades of red, yellow, orange, rose, and brown, usually with brown or maroon spotting or mottling. Start seed indoors 10 to 12 weeks prior to the last frost for transplanting to the garden after all danger of frost has passed. Plants benefit from the addition of organic matter to the soil. They require some shade and ample moisture.

Miscanthus (mis-KAN-thus)
EULALIA

USDA Hardiness: zones 5-9
AHS Heat: zones 8-1
Height: 5 to 8 feet
Plant type: ornamental grass
Soil: moist, well-drained
Light: full sun

These fine-textured grasses with their long, narrow, arching leaves and feathery fan-shaped plumes of fall flowers make striking specimens or screens. The clump-forming foliage turns golden tan to buff in winter. M. sinensis (Japanese silver grass, Chinese silver grass) grows 6 to 8 feet tall, with pale pink to reddish flower clusters blooming in fall and lasting nearly all winter; the leaves of 'Gracillimus' have a white midvein. Eulalia grows well in any ordinary garden soil, and is drought tolerant. Too-rich soil may cause stems to fall over. Although eulalia tolerates light shade, it grows best in full sun.

Miscanthus sinensis 'Zebrinus'

Mitchella repens

Mitchella (mi-CHEL-a)
PARTRIDGE-BERRY

USDA Hardiness: zones 3-9
AHS Heat: zones 9-1
Height: 2 to 4 inches
Plant type: perennial
Soil: moist, acid
Light: partial to full shade

Partridgeberry is a dainty low-growing evergreen native to woodlands and stream banks of the eastern and central United States. It provides a fine-textured year-round ground cover for shaded areas and is a lovely addition to a rock garden. *M. repens* (partridgeberry, twinberry) has pairs of white flowers in late spring and bright red berries in fall. Its trailing stems root as they creep over. Partridgeberry thrives in cool, moist, humus-rich soil in partial to full shade. Mulch lightly with leaves in winter.

Monarda didyma

Monarda (mo-NAR-da)
BEE BALM

USDA Hardiness: zones 4-9
AHS Heat: zones 9-2
Height: 2 to 4 feet
Plant type: perennial
Soil: moist or dry loam
Light: full sun to light shade

Bee balm has fragrant leaves and shaggy clusters of tiny tubular flowers growing on square stems. Attractive to bees, butterflies, and hummingbirds, these plants are easily cultivated. *M. didyma* bears scarlet flowers; 'Cambridge Scarlet' bears wine-red flowers; 'Croftway Pink' bears rose-pink blooms; 'Marshall's Delight' is mildew resistant, with pink flowers on 2-foot stems; 'Blue Stocking' blooms violet-blue; 'Snow Queen' is white. Monarda thrives in moist areas, although *M. fistulosa* (wild bergamot, with lilac to pink flowers) and *M. punctata* (spotted bee balm, with purple-spotted yellow blossoms) tolerate dry conditions. Thin plants occasionally for air circulation and to avoid mildew.

Moluccella laevis

Moluccella (mol-lew-SELL-a)
BELLS OF IRELAND

USDA Hardiness: zone 11
AHS Heat: zones 6-1
Height: 2 to 3 feet
Plant type: annual
Soil: moist, well-drained
Light: full sun

This native of the eastern Mediterranean region provides a lovely vertical accent to beds, borders, and indoor arrangements both fresh and dried. It is grown for its showy calyxes, which surround the bases of tiny flowers in late summer and fall. *M. laevis* bears flowers that are fragrant, pink or white, and surrounded by a white-veined, light green calyx that resembles a bell. In areas exposed to wind and rain, bells of Ireland may require staking.

Muhlenbergia capillaris

Muhlenbergia (myoo-len-BUR-jee-a)
MUHLY

USDA Hardiness: zones 6-11
AHS Heat: zones 12-1
Height: 1½ to 4 feet
Plant type: ornamental grass
Soil: moist, sandy to dry, rocky
Light: full sun to partial shade

The graceful foliage and airy flowers of these clump-forming perennial grasses bear softly colored seed heads that develop in fall and remain attractive through winter. *M. capillaris* (pink muhly, hair grass) is nearly evergreen with soft pink flower clusters in early fall followed by purplish seed heads; it needs full sun and adapts to moist to dry, sandy to clayey soil and tolerates occasional flooding or drought. *M. lindheimeri* (Lindheimer muhly) has blue-green leaves and purplish flower spikes in fall, followed by silvery seed heads; it prefers full sun and a moist, well-drained rocky soil, but it tolerates both drought and some shade; USDA zones 7-9.

Myosotis sylvatica

Myosotis (my-oh-SO-tis)
FORGET-ME-NOT

USDA Hardiness: zones 5-8
AHS Heat: zones 7-1
Height: 6 to 10 inches
Plant type: annual, biennial
Soil: moist, well-drained
Light: full sun to partial shade

Airy clusters of dainty flowers with prominent eyes open above the forget-me-not's low mounds of delicate foliage. *M. sylvatica* (woodland forget-me-not, garden forget-me-not) produces loose clusters of yellow-centered blue flowers from spring through early summer; 'Ultramarine' is very dwarf with dark blue flowers; 'Victoria Blue' forms neat mounds and produces early flowers of gentian blue. Start seed outdoors in late summer to early fall for flowers the following spring. Once established, forget-me-nots self-seed readily, performing like a perennial. Enrich the soil with organic matter, and water during dry periods.

Myrrhis (MIR-ris)
SWEET CICELY, MYRRH

USDA Hardiness: zones 3-8
AHS Heat: zones 8-1
Height: 2 to 3 feet
Plant type: perennial
Soil: rich, moist, organic
Light: partial shade to full sun

The finely cut leaves of *M. odorata* (sweet cicely, myrrh) perfume the garden with the scent of celery and anise when used as a filler. The fernlike fresh leaves have several culinary uses, as do the tiny white spring-blooming flowers, their ridged green seeds, which ripen to brown-black, and the anise-scented taproot. Because sweet cicely germinates erratically, the most reliable way to grow it is to divide mature plants in fall and plant the divisions.

Myrrhis odorata

Myrica pensylvanica

Myrica (mi-RYE-ka)
BAYBERRY

USDA Hardiness: zones 2-9
AHS Heat: zones 8-1
Height: 5 to 20 feet
Plant type: shrub, tree
Soil: well-drained
Light: partial shade to full sun

Aromatic bayberry (also called wax myrtle) forms a dense, upright mound covered with small gray berries from fall into winter. Useful in shrub borders and masses, it can also be clipped into a hedge. The southern species can be used as a screen or trained into a tree to expose the attractive bark. *M. cerifera* (southern bayberry, candleberry, waxberry) is an evergreen shrub or small tree; *M. pensylvanica* (northern bayberry, swamp candleberry) is deciduous to semi-evergreen, with leathery leaves and clusters of grayish white berries. Native to coastal dunes, bayberry grows well in poor, dry, sandy soils but seems adaptable to almost any other condition except high alkalinity.

Myrtus (MIR-tus)
MYRTLE

USDA Hardiness: zones 9-11
AHS Heat: zones 12-1
Height: 5 to 20 feet
Plant type: shrub
Soil: average, well-drained
Light: full sun to light shade

Myrtle's lustrous evergreen leaves, tiny flower buds, and white flowers with puffs of golden stamens share a spicy orange scent that has made the plant a favorite in wedding bouquets. Myrtle is ideal for massing into hedges or growing as container plants. Fragrant myrtle also has culinary uses. *M. communis* (sweet myrtle, Greek myrtle) has white flowers followed by blue-black berries; 'Microphylla' is a dwarf ideal for containers; 'Variegata' has leaves marbled gray-green and cream. Plant myrtle in sites protected from drying winds. Myrtle will grow in light shade but prefers full sun.

Myrtus communis

Nandina domestica
'Fire Power'

Nandina (nan-DEE-na)
HEAVENLY BAMBOO

USDA Hardiness: zones 6-9
AHS Heat: zones 9-3
Height: 2 to 8 feet
Plant type: shrub
Soil: moist, fertile
Light: full shade to full sun

Nandina's bluish green foliage, emerging pink or coppery and often turning red to reddish purple in fall and winter, splays out from bamboolike canes. In late spring or early summer, panicles of creamy flowers appear, followed by spectacular clusters of red berries that persist through winter. Although nandina grows best in acid loam, it tolerates a wide range of other soils and withstands drought. Winter sun helps redden foliage. Plant in groups to improve berrying. If left unpruned, it becomes leggy; remove old canes or cut canes to various lengths to create a dense plant. Canes cannot be forced to branch.

Narcissus 'Unsurpassable'

Narcissus (nar-SIS-us)
DAFFODIL

USDA Hardiness: zones 3-8
AHS Heat: zones 9-2
Height: 4 to 18 inches
Plant type: bulb
Soil: well-drained
Light: full sun to shade

Daffodil flowers, vibrant harbingers of spring, now come in colors ranging the spectrum. Species narcissus are renowned for their sweet, intense fragrance. Hybrids number in the thousands, and the genus is grouped into 12 divisions for identification. There are miniature cultivars within almost every division. Group them in borders, beds, and woodland or rock gardens, or scatter them to naturalize on lawns and in meadows.

Nemophila (nem-OFF-i-la)
BABY-BLUE-EYES

USDA Hardiness: zone 0
AHS Heat: zones 12-2
Height: 6 to 10 inches
Plant type: annual
Soil: moist, well-drained
Light: full sun to partial shade

Nemophila menziesii

Baby-blue-eyes hails from California and Oregon, where it grows as a wildflower. In the garden its low, mounded habit and dainty flowers make good edging plants, rock-garden specimens, and companions for spring-flowering bulbs. They are also attractive when planted so that their trailing stems spill over the edge of a wall. *N. menziesii* forms a mounding plant and has tubular, sky blue flowers with white centers; 'Pennie Black' has deep purple ¾ inch blooms edged with silvery white. Sow seed directly in the garden in early spring, enrich the soil with organic matter, and provide abundant moisture. Plants thrive in areas with cool summers and will self-seed under favorable conditions.

Nepeta (NEP-e-ta)
CATMINT

USDA Hardiness: zones 3-9
AHS Heat: zones 12-2
Height: 1 to 3 feet
Plant type: perennial
Soil: average, well-drained loam
Light: full sun

Nepeta x *faassenii*

Catmint forms loose cushions of fragrant stems lined with soft, oval, pointed leaves and tipped with spikes of tiny white, mauve, or blue flower whorls that form a haze of color above the foliage. The plant is effective massed as a dense ground cover. *N.* x *faassenii* (blue catmint) produces lavender-blue spring-to-summer-blooming flowers; 'Six Hills Giant' grows taller and is more robust than the species. *N. mussinii* (Persian catmint) has sprawling mounds with lavender summer flowers; 'Blue Wonder' has deep blue blossoms on compact plants. Plant catmint in any well-drained soil. It can be invasive.

Nerium *(NEE-ri-um)*
OLEANDER

USDA Hardiness: zones 8-10
AHS Heat: zones 12-1
Height: 6 to 20 feet
Plant type: shrub
Soil: moist, well-drained
Light: full sun to partial shade

Oleander is a tough, easy-to-grow evergreen for warm climates. It bears attractive leaves that resemble bamboo as well as clusters of fragrant flowers from spring through fall. All parts of the oleander are poisonous. *N. oleander* has long, leathery, dark evergreen leaves and flower clusters, in pink, white, or red in its long blooming season; 'Casablanca' has single white flowers; 'Little Red' bears red flowers; 'Mrs. Roeddling' flowers are salmon pink. Oleanders prefer a moist, well-drained soil but adapt to drier conditions. They tolerate drought, wind, salt spray, and air pollution.

Nerium oleander

Nigella *(nye-JEL-a)*
LOVE-IN-A-MIST

USDA Hardiness: zone 0
AHS Heat: zones 12-2
Height: 18 to 24 inches
Plant type: annual
Soil: well-drained
Light: full sun

Love-in-a-mist's leaves are fernlike, and solitary flowers with blue, white, or pink notched petals are nestled in a mist of foliage at the ends of stems throughout the summer. Start seed directly outdoors in early spring, and make additional sowings every 2 or 3 weeks until early summer to extend the flowering season. Water during dry periods. If pods are allowed to remain on plants, they will self-seed.

Nigella damascena

Nicotiana *(ni-ko-she-AN-a)*
TOBACCO

USDA Hardiness: zone 0
AHS Heat: zones 12-1
Height: 1 to 6 feet
Plant type: annual, biennial
Soil: moist, well-drained
Light: full sun to partial shade

Flowering tobacco produces clusters of fragrant, flat-faced flowers with elongated tubular throats growing at the tips of soft stems. *N. alata* (jasmine tobacco) produces 1- to 2-foot-tall clumps with flowers that bloom from spring to fall. *N. sylvestris* (woodland tobacco) bears drooping white flowers tinged pink or purple on plants 3 to 6 feet tall. Leaf juices are poisonous. Start seed indoors 6 to 8 weeks prior to the last frost, or sow directly outdoors in late spring. Nicotiana may be biennial in the South, but will be sprawling the second year.

Nicotiana sylvestris

Nymphaea *(nim-FEE-a)*
WATER LILY

USDA Hardiness: zones 2-10
AHS Heat: zones 12-1
Height: 2 to 4 inches above water
Plant type: perennial
Soil: shallow water
Light: full sun

The sweetly scented flowers of these aquatic perennials grace ponds, lakes, and ditches over much of the eastern and central United States. The flowers, each of which lasts for about 3 days, float on the surface of the water. They close at night and on cloudy days. *N. odorata* (water lily, pond lily) has white or pink flowers 3 to 5 inches across with numerous gold stamens from mid- to late summer. Flat 4- to 12-inch leaves are green on the upper surface and reddish below, and float on the surface of the water.

Nymphaea 'St. Louis Gold'

Ocimum *(OS-si-mum)*

BASIL

USDA Hardiness: zones 9-11
AHS Heat: zones 10-1
Height: 6 inches to 3 feet
Plant type: annual
Soil: rich, organic, well-drained
Light: full sun

Ocimum basilicum
'Purple Ruffles'

Pointed, oval, slightly curved leaves with mixed scents of cinnamon, clove, anise, rose, lemon, orange, thyme, mint, or camphor make basil not only a classic culinary seasoning but also a choice fragrance planting. All species do well in containers, and most are ideal for window-sill pot culture throughout winter. Many forms are available, with varying flavors and colors to suit individual tastes. *O. basilicum* (common basil) has fragrant 2- to 3-inch leaves lining stems tipped with white flowers. Basil needs soils 50°F or warmer to thrive and is vigorous only in summer heat. Provide mulch to keep roots from drying out and to keep leaves clean.

Onopordum *(o-no-POR-dum)*

SCOTCH THISTLE

USDA Hardiness: zones 6-8
AHS Heat: zones 12-7
Height: 6 to 9 feet
Plant type: annual, biennial
Soil: well-drained to dry
Light: full sun

Onopordum acanthium

Scotch thistle produces fuzzy, globular flower heads on tall, stiffly erect branching stems lined with spiny, gray-green leaves. The unusual flowers and foliage add both color and texture as vertical accents in a border. *O. acanthium* (cotton thistle, silver thistle) has stiff, enormous downy leaves on branching stems 6 to 9 feet tall tipped in late spring to summer with round, prickly purple to white flowers that have flat, fuzzy tops. Scotch thistle thrives in hot, dry locations. Plants self-sow for a display the following year.

Oenothera *(ee-no-THEE-ra)*

SUNDROP, EVENING PRIMROSE

USDA Hardiness: zones 5-9
AHS Heat: zones 12-1
Height: 6 inches to 8 feet
Plant type: biennial, perennial
Soil: well-drained
Light: full sun

Oenothera missouriensis

In this genus of mostly perennial plants are a few hardy biennials that can be treated as annuals. Showy, four-petaled, saucer-shaped flowers bloom on sundrops during the day and on evening primroses (night-blooming oenothera) at night. *O. fruticosa* (common sundrop) bears prolific clusters of bright yellow flowers. *O. missouriensis* (Ozark sundrop) has large yellow flowers. *O. speciosa* (showy evening primrose) bears white or pink blossoms on spreading stems. Good drainage is essential, as wet soil will cause rot. Evening primroses are drought tolerant.

Ophiopogon *(o-fi-o-PO-gon)*

DWARF MONDO GRASS

USDA Hardiness: zones 7-9
AHS Heat: zones 12-3
Height: 6 to 12 inches
Plant type: perennial
Soil: moist, well-drained
Light: full sun to partial shade

Ophiopogon japonicus

Dense clumps of grasslike leaves make dwarf mondo grass an excellent ground cover or edging for a bed. Stems of light blue flowers are produced in the summer, followed by metallic blue berries, though both flowers and fruit are somewhat hidden among the leaves. *O. japonicus* has dark, evergreen leaves and tiny individual lilac-blue flowers growing in clusters; the steel blue fruit is pea-size. Dwarf mondo grass is adaptable to sun or partial shade, though it prefers some protection from hot afternoon sun. It can be grown under trees and is useful for controlling erosion on slopes.

Origanum (o-RIG-a-num)
OREGANO

USDA Hardiness: zones 4-9
AHS Heat: zones 10-2
Height: 6 to 24 inches
Plant type: annual, perennial
Soil: rich, dry, well-drained
Light: full sun

Origanum vulgare

Fragrantly spicy leaves and branching clusters of tiny flowers on mounding or sprawling plants make marjorams useful in kitchen gardens. They can also be used as border edgings or ground covers. Tender perennial species grow as annuals in cooler climates; marjorams also do well in containers both indoors and out. *O. majorana* (sweet marjoram) is an essential seasoning in Greek cuisine and more intensely flavored than *O. vulgare*. Give golden-leaved cultivars light shade to prevent leaf scorch. *O. vulgare* (oregano, pot marjoram, wild marjoram, organy) can be invasive.

Osmanthus (oz-MAN-thus)
DEVILWEED

USDA Hardiness: zones 7-9
AHS Heat: zones 9-4
Height: 6 to 45 feet
Plant type: shrub, tree
Soil: moist, well-drained, acid
Light: full sun to partial shade

Osmanthus heterophyllus

This genus includes 30 to 40 species of slow-growing trees and shrubs. Commonly used as foundation shrubs, for massing, for screening or in containers; plants bear attractive leathery leaves and sweetly fragrant flowers. *O. fragrans* (sweet olive) grows to 10 feet; bears dark green leaves and fragrant white flower clusters in spring through summer. *O. heterophyllus* 'Variegatus' (variegated false holly) has a mounded habit; produces holly-like leathery leaves edged in creamy-white.

Orthocarpus (or-tho-KAR-pus)
OWL'S CLOVER

USDA Hardiness: zone 0
AHS Heat: zones 12-1
Height: 12 to 15 inches
Plant type: annual
Soil: light, well-drained
Light: full sun

Orthocarpus purpurascens

Owl's clover is native to the southwestern United States, where it covers entire hillsides with rose-purple blooms set off by red-tinged bracts. Individual flowers resemble snapdragons and are tipped with yellow or white on their lower lip. They provide a long season of color. *O. purpurascens* (escobita) bears two-lipped rose-purple or crimson flowers from early to midsummer. Owl's clovers thrive in warm weather. Water during periods of dry weather.

Osmunda (oz-MUN-da)
FLOWERING FERN

USDA Hardiness: zones 2-10
AHS Heat: zones 9-1
Height: 2 to 6 feet
Plant type: fern
Soil: moist to wet, acid, sandy loam
Light: bright full shade

Osmunda cinnamomea

These stately, deciduous ferns grow wild mostly in marshes and swamps, but they readily adapt to the home garden. Spreading slowly on rhizomes, they make excellent background plantings in borders and rock gardens or against a wall. Flowering ferns thrive in soil consisting of 1 part loam, 1 part sand, and 2 parts leaf mold or peat moss. *O. claytoniana* (interrupted fern) needs highly acid conditions. *O. cinnamomea* (cinnamon fern, fiddleheads, buckhorn) and *O. regalis* (royal fern) can tolerate part sun if the soil remains wet, as by a stream or pond.

Osteospermum
(os-ti-o-SPER-mum)

AFRICAN DAISY

USDA Hardiness: zones 9-10
AHS Heat: zones 12-9
Height: 6 to 12 inches
Plant type: perennial
Soil: well-drained
Light: full sun

Osteospermum fruticosum

The African daisy is a flowering ground cover for warm zones. It has a trailing habit and spreads rapidly to create a dense mat. Flowers bloom most heavily in late winter and early spring, and intermittently throughout the rest of the year. It makes a lovely show in containers or behind stone walls where it can spill over the edges. *O. fruticosum*'s flowers are lavender with purple centers, fading to white; 'Hybrid White' has white flowers; 'African Queen' has deep purple flowers. Because the stems root as they grow along the ground, the African daisy is well suited to covering large areas. It thrives in full sun and, once established, tolerates drought.

Oxydendrum
(ok-si-DEN-drum)

SORREL TREE

USDA Hardiness: zones 5-9
AHS Heat: zones 9-1
Height: 25 to 30 feet
Plant type: tree
Soil: moist, well-drained, acid
Light: full sun to partial shade

Oxydendrum arboreum

In spring the sorrel tree's leaves emerge a dark green. White, urn-shaped flowers hang in clusters in midsummer. The pendulous light green fruit, which appears in fall, creates a stunning display against the leaves, which turn a brilliant scarlet. The fruit turns brown and persists into winter. Incorporate generous amounts of organic matter into soil prior to planting. The trees are slow growing but attractive even when young. Although they thrive in sun or partial shade, plants grown in the sun produce more flowers and better fall color.

Pachysandra
(pak-i-SAN-dra)

PACHYSANDRA

USDA Hardiness: zones 5-9
AHS Heat: zones 8-3
Height: 6 to 12 inches
Plant type: perennial
Soil: moist, well-drained, acid
Light: partial to full shade

Pachysandra procumbens

Pachysandra is a spreading ground cover whose dark green leaves provide a lush carpet beneath trees and shrubs. In early spring short flower spikes rise from the center of each whorl of leaves. *P. procumbens* (Allegheny pachysandra, Allegheny spurge) leaves are deciduous in cooler zones and semi-evergreen to evergreen in mild areas; flowers are white or pink. *P. terminalis* (Japanese pachysandra) leaves are evergreen and dark, with white flowers. Pachysandra thrives in the shade; given too much sun, leaves will yellow. It grows well beneath trees. Incorporate organic matter into the soil prior to planting. Keep new plantings uniformly moist.

Paeonia *(pee-O-nee-a)*
PEONY

USDA Hardiness: zones 4-8
AHS Heat: zones 9-1
Height: 18 to 36 inches
Plant type: perennial, shrub
Soil: well-drained, fertile loam
Light: full sun to light shade

Paeonia 'Mitama'

Peonies are long-lived plants with large, showy flowers and attractive foliage. Peony flowers are classified by their form: Single-flower peonies have a single row of five or more petals surrounding a center of bright yellow stamens—these are the best peonies for the heat of the Deep South. Japanese and anemone peonies have a single row of petals surrounding modified stamens that resemble finely cut petals. Semidouble peonies have several rows of petals surrounding conspicuous stamens. Double-flowered peonies have multiple rows of petals crowded into ruffly hemispheres. *P.* 'Festiva Maxima' withstands heat and humidity better than most forms. Plant peonies in soil containing organic matter.

Panax quinquefolius

Panax (PAN-ax)
GINSENG

USDA Hardiness: zones 5-8
AHS Heat: zones 9-1
Height: 6 to 36 inches
Plant type: perennial
Soil: organic, moist, well-drained
Light: light to full shade

Ginseng's thick roots send up a single thin stalk with leaves arranged like the fingers on a hand. In late spring or summer, tiny yellow-green flower clusters appear, followed by red berries. In woodland gardens, ginseng slowly spreads into a lacy ground cover. Ginseng's Greek name means "all ills," reflecting its root's fame as an herbal tonic in Oriental medicine. *P. pseudoginseng* [also classified as *P. ginseng*] grows 2 to 3 feet tall; and *P. quinquefolius* (American ginseng) is 6 to 20 inches. Provide panax with organic mulch annually. When roots are at least 6 years old, dig them up in fall to use fresh or dried for teas.

Papaver (pa-PAY-ver)
POPPY

USDA Hardiness: zones 5-7
AHS Heat: zones 9-2
Height: 1 to 4 feet
Plant type: annual, tender perennial, perennial
Soil: well-drained to dry
Light: full sun to light shade

Papaver nudicaule

Poppy's showy spring petals surround prominent centers above clumps of coarse, hairy, deeply lobed leaves. The brightly colored flower petals are extremely delicate in appearance, with a tissuelike texture. Flowers may be single, with four overlapping petals, or double, with many petals forming a rounded bloom. *P. rhoeas* (corn poppy, Flanders poppy) and *P. somniferum* (opium poppy) have quality cultivars in many colors. *P. nudicaule* (Iceland poppy), with white, yellow, orange, salmon, pink, or scarlet cup-shaped flowers, can be started indoors 10 weeks prior to the last frost for transplanting in late spring. You can also sow directly in the garden in late fall or early spring.

Panicum virgatum

Panicum (PAN-i-kum)
PANIC GRASS

USDA Hardiness: zones 5-9
AHS Heat: zones 9-1
Height: 3 to 6 feet
Plant type: ornamental grass
Soil: moist, well-drained
Light: full sun

This large genus includes both annual and perennial ornamental grasses. Branching stalks bearing feathery clusters of tiny buff flowers rise from panicum's clumps of arching, attractively colored leaves in fall. The seed heads that follow remain attractive through winter. *P. virgatum* (switch grass) has loose, open flower clusters above green leaves coloring yellow and red in fall; 'Haense Herms' has red summer foliage lasting until frost and grayish dried seed heads; 'Heavy Metal' has deep blue leaves that turn yellow in fall. Switch grass thrives in moist soil but will tolerate much drier conditions, even drought, though it will spread more slowly. It will also tolerate salt spray and seaside conditions.

Parrotia (pa-ROTE-ee-a)
IRONWOOD

USDA Hardiness: zones 6-9
AHS Heat: zones 8-1
Height: 20 to 40 feet
Plant type: shrub, tree
Soil: well-drained
Light: full sun

Parrotia persica

Ironwood's trunk and horizontal branches are covered with flaky bark that peels away to give the plant an attractive, mottled green-gray-and-brown texture. Tiny, inconspicuous flowers with red stamens bloom along young branches before the leaves emerge in spring. The oval foliage colors attractively in fall. *P. persica* (Persian parrotia) has lustrous green leaves in brilliant shades of yellow and orange turning rosy pink and scarlet in fall. Use parrotia as a specimen tree or part of a shrub border. Plant Persian parrotia in slightly acidic soil.

Passiflora pfordtii

Passiflora (pas-i-FLOR-a)
PASSION-FLOWER

USDA Hardiness: zones 6-10
AHS Heat: zones 12-1
Height: to 15 to 25 feet with support
Plant type: vine
Soil: well-drained
Light: full sun to partial shade

The perennial passion-flowers are herbaceous vines native to the eastern United States with showy flowers, and lush and edible fruit. *P. incarnata* (passion-flower, maypop) bears lavender flowers followed by large apricot-colored fruit. *P. lutea* (passionflower) has greenish yellow flowers and purple-black fruit. Its leaves turn yellow in fall. *P. pfordtii* has fragrant, 4-inch flowers, white outside and pink to purple inside. Grow passionflowers in well-drained soil. *P. incarnata* adapts to either sun or partial shade, while *P. lutea* prefers partial shade. Their abundant growth requires sturdy support.

Pelargonium (pel-ar-GO-nee-um)
GERANIUM, STORKSBILL

USDA Hardiness: zone 11
AHS Heat: zones 12-1
Height: 12 inches to 6 feet
Plant type: annual, perennial, shrub
Soil: rich, moist, well-drained
Light: full sun to light shade

Pelargonium tomentosum

When brushed or rubbed, the foliage of scented geraniums emits a citrusy, floral, minty, or resinous perfume depending on the species or cultivar. Outdoors year round where they can be protected from frost, taller species grow as specimens; sprawling types can be used as ground covers. Elsewhere, scented geraniums are treated like summer bedding plants. While all scented geraniums do best in full sun, *P. crispum* (lemon geranium), *P. odoratissimum* (apple geranium), and *P. tomentosum* (peppermint geranium) will tolerate light shade. Too-rich soil tends to minimize fragrance.

Patrinia scabiosifolia

Patrinia (pat-RIN-ee-a)
PATRINIA

USDA Hardiness: zones 5-9
AHS Heat: zones 12-1
Height: 2 to 6 feet
Plant type: perennial
Soil: moist, well-drained
Light: full sun to light shade

Patrinia produces large, airy sprays of flowers late in the summer and fall. these are followed by bright yellow seedpods on orange stems. It is well suited to a natural garden, where it combines well with ornamental grasses. *P. scabiosifolia* grows to 6 feet tall and has ruffled leaves and long-lasting yellow flowers that form 2-inch clusters held well above foliage. Plant patrinias in moist, well-drained soil. Taller types often require staking. Once established, patrinias are long-lived perennials that self-sow and rarely need to be divided.

Pennisetum (pen-i-SEE-tum)
FOUNTAIN GRASS

USDA Hardiness: zones 5-9
AHS Heat: zones 9-2
Height: 2 to 4 feet
Plant type: ornamental grass
Soil: well-drained, fertile
Light: full sun

Pennisetum alopecuroides

Fountain grass forms a spray of arching leaves with bottle-brush flower heads borne on thin, arching stems in summer and fall. Stunning in masses, fountain grass graces borders, rock gardens, water features, and fall-blooming perennial beds. It is also useful as an accent plant. *P. setaceum* (annual fountain grass) is drought tolerant, self-sows readily, and is often grown as an annual in climates where it is not hardy. Divide every 5 to 10 years to prevent the center from falling open. Fountain grass is tolerant of humidity.

Penstemon (pen-STEE-mon)
BEARDTONGUE

USDA Hardiness: zones 3-9
AHS Heat: zones 9-1
Height: 18 to 36 inches
Plant type: perennial
Soil: well-drained loam
Light: full sun to light shade

Penstemon gentianoides

Clusters of tubular flowers with fine hairs covering their lower lips nod above shrubby foliage over beardtongue's long season of bloom. Low-growing varieties are well suited to rock gardens, dry walls, and the edges of beds. Taller types mix well with other perennials in the middle or back of a border or in a wildflower garden. Penstemons tolerate drought and are useful in dry areas of average fertility. They are subject to rot if the soil remains damp, but do not require a highly fertile soil.

Perovskia (per-OV-skee-a)
RUSSIAN SAGE

USDA Hardiness: zones 5-9
AHS Heat: zones 9-4
Height: 3 to 4 feet
Plant type: perennial
Soil: well-drained loam
Light: full sun

Perovskia atriplicifolia

Russian sage's mounds of fine-textured, deeply toothed aromatic gray foliage are an effective filler in the border and remain attractive through winter. In summer, spires of tiny lavender flowers tip each stem. Planted in a mass, Russian sage develops into a summer hedge, and the stems remain attractive through the winter. *P. atriplicifolia* (azure sage) has tubular, two-lipped lavender flowers growing in whorls to 4 feet tall and wide. 'Blue Spire' is upright with violet-blue flowers. Plant Russian sage 2 to 3 feet apart in full sun; shade causes floppy, sprawling growth. Soil should not be overly rich. Plants are drought tolerant.

Perilla (per-RILL-a)
BEEFSTEAK PLANT

USDA Hardiness: zone 0
AHS Heat: zones 9-1
Height: 2 to 3 feet
Plant type: annual
Soil: well-drained to dry
Light: full sun to partial shade

Perilla frutescens

This Asian native is grown for its attractive foliage, which resembles that of coleus or purple basil. The leaves of *P. frutescens* are up to 5 inches long, have a quilted texture, and are purple-bronze, green, or variegated in color; 'Crispa' develops bronze leaves with wrinkled margins; 'Atropurpurea' has very dark purple leaves. Start seed indoors 6 weeks prior to the last frost, or sow directly in the garden after the soil has warmed. Plants will tolerate poor soil.

Petroselinum (pet-ro-se-LEE-num)
PARSLEY

USDA Hardiness: zones 5-9
AHS Heat: zones 9-1
Height: 12 to 24 inches
Plant type: biennial
Soil: rich, moist, well-drained
Light: full sun

Petroselinum crispum

A biennial flowering its second year, parsley is usually grown as an annual in an herb garden, as an edging plant, or in containers indoors or out. It is a culinary staple. *P. crispum* var. *crispum* (curly parsley, French parsley), used primarily as garnish, has highly frilled leaves. *P. crispum* var. *neapolitanum* (Italian parsley, flatleaf parsley) has flat, deeply lobed celery-like leaves and is more strongly flavored than curly parsley. Sow parsley seed in soil warmed to at least 50°F.

Phacelia sericea

Phacelia (fa-SEEL-ee-a)
DESERT BELLS

USDA Hardiness: zones 5-10
AHS Heat: zones 9-1
Height: 4 to 48 inches
Plant type: annual, perennial
Soil: well-drained to dry, sandy
Light: full sun

Desert bells are annuals and perennials native to the deserts and open flats of the West. Their bell-shaped flowers bloom in clusters along one side of curved stems. *P. campanularia* (California bluebell) is an annual with deep blue flowers in spring. *P. minor* (wild Canterbury bell, whitlavia) is an annual with purple flowers in spring. *P. sericea* (silky phacelia) is a short perennial with dark blue, lavender, or purple flowers in summer. *P. tanacetifolia* (lacy phacelia, fiddleneck) is a perennial 1 to 4 feet tall with blue or lavender flowers in spring. Desert bells thrive in full sun and well-drained to dry soil.

Phellodendron (fell-o-DEN-dron)
CORK TREE

USDA Hardiness: zones 4-7
AHS Heat: zones 8-5
Height: 30 to 45 feet
Plant type: tree
Soil: adaptable
Light: full sun

Cork tree is valued for the heavily ridged and furrowed gray-brown bark, resembling cork, that cloaks the few wide-spreading horizontal main branches on old trees. Inconspicuous yellowish green flowers bloom in late spring, followed by small clusters of black berries in late fall on female trees. *P. amurense* (Amur cork tree) grows 30 to 45 feet tall, with orange-yellow stems bearing glossy dark green leaflets to 4 inches long. Cork tree tolerates drought, pollution, and a wide variety of soil types.

Phellodendron amurense

Phaseolus coccineus

Phaseolus (faz-ee-OH-lus)
BEAN

USDA Hardiness: zones 10-11
AHS Heat: zones 12-1
Height: 6 to 10 feet
Plant type: tender perennial
Soil: moist, well-drained, fertile
Light: full sun

This tender perennial twining vine from tropical America produces abundant dark green leaves that are a perfect foil for its brilliant scarlet flowers. The vine will grow quickly to cover a trellis or fence, or climb up a porch railing. The flowers attract hummingbirds. *P. coccineus* (scarlet runner bean) produces twining stems bearing bright red pealike flower clusters from early to midsummer. Both flowers and beans are edible. Plant seed outdoors in spring after danger of frost has passed. Provide support for climbing, and water when dry.

Philadelphus (fill-a-DEL-fus)
MOCK ORANGE

USDA Hardiness: zones 4-9
AHS Heat: zones 8-4
Height: 4 to 12 feet
Plant type: shrub
Soil: moist to dry, well-drained
Light: full sun to light shade

Mock orange is an old-fashioned shrub that produces delightfully fragrant blooms reminiscent of orange blossoms in late spring and early summer. This shrub adapts to a wide range of conditions and is best planted in combination with other flowering plants in a mixed shrub border. Mock orange is easily transplanted, fast-growing, and not too particular about site. Once established, mock orange is tolerant of dry soils.

Philadelphus x *virginalis*

Phlox divaricata

Phlox (flox)
PHLOX

USDA Hardiness: zones 3-9
AHS Heat: zones 9-4
Height: 3 inches to 4 feet
Plant type: annual, perennial
Soil: sandy, dry to moist, fertile loam
Light: full sun to full shade

Phlox produces flat flowers, either singly or in clusters, many with an eye at the center, and range in size from 3-inch creepers to upright border plants growing 4 feet tall. *P. divaricata* (wild blue phlox) grows well in shady, moist sites; *P. subulata* (moss phlox) thrives in sunny, dry spots. *P. stolonifera* (creeping phlox) grows in sun or shade. *P. maculata* (wild sweet William) and *P. paniculata* (summer phlox, garden phlox) thrive in full sun, provided they receive ample moisture during the growing season. *P. andicola, P. hoodii*, and *P. bryoides* are especially heat tolerant. Space phlox for good air circulation to avoid powdery mildew.

Physostegia (fy-so-STEE-gee-a)
FALSE DRAGONHEAD

USDA Hardiness: zones 2-8
AHS Heat: zones 8-4
Height: 2 to 4 feet
Plant type: perennial
Soil: moist or dry acid loam
Light: full sun to partial shade

False dragonhead produces unusual 8- to 10-inch flower spikes with four evenly spaced vertical rows of blossoms resembling snapdragons. *P. virginiana*'s pink flowers tip each stem in clumps of 4-foot stalks; 'Variegata' has pink flowers above green-and-white variegated leaves; 'Vivid', rosy pink blossoms on compact plants only 20 inches tall; 'Summer Snow', early-blooming white flowers. False dragonhead is so tolerant of varying growing conditions that it can become invasive.

Physostegia virginiana

Phormium tenax

Phormium (FOR-mee-um)
FLAX LILY

USDA Hardiness: zones 9-11
AHS Heat: zones 12-2
Height: 7 to 15 feet
Plant type: perennial
Soil: moist, well-drained
Light: full sun

Dramatic fans of stiff, evergreen leaves, sometimes split at their ends or edged with red, bear tall flower stalks lined with dull red 2-inch flowers rising above the foliage. *P. tenax* (New Zealand flax) has leathery leaves with flower stalks to 15 feet; 'Atropurpureum' has rich purple leaves; 'Bronze', deep red-brown leaves; 'Maori Sunrise', bronze leaves striped pink and cream; 'Tiny Tim' is shorter with yellow-striped bronze leaves; 'Variegatum' has creamy white striping on green leaves. Plant New Zealand flax in soil enriched with organic matter. Plants tolerate seaside conditions and pollution.

Picea (PYE-see-a)
SPRUCE

USDA Hardiness: zones 2-7
AHS Heat: zones 7-2
Height: 3 to 60 feet or more
Plant type: tree
Soil: moist, well-drained, acid
Light: full sun to partial shade

These needled evergreens form towering pyramids useful as windbreaks, screens, or single specimens. Smaller forms are good as accents or in groups. *P. abies* (Norway spruce) is a fast-growing pyramid, 40 to 60 feet tall (can reach 150 feet), that bears 4- to 6-inch cylindrical cones; 'Conica' (dwarf Alberta spruce) is a neat, very slow-growing (to 10 feet in 25 years) cone-shaped plant. *P. pungens* (Colorado spruce) grows to 100 feet or more and bears bluish green cones. Spruces prefer moist, acid, deep loam but tolerate other soils with adequate moisture, especially in the first few years. They prefer sunny sites in cold climates. *P. glauca* (white spruce) withstands heat and drought better than many other species.

Picea pungens

Pieris japonica 'Deep Pink'

Pieris (PYE-er-is)
PIERIS

USDA Hardiness: zones 5-8
AHS Heat: zones 9-6
Height: 6 to 12 feet
Plant type: shrub
Soil: moist, well-drained, slightly acid
Light: full sun to light shade

Clustered chains of greenish to red buds decorate this mounding shrub from late summer to the following spring, when they open into white or pink urn-shaped flowers. New foliage, tinged with reddish bronze, unfurls and retains that hue for weeks before turning a lustrous dark green. *Pieris japonica* (Japanese pieris) makes a beautiful four-season specimen. Caution: Pieris buds and flowers are poisonous. Japanese pieris grows best in well-drained soil well supplemented with leaf mold or peat moss. Provide light shade where summers are hot.

Pistacia (pis-TAY-shee-a)
PISTACHIO

USDA Hardiness: zones 6-9
AHS Heat: zones 12-4
Height: 30 to 35 feet
Plant type: tree
Soil: adaptable
Light: full sun

Pistacia chinensis

One of the best deciduous trees for fall foliage in the South, *P. chinensis* (Chinese pistache) has lustrous dark green compound leaves that turn a brilliant orange to orange-red even in semi-desert conditions. Chinese pistache grows 30 to 35 feet high with equal spread, eventually becoming oval to rounded. Chinese pistache grows best in moist, well-drained soil, where it may achieve 2 to 3 feet per year, but it tolerates other soil types and drought.

Pinus strobus

Pinus (PYE-nus)
PINE

USDA Hardiness: zones 2-10
AHS Heat: zones 9-1
Height: 6 to 90 feet
Plant type: tree
Soil: wet to dry
Light: full sun

This diverse genus of needle-leaved evergreen conifers includes picturesque specimen and accent plants, towering screens, and lovely single shade trees. *P. arisata* (bristlecone pine) does well in poor, dry soils but suffers in drying winds or pollution. *P. eldarica* (Afghanistan pine) and *P. cembroides* var. *edulis* (pinyon, nut pine) thrive in desert conditions; the former also tolerates salt spray. *P. nigra* (Austrian pine) tolerates alkaline soils, moderate drought, salt, and urban pollution but grows best where moisture is assured. *P. strobus* (white pine) grows best in moist loams but is also found on dry, shallow soils and wet bogs; it is intolerant of air pollutants, salt, and highly alkaline soil.

Pittosporum (pit-o-SPO-rum)
PITTOSPORUM

USDA Hardiness: zones 8-10
AHS Heat: zones 12-3
Height: 10 to 12 feet
Plant type: shrub
Soil: well-drained
Light: full sun to full shade

Pittosporum tobira

A dense, impenetrable evergreen shrub, *P. tobira* (Japanese pittosporum, mock orange) grows 10 to 12 feet high and has creamy white flowers in spring. Used in foundation beds, drifts, barriers, hedges, and windbreaks, pittosporums may be left unsheared or pruned into formal shapes. The leaves are borne in rosettes at the ends of branches, lending a soft, clean appearance to the slow-growing, symmetrical mound. Japanese pittosporums tolerate soil from dry and sandy to moist clay, requiring only that the soil be well drained. They withstand salt spray and thrive in hot, humid climates and exposed locations.

Platycodon grandiflorus

Platycodon (plat-i-KO-don)
BALLOON FLOWER

USDA Hardiness: zones 4-9
AHS Heat: zones 9-3
Height: 10 to 36 inches
Plant type: perennial
Soil: well-drained, acid loam
Light: full sun to partial shade

The balloon flower derives its common name from the fat, inflated flower buds it produces. These pop open into spectacular cup-shaped 2- to 3-inch-wide blossoms with pointed petals. *P. grandiflorus* has deep blue flowers on slender stems above neat clumps of blue-green leaves; 'Album' has white flowers; 'Shell Pink', pale pink flowers; 'Mariesii' is a compact variety with bright blue flowers; 'Double Blue' has bright-blue double flowers on 2-foot stems. Pink varieties develop the best color when grown in partial shade.

Plumbago (plum-BAY-go)
CAPE PLUMBAGO

USDA Hardiness: zones 9-11
AHS Heat: zones 12-5
Height: 6 to 8 feet
Plant type: shrub
Soil: well-drained
Light: full sun to partial shade

Plumbago auriculata

Cape plumbago is a large evergreen shrub that develops a mounded habit with long vinelike branches. Flowers are azure blue or white, and under ideal conditions they will appear year round. Cape plumbago can be maintained through pruning as a dense, low hedge or foundation plant. If trained it will climb a trellis or wall, and it is also well suited as a tall ground cover for large, well-drained slopes. Cape plumbago thrives in full sun but tolerates light shade in hot areas; it tolerates coastal conditions as well but is sensitive to frost.

Plectranthus amboinicus

Plectranthus (plec-TRAN-thus)
INDIAN BORAGE

USDA Hardiness: zones 10-11
AHS Heat: zones 12-1
Height: 12 to 36 inches
Plant type: tender perennial
Soil: rich, well-drained
Light: full sun to light shade

The fleshy lemon-scented leaves of Indian borage have a flavor reminiscent of thyme, oregano, and savory. The leaves trail attractively from hanging baskets. Use fresh leaves in cooking. *P. amboinicus* (Indian borage, Spanish thyme, French thyme, soup mint, Mexican mint, Indian mint, country borage) has round gray-green leaves and whorls of tiny mintlike blue summer flowers in spikes up to 16 inches long; 'Variegata' has gray-green leaves edged in cream. Indian borage plants stop growing at temperatures below 50°F and are quickly killed by even light frost.

Podophyllum (po-doh-FIL-um)
MAY APPLE

USDA Hardiness: zones 3-9
AHS Heat: zones 9-1
Height: 12 to 18 inches
Plant type: perennial
Soil: moist, well-drained, slightly acid, fertile
Light: full to dappled shade

Podophyllum peltatum

This woodland wildflower bears huge, deeply lobed leaves and nodding white flowers that arise in spring and mature into large berries. The foliage dies down in summer. The seeds, stem, and root are poisonous. *P. hexandrum* (Himalayan May apple) has white to pink flowers that bloom before the leaves unfurl. *P. peltatum* (common May apple, wild mandrake, raccoon berry) has less conspicuous flowers and yellow fruit. Often found in boggy, low-lying areas near woodland streams, May apple thrives in constantly moist soil to which leaf mold has been added. Mulch with leaf litter in winter.

Pogostemon cablin

Pogostemon
(po-go-STAY-mon)
PATCHOULI

USDA Hardiness: zones 10-11
AHS Heat: zones 12-4
Height: 3 to 4 feet
Plant type: tender perennial
Soil: rich, moist
Light: full sun to light shade

Patchouli's hairy triangular leaves contain a minty, cedar-scented oil valued in the making of perfume. Dried leaves gradually develop the scent and retain it for long periods in potpourri. In tropical gardens, patchouli forms mounds of fragrant foliage. *P. cablin* [also classified as *P. patchouli*] (patchouli) has lightly scalloped leaves up to 5 inches long with spikes of violet-tinged white flowers in fall. Outdoors where patchouli is not hardy, start tip cuttings to overwinter and treat plants as annuals, or grow in containers to move indoors.

Polygonatum odoratum

Polygonatum
(po-lig-o-NAY-tum)
SOLOMON'S-SEAL

USDA Hardiness: zones 3-9
AHS Heat: zones 9-1
Height: 1 to 6 feet
Plant type: perennial
Soil: moist, acid, rich
Light: partial to full shade

These woodland perennials native to the eastern half of the United States bear drooping greenish white flowers suspended from the undersides of gracefully arching stems in late spring. Blue berries follow the flowers. *P. biflorum* (small Solomon's-seal) has small, bell-shaped greenish white flowers in pairs. *P. commutatum* (great Solomon's-seal) grows to 6 feet with flowers similar to those of *P. biflorum* in clusters of two to 10. *P. odoratum* bears arching stems to 18 inches with greenish white, fragrant flowers. Solomon's-seals are easily grown in light to dense shade and a rich, moist, acid soil, where they will spread to form dense colonies.

Polemonium viscosum

Polemonium
(po-le-MO-nee-um)
JACOB'S-LADDER

USDA Hardiness: zones 2-9
AHS Heat: zones 8-1
Height: 4 to 36 inches
Plant type: perennial
Soil: moist to rocky, well-drained, rich
Light: full sun to partial shade

The polemoniums are natives of meadows, open woodlands, and stream banks. Their dark green compound leaves provide an attractive foil for their upward-facing, cup-shaped flowers. *P. carneum* (royal polemonium) has clusters of purple, pink, or salmon flowers; USDA zones 7-9. *P. occidentale* [also called *P. caeruleum* ssp. *amygdalinum*] (western polemonium) has clusters of pale blue summer flowers; USDA zones 3-9. *P. viscosum* (sky pilot) has light blue or white flower clusters; USDA zones 3-7. *P. viscosum* grows in full sun and well-drained rocky soil. The other species prefer partial shade and moist soil.

Pontederia cordata

Pontederia
(pon-te-DEER-ee-a)
PICKERELWEED

USDA Hardiness: zones 4-9
AHS Heat: zones 9-1
Height: 1 to 4 feet
Plant type: perennial
Soil: shallow water to wet soil
Light: full sun

Pickerelweed is an aquatic perennial with vivid flowers, a long blooming season, and attractive foliage that grows wild in shallow fresh water. *P. cordata* bears spikes of blue-purple funnel-shaped flowers held 1 to 2 feet above the water's surface on sturdy stems from early summer through fall. Large dark green leaves rise 2 to 4 feet above the surface on long stems. Pickerelweed will grow in wet boggy soil, but it performs best when its roots are covered by several inches of water. When setting out new plants, use stones or pebbles to hold them in place until their roots are established.

Populus tremuloides

Populus (POP-yew-lus)
POPLAR, ASPEN

USDA Hardiness: zones 4-9
AHS Heat: zones 9-3
Height: 40 to 90 feet
Plant type: tree
Soil: adaptable
Light: full sun

P. tremuloides (quaking aspen, trembling aspen, quiverleaf) is a fast-growing slender deciduous tree whose lustrous dark green leaves, turning yellow in the fall, quiver with the slightest breeze. The bark is smooth, creamy to greenish white, becoming dark and furrowed on old trees. Invasive root systems make quaking aspens good for erosion control. Quaking aspen grows in almost any site except soggy soils. Best growth occurs, however, in moist, deep, well-drained soil. The wood is weak and easily broken by storms. They tolerate drought, salt spray, and urban pollution.

Potentilla (po-ten-TILL-a)
CINQUEFOIL

USDA Hardiness: zones 3-8
AHS Heat: zones 9-4
Height: 1 to 4 feet
Plant type: perennial, shrub
Soil: adaptable
Light: full sun to partial shade

Cinquefoils offer long-blooming flowers and small compound leaves. *P. fruticosa* (bush cinquefoil, shrubby cinquefoil), a very bushy, rounded deciduous shrub, can be used as a low hedge, edging, or facer plant for a mixed border. *P. nepalensis* (Nepal cinquefoil), a sprawling perennial, is ideal for rock gardens or as a ground cover on slopes. There are many quality cultivars. Cinquefoils grow almost anywhere but perform best in moist, well-drained soil. Both species prefer full sun; bush cinquefoil tolerates partial shade.

Potentilla fruticosa

Portulaca grandiflora

Portulaca (por-tew-LAK-a)
MOSS ROSE

USDA Hardiness: zone 11
AHS Heat: zones 12-1
Height: 6 to 8 inches
Plant type: annual
Soil: well-drained to dry
Light: full sun

This low-growing annual spreads like a carpet, which sets off its brightly colored blooms. Flowers appear from early summer to frost. Portulaca is a fine choice for hot, dry sites where few other flowers will thrive. *P. grandiflora* (sun plant, eleven-o'clock) produces bowl-shaped flowers that may be single, semidouble, or double, and may be red, pink, white, yellow, orange, magenta, or striped; 'Sundance' bears semidouble flowers in a mixture of red, orange, yellow, cream, and white; 'Sundial' blooms early with double flowers. Moss rose often self-seeds. Do not fertilize; it likes poor, dry soils.

Primula (PRIM-yew-la)
PRIMROSE

USDA Hardiness: zones 5-7
AHS Heat: zones 7-3
Height: 2 to 24 inches
Plant type: perennial
Soil: moist loam
Light: partial shade

Neat, colorful primroses produce clusters of five-petaled blossoms above rosettes of tongue-shaped leaves, which are evergreen in milder climates. More than 400 species of primroses in nearly every color of the rainbow offer the gardener a multitude of choices in height and hardiness. Plant primroses in moisture-retentive soil, and water deeply during dry periods. *P. denticulata* (Himalayan primrose), *P. helodoxa* (amber primrose), and *P. japonica* (Japanese primrose) require a boglike soil. *P. vulgaris* (English primrose) and *P.* x *polyantha* (polyanthus primrose) tolerate drier conditions, while other species fall somewhere in between.

Primula x *polyantha*

Prunella (*pru-NELL-a*)
SELF-HEAL

USDA Hardiness: zones 4-9
AHS Heat: zones 8-1
Height: 12 to 20 inches
Plant type: perennial
Soil: average to dry, well-drained
Light: light shade to full sun

Prunella vulgaris

P. vulgaris (common self-heal, heal-all) slowly creeps via underground runners and rooting stems and forms dense mats useful as ground covers, especially in difficult areas such as under shrubs. From summer through fall, small spikes of purple to pale violet and sometimes pink hooded flowers rise decoratively above the foliage, attracting bees and butterflies with their sweet nectar. Common self-heal's leaves and flowers have figured in herbal medicine. Common self-heal survives in dry, average soils but can be very invasive in moist, rich soils, particularly when planted at the edges of lawns.

Pulmonaria
(*pul-mo-NAY-ree-a*)
LUNGWORT

USDA Hardiness: zones 4-8
AHS Heat: zones 8-4
Height: 6 to 18 inches
Plant type: perennial
Soil: moist, well-drained
Light: bright full shade

Pulmonaria angustifolia

Small mounds or clumps of oval leaves follow bell-shaped flowers that nod on arching stems in spring. *P. angustifolia* (blue lungwort) has pink buds opening into deep blue flowers. *P. longifolia* (long-leaved lungwort, Joseph and Mary, spotted dog) 'Ankum' has blue flowers; 'Roy Davidson' has silver-and-green foliage. *P. officinalis* 'Rubra' (blue lungwort, Jerusalem sage, Jerusalem cowslip) has white-spotted leaves and flowers that turn mottled violet. Propagate by division in the fall.

Prunus (*PROO-nus*)
CHERRY, APRICOT

USDA Hardiness: zones 4-10
AHS Heat: zones 9-1
Height: 3 to 50 feet
Plant type: shrub, small tree
Soil: moist, well-drained
Light: full sun to partial shade

Prunus laurocerasus

This huge genus ranges from shrubs and small to mid-size deciduous trees valued for their spring flowers to robust broad-leaved evergreens used for screens, foundation plants, and hedges. As a rule, plant flowering fruit trees in full sun in well-worked loam; add sand to loosen heavy clay. In warmer climates, provide afternoon shade for *P. caroliniana* (Carolina cherry laurel), even in winter. *P. laurocerasus* (common cherry laurel) is tolerant of wind and salt spray. Laurels can thrive in full sun to partial shade in soil enriched with organic matter, usually enduring drought once established.

Punica (*PEW-ni-ka*)
PUNICA

USDA Hardiness: zones 7-10
AHS Heat: zones 12-5
Height: 12 to 20 feet
Plant type: shrub, tree
Soil: moist, well-drained
Light: full sun to partial shade

Punica granatum

Small, carnation-like flowers with crumpled petals in red, orange, pink, white, or yellow adorn this multistemmed rounded deciduous shrub from early summer and sometimes into fall. Juicy yellow edible fruits up to 3 inches across, sporting thick, leathery skins, develop a reddish flush and are ready to be picked by early to midfall on *P. granatum* (pomegranate). Easily cultivated, pomegranate makes its best growth in rich, moist loam and once established is drought tolerant. It is adaptable to a range of other soils as long as they are well drained.

Puschkinia scilloides var. *libanotica* 'Alba'

Puschkinia (push-KIN-ee-a)
PUSCHKINIA

USDA Hardiness: zones 3-9
AHS Heat: zones 9-1
Height: 4 to 6 inches
Plant type: bulb
Soil: moist, well-drained
Light: full sun to light shade

Puschkinia's wands of tight, oval buds open first into loose clusters of tiny flower bells and finally into small stars on slender stems rising from tufts of narrow leaves like those of daffodils. The plants naturalize easily into drifts of blooms to carpet rockeries or beds and make an attractive border edging. *P. scilloides* var. *libanotica* (striped squill) has tiny, bluish white flowers striped darker blue above 6-inch leaves; 'Alba' is pure white.

Pyracantha (py-ra-KAN-tha)
SCARLET FIRETHORN

USDA Hardiness: zones 6-9
AHS Heat: zones 9-3
Height: 4 to 16 feet
Plant type: shrub
Soil: well-drained
Light: full sun

Pyracantha fortuneana

The scarlet firethorn is a semi-evergreen shrub with white spring flowers and stunning orange-red berries that ripen in the fall and persist into winter. It can be used effectively as a hedge or barrier. It is also a good choice as an espalier specimen, trained against a wall. *P. fortuneana* 'Graberi' is a vigorous grower noted for large red berries in midseason, lasting into winter. Plant scarlet firethorn in spring, choosing a well-drained site in full sun. Plants will grow in partial shade, but flower and fruit production will be reduced.

Pycnanthemum virginianum

Pycnanthemum (pik-NAN-thee-mum)
MOUNTAIN MINT

USDA Hardiness: zones 4-8
AHS Heat: zones 8-2
Height: 2 to 3 feet
Plant type: perennial
Soil: moist, well-drained
Light: full sun to light shade

A sharp, peppery aroma fills gardens wherever *P. virginianum* (Virginia mountain mint, wild basil, prairie hyssop) grows. The square stems lined with whorls of very narrow, pointed leaves branch into loose mounds. In summer, tufts of flowers growing at stem tips attract bees and butterflies where the plant grows in wildflower or meadow gardens. As intensely flavored as it is fragrant, Virginia mountain mint is an excellent culinary substitute for true mint. Dry the dense flower heads for arrangements, or add dried leaves and flowers to potpourri.

Pyrus (PYE-rus)
PEAR

USDA Hardiness: zones 4-8
AHS Heat: zones 9-3
Height: to 40 feet
Plant type: tree
Soil: well-drained
Light: full sun

Pyrus calleryana

P. calleryana (Callery pear) is a showy tree that bursts with white flowers in early spring. The lustrous dark green leaves form a dense, symmetrical canopy until midfall, when they turn reddish purple and finally drop. Callery pears adjust to almost any well-drained soil and tolerate drought and pollution. They tend to lose their tight form after 20 years or so, due to many branches arising close together on the trunk; 'Chanticleer' has stronger crotches than other cultivars and shows good resistance to fire blight.

Quercus (KWER-kus)
OAK

USDA Hardiness: zones 4-8
AHS Heat: zones 9-2
Height: 40 to 100 feet or more
Plant type: tree
Soil: light to heavy, well-drained
Light: full sun

Deciduous or evergreen trees that can provide the dominant structure and framework for the landscape, oaks have a central main trunk and usually stout horizontal

Quercus rubra

branches supporting a broad canopy of dark green foliage. Most species fare well in a wide range of soil types as long as there is no hardpan present. Oaks grow better and stay healthier in full sun than in partial shade. *Q. ilex* (holly oak) can withstand inland drought and salt spray. *Q. rubra* (red oak) is a deciduous species that grows to 80 feet. A good oak for desert conditions, *Q. suber* (cork oak) needs well-drained soil and is drought resistant once established.

Raphiolepis (raf-i-O-le-pis)
HAWTHORN

USDA Hardiness: zones 8-11
AHS Heat: zones 9-3
Height: 3 to 5 feet
Plant type: shrub
Soil: moist, well-drained, slightly acid
    to neutral
Light: full sun

R. indica (Indian hawthorn) is a dense, glossy-leaved evergreen shrub with showy clusters of white or pink flowers in early spring. Purplish to

Raphiolepis indica

blue-black berries ripen in fall and linger though winter. This slow-growing, sturdy shrub is often used in low hedges or as background for a flower bed. Indian hawthorn may get leggy in light shade, and it flowers best in full sun. Encourage dense growth by pinching off the tips. Once established, it withstands drought. Tolerant of salt, it grows well at the seashore.

Ranunculus
(ra-NUN-kew-lus)
BUTTERCUP, CROWFOOT

USDA Hardiness: zones 9-11 or tender
AHS Heat: zones 8-2
Height: 10 to 18 inches
Plant type: tuber
Soil: moist, very well-drained, sandy
Light: full sun

Buttercups produce quantities of saucer-shaped flowers over a long season of bloom. There are many hybrids, so

Ranunculus asiaticus

thickly doubled that flowers become colorful domes of whorled overlapping petals. *R. asiaticus* 'Tecolote Giants' (Persian buttercup) has flowers up to 5 inches across in pastel shades of pink, rose, yellow, tangerine, and white, with bi- and tricolors. Crowns are subject to rot, so sites with fast drainage are essential for success. Tubers go dormant in summer. North of USDA zone 9, treat plants as annuals, setting them out in spring and lifting them in fall for winter storage.

Ratibida (ra-ti-BID-a)
PRAIRIE CONEFLOWER

USDA Hardiness: zones 3-9
AHS Heat: zones 9-1
Height: 1½ to 5 feet
Plant type: perennial
Soil: well-drained to dry
Light: full sun to partial shade

Prairie coneflowers are sturdy perennials with brightly colored daisylike flowers that bloom in summer in the northern parts of their ranges

Ratibida columnifera

and from late spring through fall in the milder zones. *R. columnifera* (Mexican hat) has drooping yellow, red, or bicolored notched petals and a purplish brown cone; USDA zones 3-9. *R. pinnata* (gray-headed coneflower) has flowers composed of yellow petals surrounding a grayish brown cone; will tolerate partial shade; USDA zones 3-8. Prairie coneflowers thrive in well-drained soil and full sun. Gray-headed coneflower also grows in partial shade, and both species tolerate drought.

Rhexia mariana

Rhexia (REEK-see-a)
MEADOW BEAUTY

USDA Hardiness: zones 4-9
AHS Heat: zones 9-2
Height: 1 to 2 feet
Plant type: perennial
Soil: moist, acid, sandy to wet boggy
Light: full sun to partial shade

Meadow beauties are perennials that bloom all summer in their native wetlands and moist meadows in the eastern United States. The individual blossoms last less than a day. *R. mariana* (Maryland meadow beauty) bears loose clusters of white, pink, or pale rose flowers with bright yellow stamens; USDA zones 4-9. *R. virginica* (Virginia meadow beauty) has purplish red petaled flowers with bright yellow stamens; foliage is bright green; USDA zones 5-9. Rhexias thrive in boggy soil or in rich, sandy garden soil as long as moisture is abundant. They prefer full sun but tolerate light shade. Plants spread by rhizomes to form colonies.

Rhododendron (roh-doh-DEN-dron)
RHODO-DENDRON

USDA Hardiness: zones 6-8
AHS Heat: zones 9-5
Height: 2 to 12 feet
Plant type: shrub
Soil: moist, well-drained, acid, fertile
Light: partial to bright full shade

Rhododendron 'Wisahickon'

Over 900 species of rhododendrons and azaleas are included in this important genus. Most rhododendrons are evergreen, have bell-shaped flowers, and often have scaly leaves. Most azaleas are deciduous, have funnel-shaped flowers, and have leaves that are never scaly. Both are effective in borders, groupings, and naturalistic shady gardens. Mulch to conserve moisture and to keep roots cool. Water deeply in dry periods, particularly before the onset of winter. Evergreen types should be protected from hot afternoon sun and winter winds. Morning sun enhances bloom without stressing the plant.

Rhodochiton atrosanguineum

Rhodochiton (ro-DOH-ki-ton)
RHODOCHITON

USDA Hardiness: zones 9-11
AHS Heat: zones 8-2
Height: 5 to 15 feet
Plant type: tender perennial, perennial
Soil: well-drained, fertile
Light: full sun

Native to Mexico, where it is a perennial, the purple bell vine is grown as an annual north of USDA zone 9. From summer to frost, tubular deep purple flowers hang from thin stalks and are surrounded by a four-pointed fuchsia calyx. Start seed indoors in individual peat pots 3 to 4 months prior to the last frost, and transplant to the garden after soil has warmed. They thrive in warm weather. Fertilize and water regularly.

Rhus (RUSS)
SUMAC

USDA Hardiness: zones 4-9
AHS Heat: zones 9-5
Height: 2 to 30 feet
Plant type: shrub
Soil: adaptable, well-drained to dry
Light: full sun to partial shade

Rhus typhina

Sumacs are fast-growing shrubs that are useful for covering large areas of poor soil, forming dense thickets on steep banks or roadsides, where they help stabilize the soil. They are outstanding for their colorful fall foliage and bright red fruit, which is effective for many weeks. *R. typhina* (staghorn sumac) turns orange to scarlet in fall and bears crimson fruit. Sumacs prefer acid soil and do not tolerate poorly drained sites.

Ricinus *(RISS-in-us)*
CASTOR-OIL PLANT

USDA Hardiness: zone 11
AHS Heat: zones 12-1
Height: 8 to 10 feet
Plant type: annual, tender perennial
Soil: well-drained
Light: full sun

Clumps of large, glossy leaves make an effective, coarse-textured backdrop in sunny borders. The insignificant flowers are followed by prick-

Ricinus communis

ly husks filled with tiny brown seeds. These are extremely poisonous. *R. communis* (castor bean) leaves emerge red-tinged and turn glossy green until frost. Plant in loose, fertile soil, and provide ample water and fertilizer. Plants grow best in hot, humid climates; they may survive as perennials in warm climates.

Romneya *(RAHM-nee-a)*
CALIFORNIA TREE POPPY

USDA Hardiness: zones 8-10
AHS Heat: zones 9-2
Height: 4 to 8 feet
Plant type: perennial
Soil: dry, infertile
Light: full sun

The California tree poppy produces fragrant 3- to 6-inch flowers with silky white petals surrounding a bright golden center. They bloom

Romneya coulteri

throughout the summer, and though each flower lasts only a few days, they make a handsome show in both the garden and indoor arrangements. *R. coulteri*'s leaves are gray-green and deeply cut, and the fragrant summer flowers are very large, resembling crepe paper. Plant California tree poppies in poor, dry soil in full sun where invasive roots will not cause a problem. They are most successfully grown in USDA zones 8 to 10 but can survive in USDA zone 7 with a heavy winter mulch.

Rodgersia *(ro-JER-zee-a)*
RODGERSIA

USDA Hardiness: zones 5-8
AHS Heat: zones 8-1
Height: 2 to 6 feet
Plant type: perennial
Soil: moist to wet
Light: partial to full shade

The feathery plumes of rodgersia rise above huge, coarse-textured, compound leaves, often in metallic bronze-colors. *R. aesculifolia* (fingerleaf rodgersia) bears

Rodgersia aesculifolia

creamy white or pink flower plumes; USDA zones 5-6. *R. pinnata* (featherleaf rodgersia) bears plumes of buff pink flowers that emerge from late spring to midsummer; 'Superba' has very large red flowers. *R. podophylla* (bronze-leaf rodgersia) produces yellowish white 1-foot plumes; USDA zones 5-6. Space rodgersia 3 feet apart in soil that is constantly wet, such as at the edge of streams and ponds. In colder climates, provide winter protection by mulching.

Rosa *(RO-za)*
ROSE

USDA Hardiness: zones 4-9
AHS Heat: zones 9-3
Height: 1½ to 20 feet
Plant type: shrub
Soil: well-drained, organic
Light: full sun

Roses have single, double, or very double flowers, often fragrant, on thorny stems. Colorful fruit (hips) may appear in fall. Mass them for a hedge or border, let them

Rosa banksiae

ramble over a slope, or train them on a trellis or fence. Some varieties offer good fall foliage. Roses grow best in moist, slightly acid soil and prefer good air circulation. Mulch to conserve moisture, suppress weeds, and protect roots in winter. *R. banksiae* grows to 20 feet with white or yellow flowers 1 inch across. *R. rugosa* (rugosa rose) adapts to sand and salt. Heat-tolerant roses include white climber *R.* 'Sombreuil', yellow semidouble *R.* 'Alberic Barbier', pink shrub *R.* 'Complicata', and red bush *R.* 'Crimson Glory'.

Rosmarinus
(rose-ma-RY-nus)
ROSEMARY

USDA Hardiness: zones 8-10
AHS Heat: zones 12-2
Height: 6 inches to 7 feet
Plant type: perennial
Soil: well-drained, alkaline
Light: full sun

Rosmarinus officinalis

Rosemary's branching, stiff stems are lined with resinous, aromatic needlelike leaves. Small flowers cluster along the woody stems in winter. Grown as a ground cover or shrub in warm climates, rosemary is pot grown elsewhere. Rosemary's piny leaves, fresh or dried, are widely used in cooking. *R. officinalis* (garden rosemary) has gray-green leaves along branches to 6 feet outdoors, 4 feet indoors, and blue flowers; 'Arp' is very hardy, with lemon-scented leaves; 'Prostratus' is almost everblooming, with twisting branches; 'Tuscan Blue' is fast growing, with large deep blue leaves.

Ruellia (roo-EL-ee-a)
RUELLIA

USDA Hardiness: zones 4-9
AHS Heat: zones 12-6
Height: 1 to 3 feet
Plant type: perennial
Soil: dry, sandy
Light: full sun to partial shade

Ruellia x brittoniana

Ruellias are perennials found growing wild in open woods and prairies in the eastern United States. Their loose clusters of funnel-shaped flowers add a delicate touch to wildflower meadows, herbaceous borders, and woodland edges. *R.* x *brittoniana* grows to 3 feet and bears lavender flowers. *R. caroliniensis* (ruellia) bears clusters of two to four light purple flowers throughout summer; USDA zones 6-9. *R. humilis* (wild petunia) has showy lavender to purple 2-inch flowers on compact bushy plants throughout summer and fall; USDA zones 4-9. Ruellias prefer dry soils that are sandy or rocky but will adapt to other types of soil as long as they are not too moist.

Rudbeckia (rood-BEK-ee-a)
CONEFLOWER

USDA Hardiness: zones 4-9
AHS Heat: zones 9-2
Height: 1½ to 5 feet
Plant type: annual, biennial, tender
 perennial
Soil: moist, well-drained, slightly acid
Light: full sun to light shade

Rudbeckia hirta

Coneflowers, with blossoms consisting of yellow raylike petals around a raised center of another color, produce abundant bloom over a long season. They are a cheerful and reliable addition to any sunny perennial border and are excellent for cutting. *R. hirta* (black-eyed Susan) grows to 3 feet and bears flowers with deep yellow rays around black centers from midsummer into fall. Coneflowers thrive in heat and humidity and produce more flowers in full sun. Amend soil with peat moss, leaf mold, or finished compost. Stake taller forms to prevent wind damage.

Rumex (ROO-mex)
SORREL, DOCK

USDA Hardiness: zones 4-8
AHS Heat: zones 12-2
Height: 6 inches to 5 feet
Plant type: perennial
Soil: well-drained
Light: full sun to light shade

Rumex crispus

Sorrel's slightly sour, lemony, arrowhead-shaped leaves add zest to salads and accent soups and sauces. Use fresh leaves sparingly, as the high oxalic acid content can aggravate conditions such as gout. Birds love the tiny seeds produced at the tips of the stalks. *R. acetosa* (garden sorrel, sour dock) has narrow leaves. *R. crispus* (curled dock) has extremely wavy, curly leaves. *R. scutatus* (French sorrel) has thick, broad, shield-shaped leaves and grows into mats. Sorrel leaves become bitter in hot weather, but flavor returns with cooler temperatures.

Ruta graveolens

Ruta (ROO-ta)
RUE

USDA Hardiness: zones 5-9
AHS Heat: zones 9-3
Height: 12 to 36 inches
Plant type: perennial
Soil: well-drained
Light: full sun

R. graveolens (common rue) forms clumps of lacy, aromatic evergreen foliage that makes an attractive filler or low hedge in a perennial border. For several weeks in summer, frilly, spidery flowers bloom atop the foliage, followed by inflated lobed seed capsules. Once used in herbal medicine, rue is now considered poisonous. Sensitive individuals develop a blistering dermatitis after touching the leaves. *R. graveolens* bears yellow flowers in loose, open clusters; 'Jackman's Blue' is a compact, nonflowering cultivar with waxy blue foliage.

Salvia (SAL-vee-a)
SAGE

USDA Hardiness: zones 4-10
AHS Heat: zones 12-1
Height: 8 inches to 6 feet
Plant type: annual, tender perennial, perennial
Soil: sandy, dry to well-drained
Light: full sun to partial shade

Salvia coccinea

This large genus includes more than 750 species. From low-growing clumps to erect 6-foot-tall shrubs, there are sages suitable for almost every region. Whorled spikes of tiny hooded summer-to-fall-blooming flowers line the tips of salvia's erect stems above soft, sometimes downy leaves. Tender perennial salvias are grown as annuals in USDA zone 8 and colder. *S. coccinea* (Texas sage) produces heart-shaped leaves on 1-to 2-foot branching stems; *S. officinalis* (garden sage) bears bluish purple or white flowers from late spring to early summer. Propagate by division in spring or fall, from cuttings, or, except for perennial salvia, from seed. Salvias are generally drought tolerant.

Sagittaria latifolia

Sagittaria (sa-ji-TAY-ree-a)
ARROWHEAD

USDA Hardiness: zones 3-11
AHS Heat: zones 12-1
Height: to 4 feet
Plant type: perennial
Soil: shallow water to wet soil
Light: partial shade

Arrowhead, a perennial found throughout the United States and southern Canada in wet meadows, marshes, and ponds, has whorled clusters of showy flowers set off by large, leathery leaves. Arrowhead produces edible tubers relished by ducks. *S. latifolia* (wapatoo, duck potato) bears white flowers on leafless stems from mid- to late summer. The arrow-shaped leaves are up to 16 inches long. Arrowhead grows best when its roots are submerged in shallow water, but it can also be grown in the wet soil of a bog garden.

Sanguinaria (sang-gwi-NAR-ee-a)
BLOODROOT

USDA Hardiness: zones 3-9
AHS Heat: zones 8-1
Height: 6 to 14 inches
Plant type: rhizome
Soil: moist, well-drained, rich
Light: partial shade

Sanguinaria canadensis

Bloodroot is one of the loveliest spring-blooming woodland wildflowers native to eastern North America, and its large round blue-green leaves make an attractive ground cover. *S. canadensis* (bloodroot, red puccoon) has a solitary white flower with gold stamens, surrounded by a furled leaf when it emerges. Bloodroot thrives in rich, moist soil and benefits from added organic matter. It does best when planted beneath deciduous trees, where it receives bright sunshine before the trees leaf out and partial shade for the rest of the growing season. Mulch lightly with deciduous leaves in winter.

Santolina chamaecyparissus

Santolina *(san-to-LEE-na)*
LAVENDER COTTON

USDA Hardiness: zones 6-9
AHS Heat: zones 12-1
Height: 18 to 24 inches
Plant type: perennial
Soil: well-drained to dry loam
Light: full sun

Santolina forms a broad, spreading clump of aromatic leaves and tiny yellow flower buttons. The foliage makes an attractive edging for a bed or walkway. It can also be sheared into a tight, low hedge. *S. chamaecyparissus* forms a broad, cushionlike, evergreen mound with yellow flowers blooming in summer that are often removed to maintain a clipped hedge. Lavender cotton is a tough plant, well suited to adverse conditions such as drought and salt spray. It prefers dry soils of low fertility and becomes unattractive and open in fertile soils. Avoid excess moisture, especially in winter.

Sapindus *(SAP-in-dus)*
SOAPBERRY

USDA Hardiness: zones 8-10
AHS Heat: zones 10-2
Height: 25 to 50 feet
Plant type: tree
Soil: dry to adaptable
Light: full sun to light shade

Panicles of yellowish white flowers 6 to 10 inches long bloom in late spring on this graceful deciduous scaly-barked shade tree. Small yellow-orange berries, supposedly used by American Indians to make soap, emerge in fall and persist through winter, finally turning black. Soapberry is tolerant of most soils but is especially at home in the poor, dry soils of its native Southwest. It is also tolerant of urban pollution and is insect and disease resistant.

Sapindus drummondii

Sanvitalia procumbens

Sanvitalia *(san-vi-TAY-lee-a)*
CREEPING ZINNIA

USDA Hardiness: zone 0
AHS Heat: zones 12-1
Height: 5 to 6 inches
Plant type: annual
Soil: well-drained to dry
Light: full sun

This low-growing annual from Mexico produces a nonstop display of flowers from early summer to the first frost. Flowers resemble zinnias but are smaller. *S. procumbens* (trailing sanvitalia) bears flowers composed of yellow or orange rays surrounding a dark purple center and may be single, semidouble, or double; 'Gold Braid' produces double yellow blooms; 'Mandarin Orange' bears semidouble orange flowers. Start seed indoors 4 to 6 weeks prior to the last frost, or sow directly outdoors in late spring. Sanvitalia thrives in hot, humid weather and is drought tolerant.

Sarcococca *(sar-ko-KO-ka)*
SWEET BOX

USDA Hardiness: zones 5-9
AHS Heat: zones 9-5
Height: 18 inches to 5 feet
Plant type: shrub
Soil: moist, well-drained, fertile
Light: partial to bright full shade

A handsome plant with year-round ornamental value, sarcococca has shiny, narrow leaves on its roundly mounded shape. In late winter to early spring, inconspicuous but fragrant white flowers bloom, to be replaced by shiny black or red berries that linger into fall. Sarcococca spreads slowly by suckers; the low form makes a good ground cover. Best grown in USDA zone 8 in the South and along the Pacific Coast; *S. confusa* and *S. ruscifolia* need shelter in USDA zone 7. Protect from winter winds. Add leaf mold or peat moss to the soil to improve drainage. Mulch to conserve moisture.

Sarcococca hookerana var. *humilis*

Satureja (sat-yew-REE-jia)
SAVORY

USDA Hardiness: zones 6-11
AHS Heat: zones 12-1
Height: 3 to 18 inches
Plant type: annual, perennial
Soil: well-drained, slightly alkaline
Light: full sun

Savory's aromatic needlelike leaves line erect stems tipped with whorls of tiny blossoms from summer through fall. Plant savories as border edg-

Satureja montana

ings, in kitchen or rock gardens, or in pots for the window sill. Use leaves fresh, dried, or frozen as fines herbes. Savory also figures in traditional herbal medicine. *S. hortensis* (summer savory) is a hardy annual with pink flowers. *S. montana* 'Nana' (pygmy winter savory) has peppery leaves and white or lilac blooms; USDA zones 5-8. *S. spicigera* (creeping savory) forms evergreen mats with white flowers; USDA zones 7-8.

Scabiosa (skab-ee-O-sa)
SCABIOUS

USDA Hardiness: zones 4-11
AHS Heat: zones 8-3
Height: 18 inches to 3 feet
Plant type: annual, perennial
Soil: well-drained, fertile
Light: full sun

Scabiosa is easy to grow and produces long-lasting flowers that resemble pins stuck in a pincushion; colors include lavender, pink, purple, maroon, red, and white. *S. atro-*

Scabiosa columbaria

purpurea has domed flower heads; *S. columbaria* 'Butterfly Blue' is a prolific compact form with samll flowers on 15-inch stems; *S. stellata* (paper moon) bears pale blue flowers that become papery when dry. Start seed indoors 4 to 6 weeks prior to the last frost and transplant to the garden after danger of frost has passed, or sow directly outdoors in late spring. Water during dry periods.

Saxifraga (saks-IF-ra-ga)
SAXIFRAGE, ROCKFOIL

USDA Hardiness: zones 6-9
AHS Heat: zones 8-1
Height: 4 to 24 inches
Plant type: perennial
Soil: moist, well-drained, neutral, fertile
Light: full to dappled shade

An ideal plant for rock gardens, saxifrage has rosettes of leaves that form a mat from

Saxifraga x 'Carnival'

which runners spread. Delicate flowers rise above foliage in spring. *S. stolonifera* (strawberry geranium, beefsteak geranium) bears white flowers. *S.* x 'Carnival' bears small daisy-like rose-red flowers in early spring above clumps of bright green leaves. Saxifrages grow best in neutral, rocky soil but will tolerate other soils as long as they are very well drained but evenly moist. Generously enrich the soil with leaf mold or peat moss. Mulch lightly to overwinter, and apply an all-purpose fertilizer in spring.

Schizachyrium (ski-ZAK-e-reé-um)
LITTLE BLUESTEM

USDA Hardiness: zones 5-10
AHS Heat: zones 9-2
Height: 2 to 5 feet
Plant type: ornamental grass
Soil: well-drained to dry
Light: full sun

This clump-forming perennial grass can be massed as a ground cover, used in a meadow garden, or planted

Schizachyrium scoparium

singly in a perennial border. Its flowers and seed heads are attractive in arrangements. *S. scoparium* (little bluestem, prairie beard grass) has narrow blue-green foliage that turns mahogany brown in fall. Tiny flower clusters open from late summer to fall and are followed by shiny white seed heads. Little bluestem is adaptable and easy to grow, thriving in most dry or well-drained soils, including those of low fertility. It does not, however, tolerate wet conditions.

Sedum (SEE-dum)
STONECROP

USDA Hardiness: zones 3-10
AHS Heat: zones 8-3
Height: 8 to 24 inches
Plant type: tender perennial,
    perennial
Soil: well-drained
Light: full sun to light shade

Stonecrops form neat, bushy globes of thick, succulent foliage covered with clusters of tiny star-shaped flowers. The broccoli-like blooms often re-

Sedum spurium

main attractive into winter. Numerous species and cultivars are available, including S. x 'Autumn Joy' with flower color ranging from pink to rust to golden brown and S. *spurium* with fleshy tiny oval leaves on 4- to 6-inch ground hugging stems and pink flowers on 6- to 9-inch stalks in summer. Sedum is extremely drought tolerant and grows well in almost any well-drained soil, even poor and dry. Propagate by division or by rooting leaf or stem cuttings.

Sesamum (SES-am-um)
SESAME

USDA Hardiness: zone 11
AHS Heat: zones 12-7
Height: 18 to 36 inches
Plant type: annual, tender perennial
Soil: well-drained
Light: full sun

Each of sesame's bell-shaped flowers, which grow where leaves join the stem, produces an upright, pointed, oval capsule that bursts when ripe to release tiny,

Sesamum indicum

nutty-tasting, oily seeds, prized in Middle Eastern cuisine. The seeds, whole or ground, have many uses in cooking. S. *indicum* (sesame, benne, gingili) has square, sticky stems lined with oval, pointed 3- to 5-inch leaves and 1-inch white flowers tinged pink, yellow, or red. Sesame plants need at least 120 days of hot weather to set seed.

Senecio (se-NEE-see-o)
GROUNDSEL, SENECIO

USDA Hardiness: zones 4-10
AHS Heat: zones 8-4
Height: 1 to 5 feet
Plant type: tender perennial,
    perennial
Soil: moist to dry, sandy
Light: full sun to partial shade

Perennial groundsels add a golden glow to their native grasslands or wooded areas for several weeks. S. *aureus*

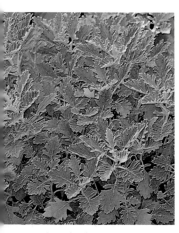

Senecio cineraria

(golden groundsel, golden ragwort) has clusters of deep golden yellow flowers in late spring and summer. It spreads rapidly by horizontal offshoots to form an attractive ground cover; plant it in moist, acid soil and full sun to partial shade in USDA zones 4-8. S. *cineraria* (dusty-miller) bears stiff, woolly white leaves with yellow or cream flowers. S. *douglasii* (shrubby senecio) has yellow flowers in summer and fall and fuzzy white foliage; it grows in full sun and prefers a well-drained sandy or rocky soil; USDA zones 6-10.

Sidalcea (sy-DAL-see-a)
CHECKER-MALLOW

USDA Hardiness: zones 4-10
AHS Heat: zones 8-2
Height: 2 to 4 feet
Plant type: perennial
Soil: wet to dry
Light: full sun to partial shade

Perennials from the western United States, the checkermallows have showy flowers resembling hollyhocks and provide a colorful vertical ac-

Sidalcea malviflora

cent in mixed herbaceous borders or meadow plantings. S. *malviflora* (checkermallow, checkerbloom) has pink or purple flowers, which open in the morning and close up in the evening in spring and summer; it prefers soil that is moist in winter and well drained to dry in summer and grows in full sun to partial shade; USDA zones 5-10. S. *neomexicana* (prairie mallow) bears mauve flowers in spring and early summer; plant it in moist, well-drained to wet soils in full sun; USDA zones 4-10.

Silene (sy-LEE-ne)
CAMPION, CATCHFLY

USDA Hardiness: zones 4-8
AHS Heat: zones 9-3
Height: 4 inches to 2 feet
Plant type: annual, perennial
Soil: well-drained, sandy loam
Light: full sun to light shade

Silene schafta

Campions produce star-shaped, five-petaled flowers on branching stems for several weeks during the growing season. *S. schafta* (moss campion) has rose-pink or purple flowers above rosettes of hairy, oblong, light green leaves. *S.* 'Robin's White Breast' bears white flower bells above dense mounds of silvery gray leaves. *S. virginica* (fire-pink catchfly) has clusters of pink to red flowers on sticky 2-foot stems above flat rosettes of evergreen leaves. Campions require good drainage and perform well in sun or shade.

Sisyrinchium (sis-i-RINK-ee-um)
BLUE-EYED GRASS

USDA Hardiness: zones 3-10
AHS Heat: zones 8-3
Height: 3 to 18 inches
Plant type: perennial
Soil: moist to seasonally dry
Light: full sun to partial shade

Sisyrinchium bellum

Sisyrinchiums are dainty-looking perennials with starry six-petaled flowers and clumps of grasslike leaves. *S. angustifolium* (narrow-leaved blue-eyed grass) has light blue flowers from spring to summer; it needs a poor to average, evenly moist soil; USDA zones 3-10. *S. bellum* (California blue-eyed grass) bears great numbers of blue, violet, or white flowers in spring; foliage may be evergreen; USDA zones 8-10. *S. douglasii* (Douglas blue-eyed grass) has reddish purple flowers in spring; USDA zones 4-9. Sisyrinchiums thrive in full sun or light shade. *S. bellum* and *S. douglasii* need soil that is moist in spring and dry in summer.

Silybum (sil-LY-bum)
BLESSED THISTLE

USDA Hardiness: zones 7-9
AHS Heat: zones 5-1
Height: to 4 feet
Plant type: annual, biennial
Soil: well-drained
Light: full sun

Silybum marianum

Silybum is grown primarily for its spiny, glossy foliage, which is dark green with silvery white spots. Thistlelike flowers rise in late summer. The roots, leaves, and flower heads can be eaten as a vegetable. *S. marianum* produces flowers ranging in color from rose to purple, surrounded by curved, spiny bracts. Sow seed directly outdoors in early spring. Once established, plants often self-seed and may become weedy. They tolerate poor soil and dry conditions.

Skimmia (SKIM-ee-a)
SKIMMIA

USDA Hardiness: zones 7-9
AHS Heat: zones 8-4
Height: 3 to 4 feet
Plant type: shrub
Soil: moist, well-drained, acid
Light: partial to bright full shade

Skimmia japonica

Skimmia forms a low mound of leathery leaves decorated in spring with clusters of flowers and in fall with bright berries that remain into the next spring. In order for a female bush to produce berries, a male bush has to be located within 100 feet. *S. japonica* (Japanese skimmia) may be planted in USDA zone 9 on the West Coast and north to USDA zone 7 on the East Coast if given a protected location. In hot climates, site it out of afternoon sun. Foliage may discolor in winter sun. Add 1 part peat moss or leaf mold to every 2 parts of soil to improve drainage.

Smilacina racemosa

Smilacina (smy-la-SEE-na)
FALSE SOLOMON'S-SEAL

USDA Hardiness: zones 2-8
AHS Heat: zones 8-3
Height: 1 to 3 feet
Plant type: perennial
Soil: moist, deep, rich
Light: partial to full shade

The arching stems, spring flowers, and fall berries of these perennial woodland natives make them an outstanding choice for a shady garden. *S. racemosa* (false Solomon's-seal, false spikenard) has conical flower clusters. The berries that follow the flowers are green in summer, turning pinkish red in fall; USDA zones 4-8. *S. stellata* (starry false Solomon's-seal) has terminal clusters of star-shaped flowers and dark green leaves; berries are dark red in fall; it tolerates somewhat drier soil and more sun, but its growth will be stunted; USDA zones 2-7. Smilacina grows best in moist, deep, humus-rich soil in shade.

Solidago sphacelata

Solidago (sol-i-DAY-go)
GOLDENROD

USDA Hardiness: zones 3-10
AHS Heat: zones 9-6
Height: 1 to 10 feet
Plant type: perennial
Soil: moist, well-drained to dry
Light: full sun to partial shade

The upright stems of goldenrods are tipped with eye-catching clusters of yellow flowers in summer and fall. These tough, dependable perennials are native to meadows and prairies in Canada and throughout most of the United States. They make excellent cut flowers, and butterflies feed on their nectar. Goldenrods thrive in full sun in soils of average fertility. Most goldenrods are aggressive growers. If it threatens to take over the garden, prune the underground rhizomes in the fall. Many species tolerate heat and dry conditions.

Sphaeralcea (sfee-RAL-see-a)
GLOBE MALLOW

USDA Hardiness: zones 3-11
AHS Heat: zones 12-8
Height: 2 to 3 feet
Plant type: perennial
Soil: dry, rocky
Light: full sun

Sphaeralcea coccinea

Globe mallows are drought-resistant perennials native to dry, rocky slopes and desert plains of the western United States. They bear brightly colored cupped flowers and are pretty choices for sunny rock gardens. *S. ambigua* (desert mallow) bears wandlike clusters of apricot-orange flowers in spring; USDA zones 6-10. *S. coccinea* (prairie mallow, scarlet globe mallow) has orange-pink flowers surrounded by red bracts in spring, summer, or fall; USDA zones 3-10. *S. munroana* (Munro's globe mallow) bears bright pink to deep apricot flowers and gray-green foliage; USDA zones 4-10. Plant globe mallow in full sun and dry, rocky soil.

Spigelia (spy-JEE-li-a)
PINKROOT, INDIAN PINK

USDA Hardiness: zones 5-9
AHS Heat: zones 9-2
Height: 1 to 2 feet
Plant type: perennial
Soil: moist, well-drained, acid
Light: partial shade

Spigelia marilandica

Pinkroot bears interesting trumpet-shaped red flowers with yellow throats along one side of an arching stem. *S. marilandica* has pinkish red flowers with yellow throats in elongated clusters, blooming in late spring to early summer. Plant pinkroot in a well-drained, slightly acid soil amended with organic matter. It thrives in partial shade, especially in warmer climates, but tolerates full sun if adequate moisture is supplied. It does not compete well with surface tree roots.

Spiraea (spy-REE-a)
SPIREA

USDA Hardiness: zones 4-9
AHS Heat: zones 10-2
Height: 2 to 8 feet
Plant type: shrub
Soil: well-drained
Light: full sun to partial shade

Hardy deciduous shrubs, spireas produce showy clusters of dainty flowers in spring or summer. Many quality forms are available, including *S.* x *bumalda* (Bum-

Spiraea x *bumalda*

ald spirea), which bears white to deep pink flower clusters in summer; 'Gold Flame' has reddish orange new leaves that turn yellow-green in summer and bright red-orange in fall, with pinkish blooms. Spireas are easy to grow in any garden soil. Prune summer bloomers in late winter, spring bloomers after flowering.

Stachys (STAY-kis)
LAMB'S EARS, BETONY

USDA Hardiness: zones 4-9
AHS Heat: zones 9-1
Height: 1 to 3 feet
Plant type: perennial
Soil: average, moist, well-drained
Light: full sun to light shade

Lamb's ears forms low rosettes of soft, silvery heart-shaped leaves with tall flower stems carrying spikes of small tubular flowers above

Stachys byzantina

them. It gradually spreads into low mats that provide a colorful filler in the perennial border when plants are blooming. Use the flowers in fresh bouquets. Steep the fresh or dried leaves for tea. *S. byzantina* (lamb's ears) bears woolly white leaves to 4 inches long and whorls of pink or purple flowers in 1- to 3-inch spikes. Stachys is an easy plant to grow in full sun and well-drained soil, but high heat and humidity may wilt it.

Sporobolus (spor-OB-o-lus)
DROPSEED

USDA Hardiness: zones 3-8
AHS Heat: zones 10-2
Height: 2 feet
Plant type: perennial
Soil: dry, sandy
Light: full sun

Native to the prairies of the central United States and Canada, this perennial grass forms a fountainlike clump of fine-textured, gracefully arching leaves. It is ideal for

Sporobolus heterolepis

small and large meadow gardens, for herbaceous borders, and as a ground cover in dry, sunny sites. *S. heterolepis* (northern prairie dropseed) has narrow rich green leaves 20 inches long, and loose clusters of dark green flowers that bloom in summer and fall. The entire plant, including the seed heads, turns an attractive tan-bronze in fall. Northern prairie dropseed prefers dry, sandy soil and full sun, but it will tolerate a little shade.

Stephanandra (stef-a-NAN-dra)
LACE SHRUB

USDA Hardiness: zones 3-8
AHS Heat: zones 9-4
Height: 1½ to 3 feet
Plant type: shrub
Soil: moist, well-drained, acid
Light: full sun to light shade

Lace shrub is a tidy plant with a gracefully mounding habit. It may be grown on banks to prevent erosion or may be used as a low hedge

Stephanandra incisa

or tall ground cover. Its dense foliage and low habit make it well suited to growing under low windows or among tall, leggy shrubs in a mixed border. *S. incisa* 'Crispa' foliage is bright green, turning reddish purple or red-orange in the fall; inconspicuous pale yellow flowers appear in early summer. Plant lace shrub in moist, acid soil in full sun or light shade. Add generous amounts of organic matter to the soil prior to planting to help retain moisture.

Stewartia pseudocamellia

Stewartia (stew-AR-tee-a)
STEWARTIA

USDA Hardiness: zones 3-9
AHS Heat: zones 8-1
Height: 10 to 40 feet
Plant type: shrub, tree
Soil: moist, well-drained, acid, organic
Light: partial shade to full sun

Stewartia has camellia-like summer flowers and colorful fall foliage. *S. pseudocamellia* (Japanese stewartia) has exfoliating bark in cream, rusty red, and gray. *S. ovata* (mountain stewartia, mountain camellia) bears creamy white flowers on spreading branches of a bushy shrub or small tree. Provide stewartia with a summer mulch and acid soil to keep the roots moist. Amend the soil liberally with peat moss, leaf mold, or compost. In warmer climates, provide some afternoon shade.

Styrax (STY-racks)
SNOWBELL, STORAX

USDA Hardiness: zones 5-9
AHS Heat: zones 9-4
Height: 20 to 30 feet
Plant type: shrub, tree
Soil: moist, well-drained, acid, organic
Light: full sun to partial shade

This genus includes deciduous or evergreen tall shrubs or small trees with a profusion of delicate white bell-like flowers that dangle from wide-spreading branches. Snowbell is an ideal candidate to shade a patio or garden bench or to plant on slopes above walkways. *S. obassia* (fragrant snowbell) is a small tree with fragrant, showy white flowers; grows to 30 feet. Provide partial shade in warmer climates, and shelter from winter winds and low areas in colder climates. Amend soil with generous amounts of leaf mold or peat moss. Japanese snowbell is a remarkably pest-free plant.

Styrax obassia

Stokesia laevis

Stokesia (sto-KEE-zi-a)
STOKES' ASTER

USDA Hardiness: zones 5-9
AHS Heat: zones 8-4
Height: 12 to 18 inches
Plant type: perennial
Soil: well-drained, sandy loam
Light: full sun

The fringed flowers of Stokes' aster bloom on branched flower stalks rising from neat rosettes of shiny, narrow, straplike leathery leaves that are evergreen in warmer climates. Stokes' aster is excellent in bouquets. *S. laevis* has solitary flower heads 2 to 5 inches across, blooming over a 4-week season in summer; 'Blue Danube' has 5-inch clear blue flowers; 'Blue Moon', lilac flowers; 'Jelitto' has 4-inch deep blue blossoms; 'Silver Moon' blooms white. Mulch Stokes' aster in winter in colder climates. It tolerates heat, drought, and poor soil conditions.

Symphytum (SIM-fit-um)
COMFREY

USDA Hardiness: zones 5-9
AHS Heat: zones 9-4
Height: 3 to 5 feet
Plant type: perennial
Soil: rich, moist
Light: full sun to light shade

Comfrey forms bold clumps of coarse, hairy oval leaves and is useful as a backdrop in large borders or meadow gardens. From spring through fall, drooping clusters of funnel-shaped flowers decorate the plants. The leaves can be steeped for liquid fertilizer, or added to the compost heap. *S. officinale* (common comfrey) has blue, white, purple, or rose tubular flowers. *S. x uplandicum* (Russian comfrey) is free-flowering with blue or purple blossoms; 'Variegatum' has leaves marbled cream and green. Choose sites carefully, as comfrey is difficult to eradicate once established.

Symphytum officinale

Syringa vulgaris

Syringa (si-RING-ga)
LILAC

USDA Hardiness: zones 3-8
AHS Heat: zones 8-3
Height: 3 to 30 feet
Plant type: shrub, tree
Soil: moist, well-drained
Light: full sun

Deciduous staples of gardens past, lilacs produce highly scented flower clusters after their dark green pointed-oval leaves have appeared. Lilacs grow best in loose, slightly acid loam, but they adjust to both acid or slightly alkaline soil. They will not flower without full sun. Lilacs need good air circulation to resist mildew. *S. vulgaris* (common lilac) bears sweetly fragrant blooms in midspring in a variety of colors. *S. reticulata* (Japanese tree lilac) is unusually pest free and resistant to mildew.

Tanacetum (tan-a-SEE-tum)
TANSY

USDA Hardiness: zones 4-9
AHS Heat: zones 9-1
Height: 8 inches to 4 feet
Plant type: perennial
Soil: average to poor, dry,
       well-drained
Light: full sun to light shade

Tanacetum vulgare var. *crispum*

Tansy bears dainty flowers with conspicuous button-shaped centers surrounded by a fringe of narrow, often inconspicuous white or yellow petals. Singly or in clusters, the flowers grow on branching stalks above pungent foliage that is semi-evergreen in milder climates. *T. vulgare* var. *crispum* (fern-leaved tansy) bears leaves like small fern fronds in mounds to 4 feet high and flowers with yellow centers surrounded by insignificant petals. While tanacetums grow best in full sun, fern-leaved tansy tolerates partial shade. Rich soils produce floppy stems; trim plants back to prevent legginess. Provide a winter mulch in colder zones.

Tagetes (ta-JEE-tez)
MARIGOLD

USDA Hardiness: zone 0
AHS Heat: zones 12-1
Height: 6 inches to 3 feet
Plant type: annual, tender perennial
Soil: moist, well-drained
Light: full sun

Marigolds are easy to grow, provide a reliable display, and are available in a wide range of heights. Their flowers range from pale yellow to orange and burgundy and are pro-

Tagetes patula

duced nonstop from early summer to frost in many varieties. Some species are grown for their fernlike foliage, which is often quite aromatic. *T. patula* (French marigold) grows 6 to 18 inches tall with a rounded habit and bears flowers in shades of yellow, orange, maroon, and bicolors. Start seed indoors 6 to 8 weeks prior to the last frost, or sow directly outdoors 2 weeks before that date. Marigolds thrive in a moist, well-drained soil but tolerate dry conditions. Remove dead blossoms to encourage continuous flowering. Avoid overwatering.

Taxodium (taks-ODE-ee-um)
CYPRESS

USDA Hardiness: zones 5-11
AHS Heat: zones 10-3
Height: 50 to 70 feet or more
Plant type: tree
Soil: moist, sandy, acid
Light: full sun

These stately deciduous conifers have sage green needle-like foliage that turns bright orange-brown in fall and is shed. Inconspicuous flowers bloom in spring, and fragrant

Taxodium distichum

green to purple cones 1 inch across mature to brown. Although *T. distichum* (common bald cypress) makes its best growth in moist to wet deep, sandy loams, it is surprisingly tolerant of dry soil and low fertility. It is also very resistant to strong winds, and is seldom seriously bothered by disease or insects.

Taxus x *media*

Taxus (TAKS-us)
YEW

USDA Hardiness: zones 4-7
AHS Heat: zones 7-1
Height: 2 to 60 feet
Plant type: shrub, tree
Soil: well-drained
Light: light shade to full sun

The dense, needled foliage of yews provides a consistent year-round anchor to the landscape. Female plants produce bright red berries if a male is nearby. (Caution: The berries are poisonous.) Smaller forms make superb foundation plants or entrance shrubs, or they may be clipped into hedges. Yews adapt to almost any soil as long as it is well drained but prefer slightly acid, sandy loam. Keep the soil moist (but not wet—the roots will rot) in hotter climates, and place the tree so as to protect it from wind.

Ternstroemia (tern-STRO-mee-a)
TERNSTROEMIA

USDA Hardiness: zones 7-11
AHS Heat: zones 12-3
Height: to 20 feet
Plant type: shrub
Soil: moist, well-drained, organic
Light: full to partial shade

Ternstroemia gymnanthera

Leathery leaves that open brownish red and mature to rich, glossy green clothe gracefully arching branches. In early summer, small clusters of fragrant creamy white flowers put on a modest display. Small red berries turn black and last through winter. Although *Ternstroemia gymnanthera* grows best in rich, slightly acid soil that stays moist, it tolerates occasional drought.

Tephrosia virginiana

Tephrosia (te-FROH-zee-a)
TEPHROSIA

USDA Hardiness: zones 5-10
AHS Heat: zones 9-3
Height: 1 to 2 feet
Plant type: perennial
Soil: dry, sandy
Light: full sun

Tephrosia is a perennial native to open woods and sandy fields of the eastern and central United States. Its pretty two-toned flowers resemble sweet peas, and the finely cut foliage is appealing all season long. *T. virginiana* (goat's rue) has compact clusters of flowers composed of yellowish upper petals and purplish pink lower petals from late spring to early summer above a mound of attractive silvery foliage. The pinnately compound leaves have eight to 15 pairs of small leaflets covered with silky white hairs. Plant *T. virginiana* in a sunny location with dry, sandy soil.

Teucrium (TEWK-ree-um)
GERMANDER

USDA Hardiness: zones 8-11
AHS Heat: zones 12-4
Height: 6 to 18 inches
Plant type: shrub
Soil: well-drained, slightly acid
Light: full sun to light shade

Teucrium aureum

Germanders are used as ornamentals, edging plants, or dwarf hedges. Germander grows to 1 foot, with toothed leaves and whorls of red-purple to rose flowers in the summer. *T. aureum* is a dwarf shrub with stems to 18 inches long covered with white, green, or golden hairs. *T. chamaedrys* (wall germander) has trailing, then erect, stems and whorls of white-dotted purple-pink flowers. Provide germander with protection from drying winter winds. Propagate by seed, cuttings, or division.

Thalictrum flavum
spp. *glaucum*

Thalictrum (thal-IK-trum)
MEADOW RUE

USDA Hardiness: zones 3-10
AHS Heat: zones 9-1
Height: 8 inches to 8 feet
Plant type: perennial
Soil: moist, rich
Light: full sun to full shade

Meadow rues, native to woodlands, meadows, and prairies, are prized for their finely cut leaves and delicate flowers. *T. dasycarpum* (purple meadow rue) bears green flowers in loose terminal clusters; USDA zones 3-6. *T. dioicum* (early meadow rue) is short with beautiful long-stalked foliage. Male and female plants bear different flowers. *T. flavum* is a creeping plant with stems to 4 feet. *T. polycarpum* (meadow rue) is grown mainly for its attractive foliage; USDA zones 6-10. *T. polygamum* (tall meadow rue) bears showy cream-colored flowers in summer and feathery blue-green foliage; USDA zones 4-7.

Thuja (THOO-ya)
ARBORVITAE

USDA Hardiness: zones 3-8
AHS Heat: zones 9-2
Height: 3 to 30 feet
Plant type: shrub, tree
Soil: moist, well-drained, fertile
Light: full sun to light shade

Thuja occidentalis

Arborvitae's fine-textured evergreen foliage develops along dense pyramids of branches in shades of green, yellow-green, and blue-green. *T. occidentalis* (American or eastern arborvitae, white cedar) has shiny green needles that turn brown in winter; 'Hetz Midget' is a small, dense globe; 'Lutea' forms a golden yellow pyramid to 30 feet; 'Rheingold' has deep gold foliage on oval shrubs to 5 feet. *T. orientalis* [also called *Platycladus orientalis*] (Oriental arborvitae) has bright green or yellow-green young foliage maturing to dark green and holding its color through winter; hardy to USDA zone 5 or 6. Arborvitaes located in shade will grow loose and open.

Thermopsis montana

Thermopsis (ther-MOP-sis)
FALSE LUPINE

USDA Hardiness: zones 3-9
AHS Heat: zones 8-1
Height: 1½ to 5 feet
Plant type: perennial
Soil: dry, rocky to moist, rich
Light: full sun to partial shade

The false lupines, which inhabit open woodlands, meadows, and stony flats, are perennials with dense clusters of yellow lupinelike flowers. *T. montana* (golden pea) bears dense clusters of bright yellow flowers in spring, followed by velvety pods; USDA zones 3-8. *T. villosa* (bush pea) has deep yellow flowers in dense clusters up to a foot long from spring to summer, followed by hairy pods; USDA zones 4-9. Grow *T. montana* in full sun in a well-drained, sandy soil. *T. villosa* adapts to full sun or light shade and prefers a humus-rich soil and supplemental watering during dry periods.

Thunbergia (thun-BER-jee-a)
CLOCK VINE

USDA Hardiness: zones 10-11
AHS Heat: zones 12-5
Height: 3 to 6 feet
Plant type: tender perennial
Soil: moist, well-drained, fertile
Light: full sun to partial shade

Thunbergia alata

Thunbergia is a climbing or trailing vine that produces a mass of neat, triangular leaves and trumpet-shaped flowers in shades of yellow, orange, and cream, usually with a very dark center, throughout the summer. *T. alata* (black-eyed Susan vine) has solitary flowers with a black or dark purple center. Start seed indoors 6 to 8 weeks prior to the last frost, or sow directly outdoors after danger of frost has past. Plants thrive where summer temperatures remain somewhat cool. Water during dry periods.

Thymus quinquecostatus

Thymus (TY-mus)
THYME

USDA Hardiness: zones 3-9
AHS Heat: zones 9-1
Height: 2 to 18 inches
Plant type: perennial, shrub
Soil: average to poor, dry,
　　well-drained, alkaline
Light: full sun

This large genus includes over 300 species of aromatic small shrubs or perennial herbs. Thyme adds pungent aroma, fine texture, and soft color to borders, rock gardens, and garden paths. Small clusters of summer-long flowers are attractive to bees. The tiny leaves are used widely in cooking. Both leaves and flowers are used in potpourris and toiletries. *T. quinquecostatus* is a prostrate desert shrub that grows to 4 inches with spiked, rose-purple flowers. Select sites with average to poor soil and incorporate a small amount of bone meal at planting time; rich or wet soils invite fungus and winter kill. Thyme is tolerant of both heat and drought.

Tithonia (ti-THO-nee-a)
MEXICAN SUNFLOWER

USDA Hardiness: zone 0
AHS Heat: zones 12-2
Height: 2 to 6 feet
Plant type: annual
Soil: well-drained
Light: full sun

Tithonia rotundifolia

This native of Mexico and Central America, with daisy-like flowers ranging in color from yellow to red, is exceptional in its ability to withstand heat and dry conditions. Flowers are borne atop erect stems with coarse-textured leaves. Plants are suitable for the back of borders and for cutting; they can also be used as a fast-growing summer screen. Start seed indoors 6 to 8 weeks prior to the last frost, or sow directly outdoors after all danger of frost has passed. Do not cover seed. Plants tolerate poor soil, heat, and drought.

Tiarella wherryi

Tiarella (ty-a-REL-a)
FOAMFLOWER

USDA Hardiness: zones 3-9
AHS Heat: zones 8-4
Height: 6 to 12 inches
Plant type: perennial
Soil: moist, well-drained, rich
Light: partial shade to shade

Foamflowers are low-growing perennials found in cool, moist woodlands and on the banks of streams. *T. cordifolia* (foamflower) has compact clusters of tiny star-shaped white flowers from midspring to early summer; mature plants spread by runners; USDA zones 3-8. *T. unifoliata* (western foamflower, sugar scoop) has white bell-shaped flowers from midspring to summer above evergreen leaves. *T. wherryi* (pink foamflower) is noted for its foliage and spikes of pink spring flowers; USDA zones 3-9. Foamflowers thrive in full or partial shade and moist, rich, slightly acid soil with a high organic content. Water during dry spells.

Tradescantia (trad-e-SKAN-shee-a)
SPIDERWORT

USDA Hardiness: zones 3-10
AHS Heat: zones 12-1
Height: 10 to 36 inches
Plant type: perennial
Soil: well-drained
Light: full sun to partial shade

Tradescantia x *andersoniana*

Found in open woods and on prairies, spiderworts are upright or trailing perennials whose flowers have three wide petals and showy stamens. *T. bracteata* (bracted spiderwort) has clusters of blue-violet flowers in late spring to early summer; USDA zones 3-8. *T. virginiana* (Virginia spiderwort) has blue to blue-violet flowers from spring to summer; USDA zones 4-10. *T.* x *andersoniana* is a hybrid with larger, more colorful flowers than the parent species. Plant spiderworts in full sun or partial shade in well-drained soil. It may become invasive when grown in rich garden soil.

Trillium (TRIL-ee-um)
TRILLIUM, WAKE-ROBIN

Trillium grandiflorum

USDA Hardiness: zones 2-9
AHS Heat: zones 8-1
Height: 6 to 18 inches
Plant type: perennial
Soil: moist, acid, rich
Light: partial shade to shade

Trilliums are woodland perennials whose solitary flowers consist of three broad petals and three greenish sepals. Below each flower is a whorl of three leaves. *T. cernuum* (nodding trillium) has nodding white flowers with deep rose anthers; USDA zones 3-7. *T. erectum* (purple trillium, squawroot) has maroon flowers; USDA zones 2-6. *T. grandiflorum* (large-flowered trillium, white wake-robin) bears long-lasting white flowers 3 to 4 inches across that turn pink with age; USDA zones 3-8. Trilliums require at least partial shade and moist, humus-rich soil.

Tsuga (TSOO-ga)
HEMLOCK

Tsuga canadensis

USDA Hardiness: zones 3-8
AHS Heat: zones 7-3
Height: 40 to 70 feet
Plant type: tree
Soil: moist, well-drained, acid
Light: full shade to full sun

Hemlocks are softly pyramidal evergreens whose graceful, drooping branches and small needles lend a fine texture to the shade garden. *T. canadensis* (Canadian hemlock, eastern hemlock) makes a beautiful hedge or screen. *T. caroliniana* (Carolina hemlock) is more tolerant of urban conditions. Unlike many other conifers, hemlocks tolerate shade well. They are shallow-rooted plants that are intolerant of wind, drought, and heat; add organic matter to sandy soils to aid in moisture retention, and mulch to keep soil moist and cool. Sunscald occurs at 95°F and above.

Tropaeolum (tro-PEE-o-lum)
NASTURTIUM

Tropaeolum majus

USDA Hardiness: zone 11
AHS Heat: zones 12-1
Height: 6 inches to 8 feet
Plant type: tender perennial
Soil: poor, well-drained to dry
Light: full sun

Nasturtiums' bright flowers and attractive shieldlike leaves make them excellent fast-growing screens or bedding plants. Blooms appear from summer through frost. *T. majus* (common nasturtium) may be bushy or climbing, with showy flowers in red, yellow, white, or orange. *T. minus* (dwarf nasturtium) 'Alaska Mixed' has a wide range of flower colors. *T. peregrinum* (canary creeper, canarybird vine) is a climbing vine with pale yellow fringed flowers. Sow seed directly outdoors after danger of frost has passed. In hot climates, nasturtiums will self-sow from year to year. Do not fertilize.

Tulbaghia (tul-BAJ-ee-a)
SOCIETY GARLIC

Tulbaghia violacea

USDA Hardiness: zones 9-11
AHS Heat: zones 12-4
Height: 1 to 2½ feet
Plant type: bulb
Soil: average, moist, well-drained
Light: full sun to light shade

In summer, society garlic carries large clusters of starry flowers above clumps of grassy evergreen leaves. Use society garlic's neat mounds as a specimen, or grow the plant as an edging. In cooler climates, society garlic grows well as a potted plant and can be wintered over on a sunny window sill. Use the flowers in fresh bouquets. The leaves have an onion or garlic aroma and a mild taste that does not linger on the breath, and can be chopped and used like garlic chives in cooking. *T. violacea* bears white or violet flowers in clusters.

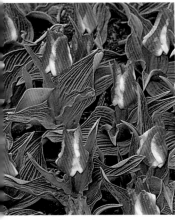

Tulipa greigii

Tulipa (TOO-lip-a)
TULIP

USDA Hardiness: zones 4-8
AHS Heat: zones 8-1
Height: 6 to 28 inches
Plant type: bulb
Soil: well-drained, sandy, fertile
Light: full sun

Tulips' buds unfold into a profusion of forms ranging from inverted bells to flat saucers, stars, urns, deep cups, and lilylike shapes. Petals may be smooth, curled, frilled, crisped, ruffled, flared, doubled, or waved. Tulips come in every color except true blue and are often striped, edged, flecked, flushed with contrasting color, or "flamed" in a zigzag variegated pattern. The hundreds of tulip species and thousands of hybrids are sorted into groups with similar origins, shapes, and bloom times. Allow the foliage to ripen before mowing or removing it. Tulips tend to disappear over time; either treat them as annuals or dig and replant bulbs every 2 to 3 years as flowering diminishes.

Vaccinium (vak-SIN-i-um)
BLUEBERRY

USDA Hardiness: zones 2-8
AHS Heat: zones 8-2
Height: 6 inches to 12 feet
Plant type: shrub
Soil: moist, well-drained, acid
Light: full sun to partial shade

Vaccinium crassifolium

The blue-green summer leaves of blueberries become a riot of color in fall. Delicate spring flowers and delicious blue-black berries add to the landscape value of this native shrub. *V. corymbosum* (highbush blueberry) is a rounded shrub with leaves turning red, orange, yellow, and bronze in fall; flowers are white; USDA zones 3-8. *V. crassifolium* (creeping blueberry) is an evergreen, prostrate shrub forming mats up to 6 feet across. Plant blueberries in moist, well-drained soil with a pH of 4.5 to 5.5. Add generous amounts of organic matter prior to planting. Mulch to preserve moisture.

Ulmus glabra

Ulmus (UL-mus)
ELM

USDA Hardiness: zones 3-9
AHS Heat: zones 8-2
Height: 40 to 70 feet
Plant type: tree
Soil: moist, well-drained
Light: full sun

Exfoliating, mottled gray, green, orange, or brown bark is this graceful, durable shade tree's most outstanding feature. Elms are widely used in streets, and parks, and for landscaping large properties. *U. glabra* (Scotch elm) is a wide-spreading tree. *U. parvifolia* (lacebark elm, Chinese elm, evergreen elm) has a spreading, rounded crown and grows best in moist, well-drained loams but adapts well to poor, dry soils, both acid and alkaline. Soil should be deep to accommodate the extensive root system. *U. parvifolia* 'Sempervirens' and 'Drake' can be semi-evergreen in warmer climates.

Valeriana (va-leer-ee-AY-na)
VALERIAN

USDA Hardiness: zones 3-9
AHS Heat: zones 9-1
Height: 3 to 5 feet
Plant type: perennial
Soil: average, moist, well-drained
Light: full sun to light shade

Valeriana officinalis

Valerian carries small flat-topped tufts of tiny flowers in summer in an open, branching cluster of lacy leaves. Both cats and butterflies find the plants attractive. The flowers, scented of honey and vanilla, are good in fresh bouquets. The roots yield a sedative compound used in herbal medicine. Add the mineral-rich leaves to compost. *V. officinalis* (common valerian, garden heliotrope) has light green ferny leaves and tubular white, pink, red, or lavender-blue flower clusters. Grow valerian from seed, and provide a moisture-retaining mulch.

Verbascum *(ver-BAS-cum)*
MULLEIN

USDA Hardiness: zones 5-9
AHS Heat: zones 7-2
Height: 2 to 8 feet
Plant type: biennial, perennial
Soil: well-drained
Light: full sun

Mulleins develop a rosette of coarse leaves and tall, sturdy spikes of long-lasting summer flowers followed by attractive dried seedpods. *V. blattaria* (moth mullein) de-

Verbascum bombyciferum

velops slender spikes of pale yellow flowers with a lavender throat. *V. bombyciferum* (silver mullein) produces sulfur yellow flowers; *V. thapsus* (flannel mullein) bears 3-foot spikes of yellow flowers. Sow seed directly outdoors in spring to bloom the following year. Established plants will self-seed. Plants tolerate dry conditions.

Veronica *(ve-RON-i-ka)*
SPEEDWELL

USDA Hardiness: zones 4-8
AHS Heat: zones 8-2
Height: 6 inches to 4 feet
Plant type: perennial
Soil: well-drained loam
Light: full sun to light shade

Clumps of spreading stems lined with soft-textured, narrow leaves and tipped with long spikes of tiny spring-to-summer flowers make speedwell a good choice for fillers

Veronica longifolia

or naturalizing. *V. longifolia* (long-leaf speedwell) 'Icicle' has white flowers; var. *subsessilis*, lilac blooms. *V. spicata* (spike speedwell) 'Blue Fox' has lavender-blue flower spikes; 'Red Fox', rose-to-pink blooms. *V. spicata* 'Sunny Border Blue' is particularly heat tolerant. *V. teucrium* [also called *V. austriaca* ssp. *teucrium*] 'Crater Lake Blue' has wide spikes of deep blue flowers. A tough plant, speedwell tolerates heat and humidity, severe winters, and drought.

Verbena *(ver-BEE-na)*
VERVAIN

USDA Hardiness: zones 8-11
AHS Heat: zones 12-1
Height: 6 inches to 4 feet
Plant type: annual, tender perennial
Soil: moist, well-drained
Light: full sun

From summer through frost, small, vividly colored flowers bloom in clusters on wiry stems with soft green foliage. *V. bonariensis* (Brazilian verbena) grows fragrant rosy violet flower clusters. *V. x*

Verbena x hybrida Purple Spreader ™

hybrida (garden verbena) bears small flowers in shades of pink, red, blue, purple, and white; 'Peaches and Cream' bears flowers in shades of apricot, orange, yellow, and cream; flowers of 'Silver Ann' open bright pink and fade to blended pink and white. Start seed indoors 12 weeks prior to the last frost and transplant outdoors after all danger of frost has passed. Verbena thrives in poor soil and full sun, and tolerates drought conditions.

Veronicastrum *(ve-ro-ni-KAS-trum)*
CULVER'S ROOT

USDA Hardiness: zones 4-8
AHS Heat: zones 8-3
Height: 3 to 6 feet
Plant type: perennial
Soil: well-drained, acid loam
Light: full sun to partial shade

Culver's root produces branched clusters of tiny flower spikes on tall, erect stems. Its leaves are arranged in tiered whorls that ascend

Veronicastrum virginicum

the stem. *V. virginicum* (blackroot) produces tiny tubular flowers that are packed densely along 6- to 9-inch flower spikes on stems 6 feet tall in clumps 18 to 24 inches wide; 'Roseum' grows pink flowers; 'Album', white flowers. Veronicastrum is a good background plant for the garden. Place veronicastrum in moderately acid soil. It is somewhat heat and drought tolerant.

Vetiveria zizanioides
(in winter)

Vetiveria (vet-i-VERR-ee-a)
VETIVER

USDA Hardiness: zone 11
AHS Heat: zones 12-9
Height: 6 to 9 feet
Plant type: perennial grass
Soil: average to rich, moist to wet
Light: full sun

Vetiver forms fountains of narrow, rough-edged leaves. Because its fibrous roots grow 10 feet deep, it is often planted to hold soil along the edges of streams and rivers. Flowers develop as flat spikelets in plumes on tall stems above the leaf clumps. The fragrant roots, can be dried to scent sachets. *V. zizanioides* (vetiver, khus-khus) has foot-long flowering spikes on stalks to 9 feet.

Viola (vy-O-la)
PANSY

USDA Hardiness: zones 3-9
AHS Heat: zones 12-1
Height: 3 to 12 inches
Plant type: annual, perennial
Soil: moist, well-drained, fertile
Light: full sun to partial shade

Although many pansies are technically short-lived perennials, they are considered annuals because they bloom their first year from seed and their flowers decline in quality afterward. They may also be treated as biennials, sown in late summer for bloom early the following spring. *V. tricolor* (Johnny-jump-up) bears violet-blue-and-yellow flowers. A bit of shade and water may encourage the blossoms to continue throughout most of the summer. Pansies started in late summer should be protected over the winter in a cold frame or with a light mulch. They can also be started indoors in midwinter to transplant to the garden in midspring. Pansies prefer a cool soil. Keep plants well watered to extend flowering.

Viola tricolor

Vitex agnus-castus

Viburnum (vy-BUR-num)
ARROWWOOD

USDA Hardiness: zones 5-8
AHS Heat: zones 8-1
Height: 3 to 12 feet
Plant type: shrub
Soil: moist, well-drained
Light: full sun to partial shade

Mostly deciduous, highly ornamental viburnums offer snowy clouds of flowers in spring and often colorful berries that may persist well into winter, as well as fragrance, reddish fall foliage, or attractive branching patterns. Viburnums are useful in shrub borders, as screens, or as specimens. Some of the better species and varieties are *V. carlesii* (Korean spice viburnum), evergreen *V. davidii* (David viburnum), and *V. setigerum* (tea viburnum). Viburnums grow best in slightly acid loam but tolerate slightly alkaline soils. Amend the soil with peat moss or leaf mold to increase moisture retention, and add mulch to cool roots in summer heat.

Viburnum carlesii

Vitex (VY-tex)
VITEX

USDA Hardiness: zones 7-10
AHS Heat: zones 10-1
Height: to 20 feet
Plant type: shrub, small tree
Soil: moist, well-drained, neutral
Light: full sun

A vase-shaped deciduous shrub or small tree with an airy, open habit and leaves that are aromatic when bruised, *V. agnus-castus* (chaste tree, hemp tree) produces fragrant flowers in foot-long mounded clusters. Chaste tree is multistemmed with showy lilac or pale violet flower panicles from midsummer to fall; 'Rosea' has pink flowers; 'Silver Spire' has white blooms throughout summer. Chaste tree thrives in hot weather. Too much fertilizer creates paler flowers.

Vitis *(VY-tis)*
GRAPE

USDA Hardiness: zones 5-9
AHS Heat: zones 9-1
Height: 20 to 50 feet
Plant type: vine
Soil: well-drained
Light: full sun

Vitis labrusca

With their twining tendrils, grapes quickly scramble over arbors and trellises. The broad leaves, attractively lobed and incised, color brilliantly in fall. Older stems have shredding, peeling bark. *V. amurensis* (Amur grape) has leaves coloring crimson to purple in fall. *V. coignetiae* (crimson glory vine) is an extremely fast-growing vine, with leaves turning scarlet in fall. *V. labrusca* (American grape) is suited for short seasons and high elevation growing areas. Plant grapes in deeply cultivated soil enriched with organic matter. When growing for shade or an arbor, cut canes back in winter to control spread.

Xeranthemum *(zer-RAN-the-mum)*
EVERLASTING

USDA Hardiness: zone 0
AHS Heat: zones 9-2
Height: 18 inches to 3 feet
Plant type: annual
Soil: moist, well-drained to average
Light: full sun

Xeranthemum annuum

Everlasting's fluffy flower heads in purple, pink, and white are displayed on long stems from summer to early fall. *X. annuum* has single or double flowers, surrounded by papery bracts that are the same color as the true flowers at the center of the head. In colder zones, start seed indoors in individual peat pots 6 to 8 weeks prior to the last frost, but handle carefully because they are difficult to transplant. In warmer climates, sow seed directly in the garden in spring after all danger of frost has passed. Allow 6 to 9 inches between plants. They adapt to most soils.

Wisteria *(wis-TEE-ree-a)*
WISTERIA

USDA Hardiness: zones 5-9
AHS Heat: zones 9-4
Height: 30 feet
Plant type: vine
Soil: moist, well-drained
Light: full sun

Wisteria floribunda

Panicles of flowers drip from this vigorous, twining vine. Lovely near patios and porches, where its bright green foliage provides dense shade for the rest of the growing season, wisteria needs a sturdy support, since the vines can eventually crush wood. *W. floribunda* (Japanese wisteria) has fragrant flowers; cultivars bear white, pale pink, and violet-purple flowers; *W. sinensis* (Chinese wisteria) include white, dark purple, and double varieties. Amend soil to create a deep, well-drained loam, and add lime if soil is very acid. Prune roots before planting.

Yucca *(YUK-a)*
YUCCA

USDA Hardiness: zones 4-9
AHS Heat: zones 9-1
Height: 2 to 12 feet
Plant type: shrub
Soil: light, well-drained
Light: full sun

Yucca filamentosa

Yucca's rosette of stiff, lance-shaped evergreen leaves accents rock gardens and entranceway designs. In early to midsummer, 3- to 12-foot-tall stalks bear erect panicles of waxy, drooping, creamy or yellowish white flowers that emit a lemony fragrance in the evening. *Y. filamentosa* 'Bright Edge' has gold leaf margins; 'Golden Sword' leaves have yellow centers and green margins; *Y. recurvifolia* (soft-leaf yucca) has blue-green foliage and large white flower panicles. Yucca grows best in fast-draining soils. It easily tolerates drought and is seldom bothered by insects or disease.

Zauschneria californica

Zauschneria (zawsh-NEER-ee-a)
CALIFORNIA FUCHSIA

USDA Hardiness: zones 8-11
AHS Heat: zones 12-8
Height: 12 to 36 inches
Plant type: perennial
Soil: moist, well-drained to dry
Light: full sun

Zauschnerias are shrubby perennials native to the western United States, where they are found in rocky slopes and canyons. Their large fuchsialike flowers attract hummingbirds. *Z. californica* (California fuchsia) bears trumpet-shaped, brilliant scarlet flowers from late summer through fall. *Z. latifolia* [also called *Epilobium canum* ssp. *latifolium*] (California fuchsia, hummingbird trumpet) has trumpet-shaped scarlet flowers from early summer through fall. Grow *Z. californica* in well-drained soil. It tolerates drought. *Z. latifolia* prefers a moist soil. Both species require full sun. Mulch for winter protection.

Zingiber (ZIN-ji-ber)
GINGER

USDA Hardiness: zones 9-11
AHS Heat: zones 12-8
Height: 3 to 4 feet
Plant type: perennial
Soil: rich, moist, well-drained
Light: light shade

Zingiber officinale

Ginger's aromatic branching roots with a spicy, citrusy bite have been prized by cooks for centuries. Grow ginger outdoors in hot, humid regions or as a container plant elsewhere. *Z. officinale* (common ginger) has 2- to 4-foot flat leaves composed of pointed leaflets lining reedlike stems and, rarely, yellow-petaled summer flowers with yellow-streaked purple lips in conical spikes. Ginger plants grow best in warm temperatures with constant humidity and soil moisture.

Zelkova serrata

Zelkova (zel-KOH-va)
ZELKOVA

USDA Hardiness: zones 5-8
AHS Heat: zones 8-2
Height: 50 to 80 feet
Plant type: tree
Soil: moist, well-drained
Light: full sun

Z. serrata (Japanese zelkova) is an elmlike deciduous tree resistant to Dutch elm disease. Vase shaped and often multistemmed, it frequently develops attractive exfoliating bark as it ages. Sharply toothed dark green leaves turn yellow or russet in fall. *Z. serrata* (Japanese zelkova, saw-leaf zelkova) grows best in deep, moist, fertile soil and adjusts to either alkalinity or acidity. Mulch to conserve moisture when the tree is young and to prevent mower damage. Once established, the tree tolerates wind, drought, and pollution.

Zinnia (ZIN-ee-a)
ZINNIA

USDA Hardiness: zone 0
AHS Heat: zones 12-1
Height: 8 to 36 inches
Plant type: annual
Soil: well-drained
Light: full sun

Zinnia elegans

Zinnias brighten the border with blooms whose petal-like rays may be flat and rounded, rolled into fringes, or crowded around yellow or green centers that are actually the true flowers. Hues range from yellows, oranges, and reds to pinks, roses, salmons, and creams, and maroon and purple. Flowers bloom from summer through frost. *Z. elegans* (common zinnia) grows 1 to 3 feet with showy flowers in many colors up to 6 inches across. Start seed indoors 6 weeks prior to the last frost, or sow directly outdoors after all danger of frost has passed. Zinnias thrive in hot weather but benefit from regular watering. Zinnias are prone to mildew in hot, humid climates.

SOURCES

To order a copy of the
AHS PLANT HEAT-ZONE MAP
contact:
American Horticultural Society
  7931 East Boulevard Dr.
  Alexandria, VA 22308-1300
  1-800-777-7931
  E-mail:
  gardenahs@aol.com

*For information on native
plants contact:*

National Wildflower Research
  Center
  4801 LaCrosse Ave.
  Austin, TX 78739
  (512) 292-4200

New England Wildflower
  Society
  180 Hemenway Rd.
  Framingham, MA
  01701-2699
  (508) 877-7630

**Mail-Order Native Plant
Nurseries**
NORTHEAST:
F.W. Schumacher Co., Inc.
  36 Spring Hill Rd.
  Sandwich, MA 02563
  (508) 888-0659
Vermont Wildflower Farm
  P.O. Box 5, Ferry Rd.
  Charlotte, VT 05445-0005
  (802) 425-3931
SOUTHEAST:
Niche Gardens
  1111 Dawson Rd.
  Chapel Hill, NC 27516
  (919) 967-0078
Suncoast Native Plants
  P.O. Box 248
  Palm View Rd.
  Palmetto, FL 34220
  (813) 729-5015
Woodlanders
  1128 Colleton Ave.
  Aiken, SC 29801
  (803) 648-7522

SOUTHWEST:
Clyde Robin Seed Co.
  P.O. Box 2366
  Castro Valley, CA 94546
  (415) 785-0425
Plants of the Southwest
  930 Baca St.
  Santa Fe, NM 87501
  (505) 983-1548
Wildseed Farms
  1101 Campo Rosa Rd.
  P.O. Box 308
  Eagle Lake, TX 77434
  (800) 848-0078
MIDWEST:
Native Seed Foundation
  Star Route
  Moyie Springs, ID 83845
  (208) 267-7938
Prairie Nursery
  P.O. Box 306
  Westfield, WI 53964
  (608) 296-3679

MID-ATLANTIC:
Appalachian Wildflower Nursery
  Route 1, Box 275A
  Reedsville, PA 17084
  (717) 667-6998
Windy Hill Plant Farm
  40413 John Mosby Highway
  Aldie, VA 20105-2827
  (703) 327-4211
NORTHWEST:
Abundant Life Seed
  Foundation
  P.O. Box 772
  Port Townsend, WA 98368
Forest Farm
  990 Tetherow Rd.
  Williams, OR 97544-9599
Siskiyou Rare Plant Nursery
  2825 Cummings Rd.
  Medford, OR 97501
  (503) 772-6846

BIBLIOGRAPHY

Books

Chaplin, Lois Trigg. *The Southern Gardener's Book of Lists.* Dallas, Texas: Taylor Publishing Company, 1994.

Christopher, Thomas. *Water-Wise Gardening.* New York: Simon and Schuster, 1994.

DeFreitas, Stan. *The Water-Thrifty Garden.* Dallas, Texas: Taylor Publishing Company, 1993.

Druse, Ken. *The Natural Habitat Garden.* New York: Clarkson Potter, 1994.

Ellefson, Connie, Tom Stephens, and Doug Welsh. *Xeriscape Gardening.* New York: Macmillan Publishing Company, 1992.

Lawrence, Elizabeth. *A Southern Garden.* Chapel Hill, North Carolina: The University of North Carolina Press, 1942.

The Ortho Gardening in Dry Climates. San Ramon, California: Ortho Books, 1989.

Ottesen, Carole. *The Native Plant Primer.* New York: Harmony Books, 1995.

Pleasant, Barbara. *Warm-Climate Gardening.* Pownal, Vermont: Storey Communications, Inc., 1993.

Rumary, Mark. *The Dry Garden.* New York: Sterling Publishing Co., Inc., 1995.

Springer, Lauren. *Waterwise Gardening.* New York: Prentice Hall, 1994.

Taylor, Jane. *Drought Tolerant Plants.*

New York: Prentice Hall, 1993.

Taylor, Jane. *Weather in the Garden.* London: John Murray Ltd., 1996.

Taylor, Patricia. *Easy Care Native Plants.* New York: Henry Holt and Company, 1996.

Taylor's Guide to Natural Gardening. Boston: Houghton Mifflin, 1993.

Taylor's Guide to Gardening in the South. Boston: Houghton Mifflin, 1992.

Taylor's Guide to Water-Saving Gardening. Boston: Houghton Mifflin, 1990.

Periodicals

Gregory, Jonathan, Thomas R.Karl, and Neville Nicholls. "The Coming Climate." Scientific American, May 1997.

PICTURE CREDITS

Virtual Garden ©1996 Time-Life Books, Inc.; Monrovia—Jerry Pavia from Virtual Garden ©1996 Time-Life Books, Inc. 129: Monrovia—Jerry Pavia; Monrovia. 130: Monrovia—Monrovia; Jerry Pavia from Virtual Garden ©1996 Time-Life Books, Inc.; Jerry Pavia from Virtual Garden ©1996 Time-Life Books, Inc.; Joanne Pavia—Monrovia; Jerry Pavia from Virtual Garden ©1996 Time-Life Books, Inc. 132: Monrovia; Jerry Pavia from Virtual Garden ©1996 Time-Life Books, Inc.—Monrovia; Jerry Pavia from Virtual Garden ©1996 Time-Life Books, Inc. 133: Monrovia—Jerry Pavia from Virtual Garden ©1996 Time-Life Books, Inc. 134: Monrovia; Jerry Pavia from Virtual Garden ©1996 Time-Life Books, Inc.—Monrovia. 135: Monrovia; © Walter Chandoha—Jerry Pavia from Virtual Garden ©1996 Time-Life Books, Inc. 136: Jerry Pavia; Monrovia—Monrovia. 137: Jerry Pavia from Virtual Garden ©1996 Time-Life Books, Inc.; Monrovia—Jerry Pavia from Virtual Garden ©1996 Time-Life Books, Inc. 138: Jerry Pavia from Virtual Garden ©1996 Time-Life Books, Inc.—Jerry Pavia from Virtual Garden ©1996 Time-Life Books, Inc.; M. W. Carlton/National Wildflower Research Center. 139: Jerry Pavia from Virtual Garden ©1996 Time-Life Books, Inc.; Jerry Pavia—Monrovia. 140: Monrovia; John A. Lynch—Jerry Pavia from Virtual Garden ©1996 Time-Life Books, Inc. 141: Jerry Pavia from Virtual Garden ©1996 Time-Life Books, Inc. 142: Jerry Pavia from Virtual Garden ©1996 Time-Life Books, Inc.; © Walter Chandoha—Jerry Pavia from Virtual Garden ©1996 Time-Life Books, Inc.;

Monrovia. 143: Jerry Pavia from Virtual Garden ©1996 Time-Life Books, Inc.—© Walter Chandoha; Carole Ottesen. 144: Jerry Pavia from Virtual Garden ©1996 Time-Life Books, Inc.; Joanne Pavia—C. Colston Burrell; Jerry Pavia from Virtual Garden ©1996 Time-Life Books, Inc. 145: Monrovia; Jerry Pavia—Jerry Pavia from Virtual Garden ©1996 Time-Life Books, Inc.; Monrovia. 146: Monrovia; Jerry Pavia—Jerry Pavia from Virtual Garden ©1996 Time-Life Books, Inc. 147: Jerry Pavia from Virtual Garden ©1996 Time-Life Books, Inc.; Jerry Pavia—Monrovia. 148: Jerry Pavia from Virtual Garden ©1996 Time-Life Books, Inc.—© Charles Mann; Jerry Pavia from Virtual Garden ©1996 Time-Life Books, Inc. 149: Jerry Pavia; Jerry Pavia from Virtual Garden ©1996 Time-Life Books, Inc.—Jerry Pavia from Virtual Garden ©1996 Time-Life Books, Inc. 150: Tom Ulrich/Oxford Scientific Films, Long Hanborough, Oxfordshire, U.K.; Jerry Pavia from Virtual Garden ©1996 Time-Life Books, Inc.—Jerry Pavia from Virtual Garden ©1996 Time-Life Books, Inc. 151: Monrovia; Jerry Pavia from Virtual Garden ©1996 Time-Life Books, Inc.—Jerry Pavia; Monrovia. 152: Monrovia—Jerry Pavia; Jerry Pavia from Virtual Garden ©1996 Time-Life Books, Inc. 153: Jerry Pavia; © R. Todd Davis—Jerry Pavia from Virtual Garden ©1996 Time-Life Books, Inc.; Monrovia. 154: Monrovia—Jerry Pavia from Virtual Garden ©1996 Time-Life Books, Inc.; Monrovia. 155: Monrovia—Monrovia; Jerry Pavia from Virtual Garden ©1996 Time-Life Books, Inc. 156: Monrovia; Jerry Pavia—©

Dency Kane; Carole Ottesen. 157: Rita Buchanan; Jerry Pavia from Virtual Garden ©1996 Time-Life Books, Inc.— Jerry Pavia from Virtual Garden ©1996 Time-Life Books, Inc.; Jerry Pavia. 158: Monrovia; Jerry Pavia from Virtual Garden ©1996 Time-Life Books, Inc.— Jerry Pavia from Virtual Garden ©1996 Time-Life Books, Inc. 159: Jerry Pavia from Virtual Garden ©1996 Time-Life Books, Inc.—Monrovia. 160: Jerry Pavia; Monrovia—Jerry Pavia; Monrovia. 161: Monrovia—Jerry Pavia; Jerry Pavia from Virtual Garden ©1996 Time-Life Books, Inc. 162: Virginia R. Weiler; Monrovia—Jerry Pavia; Jerry Pavia from Virtual Garden ©1996 Time-Life Books, Inc. 163: Jerry Pavia from Virtual Garden ©1996 Time-Life Books, Inc.—Jerry Pavia from Virtual Garden ©1996 Time-Life Books, Inc.; Monrovia. 164: Monrovia—Jerry Pavia from Virtual Garden ©1996 Time-Life Books, Inc.; Joanne Pavia. 165: Jerry Pavia from Virtual Garden ©1996 Time-Life Books, Inc.—Sally Kurtz; Jerry Pavia from Virtual Garden ©1996 Time-Life Books, Inc. 166: Jerry Pavia from Virtual Garden ©1996 Time-Life Books, Inc.; Michael Dirr—Jerry Pavia; Jerry Pavia from Virtual Garden ©1996 Time-Life Books, Inc. 167: Jerry Pavia from Virtual Garden ©1996 Time-Life Books, Inc.—Monrovia; ©Richard Day/Daybreak Imagery. 168: Monrovia; Holly H. Shimizu—Jerry Pavia from Virtual Garden ©1996 Time-Life Books, Inc.; Joanne Pavia. 169: Jerry Pavia from Virtual Garden ©1996 Time-Life Books, Inc.—Jerry Pavia; Monrovia. 170: Jerry Pavia from Virtual Garden ©1996 Time-Life Books, Inc.; Joanne

Pavia—Jerry Pavia from Virtual Garden ©1996 Time-Life Books, Inc.; Jerry Pavia. 171: Monrovia; Jerry Pavia from Virtual Garden ©1996 Time-Life Books, Inc.—Jerry Pavia from Virtual Garden ©1996 Time-Life Books, Inc.; Steven Still. 172: Jerry Pavia from Virtual Garden ©1996 Time-Life Books, Inc.— Jerry Pavia from Virtual Garden ©1996 Time-Life Books, Inc.; Joanne Pavia. 173: Monrovia; Jerry Pavia from Virtual Garden ©1996 Time-Life Books, Inc.— Jerry Pavia from Virtual Garden ©1996 Time-Life Books, Inc. 174: Monrovia; Thomas E. Eltzroth—C. Colston Burrell; Monrovia. 175: Jerry Pavia; Monrovia—Joanne Pavia; © Walter Chandoha. 176: Jerry Pavia from Virtual Garden ©1996 Time-Life Books, Inc.; Jerry Pavia—Jerry Pavia from Virtual Garden ©1996 Time-Life Books, Inc. 177: Jerry Pavia; Monrovia; Jerry Pavia; Monrovia. 178: Jerry Pavia from Virtual Garden ©1996 Time-Life Books, Inc.; Monrovia—Monrovia; Harry Smith, Horticultural Photographic Collection, Wickford, Essex, U.K. 179: Jerry Pavia; Jerry Pavia from Virtual Garden ©1996 Time-Life Books, Inc.— Monrovia; Jerry Pavia from Virtual Garden ©1996 Time-Life Books, Inc. 180: Jerry Pavia from Virtual Garden ©1996 Time-Life Books, Inc.—Monrovia. 181: Monrovia; Joanne Pavia—Monrovia. 182: Joanne Pavia; Jerry Pavia—© Runk/Schoenberger/ Grant Heilman Photography, Inc.; Jerry Pavia from Virtual Garden ©1996 Time-Life Books, Inc.

INDEX